D0105562

THE DESERT AND THE STARS

THE *Desert* AND *The Stars*

A Biography of Lawrence of Arabia

by Flora Armitage

Illustrated with Photographs

Henry Holt and Company New York

In Canada, George J. McLeod, Ltd.

FIRST EDITION

Library of Congress Catalog Card Number:
55-9223

80513-0115
Printed in the United States of America

ACKNOWLEDGMENTS

The author and the publishers wish to acknowledge their indebtedness to the following for permission to quote from their books:

Robert Graves, for extracts from *T. E. Lawrence to His Biographers* (New York, Doubleday, Doran, 1938) and *Lawrence and the Arabian Adventure* (New York, Doubleday, Doran, 1928); B. H. Liddell Hart, for extracts from *T. E. Lawrence to His Biographers*, and *Colonel Lawrence, the Man Behind the Legend* (New York, Dodd, Mead, 1934).

Thanks are also due to Doubleday and Company, New York, for their permission to quote from *The Seven Pillars of Wisdom* and *The Letters of T. E. Lawrence;* to Jonathan Cape, London, for permission to quote from *T. E. Lawrence by His Friends* and *The Mint;* to Basil Blackwell, Oxford, for permission to include extracts from *The Home Letters of T. E. Lawrence and His Brothers;* as well as to Constable and Company, Ltd., Hutchinson and Company, Ltd., and the Macmillan Company for their permission to quote from books published by them, and to the Society of Authors and the Public Trustee, London, for permission to use extracts from George Bernard Shaw's *Man and Superman* and *Too True to Be Good.*

The author wishes also to acknowledge her indebtedness to David Garnett, the editor of *The Letters of T. E. Lawrence*, and to express her gratitude to Colonel S. F. Newcombe and Captain B. H. Liddell Hart for their invaluable letters and assistance; to Eric Kennington for his permission to use the drawing, *The Cheshire Cat*, and to Colonel Ralph H. Isham and Bruce Rogers for their shared recollections.

PREFACE

A preface to a book is a pernicious thing, to write and to read. It seems to augur either an afterthought or an apology: something omitted from the text which ought to have been included; something said which was better left unsaid. An author, thinks the reader, ought to be able to say all he or she wishes to say in the compass of 300 pages, and whatever oddments are left over should be gathered into footnotes. Regard this, then, as a footnote too large to fit the page on which it should have appeared, and a modest effort to clarify a confused situation.

When this book was written, out of courtesy to members of the Lawrence family still living, it was not intended to make more than a veiled reference to the circumstances of Lawrence's birth, even though not to do so is a serious handicap for anyone writing of him. By January, 1955, however, the circumstances had already become public property, thanks to Richard Aldington; to withhold them here would serve no purpose therefore, and they have not been withheld. Their disclosure during the lifetime of Mrs. Lawrence was not laudable, but neither is it the sensational coup it has been made to appear. The facts had already been made public, quietly and without ostentation, in *Diary with Letters, 1931–1950,* by Thomas Jones, published the previous October, and the importance given the later revelation is both exaggerated and misleading.

That Thomas Edward Lawrence and his four brothers were the sons of an irregular union, were illegitimate, was never any secret to those who were Lawrence's close friends; that it should have been presented as some altogether new and scandalous fact is a clever but not very convincing journalistic trick. Other writers on Lawrence, both during and after his lifetime, could have produced the same fact, had they been less considerate, though perhaps none of them would have cared to expend so much effort on genealogical research to prove their point.

This author first learned the circumstances of Lawrence's birth in 1946, from a letter in the possession of Bruce Rogers for whom Lawrence undertook the translation of *The Odyssey* in 1928. There was nothing either guarded or reticent in this detailed recital of family affairs; and when in the following year the facts were confirmed verbally from another source, nothing new could be added. This is a simple matter which has been made much of; it should now be allowed to fall into its proper perspective and treated as a single element—a very powerful element to be sure—in the shaping of Lawrence's mind and attitudes, but not treated as a *mauvaise affaire.*

A man who has been in the grave for twenty years cannot be hurt by posthumous scandals and innuendoes. One of the benefactions of death is its inexorable cancellation of concern for mundane affairs. The evil—and the good—that men do may live on after them, but it seems reasonably certain that neither the praise nor the criticism can follow them into the grave. As for the sport of toppling heroes from their pedestals, it is an old one, as old at least as Athens and the elder Greeks. There are some of Lawrence's friends who feel he would have enjoyed hugely this spectacle of his toppling and the rumpus that followed; it may well be. Shorn of its cumbersome detail, the main indictment of Aldington's *Biographical Enquiry* does not contain any strictures harder than those Lawrence imposed on himself and his actions. We are all imposters of sorts, and would be greater ones, probably, if we had a larger stage to play on.

"Is he telling the truth?" asked E. M. Forster in his B.B.C. broadcast on Lawrence on February 14, 1955, and himself answered: "He did not always, so he will always bewilder those excellent people who identify telling the truth and being true." True he was, very real, and a great man for all his foibles and fallibilities. Let us accept him for what he is and enjoy him for what he is, one of the most romantic, provocative figures of our time. If this book adds to that enjoyment it will have been well worth the labor that has gone into it.

The author has endeavored to adopt a uniform spelling for Arabic place names, titles, and proper names throughout; but where variants occur in the writings of T. E. Lawrence and others in quoted material, those variants have been preserved in their original form. The number of accepted systems of Arabic transliteration make all these forms correct, and it is a question therefore only of uniformity and preference.

Flora Armitage

July, 1955

CONTENTS

Preface vii

1 THE WEB OF YOUTH 15

2 THE GARDEN OF PARADISE 56

3 THE LOTUS EATER 77

4 THE WILDERNESS 102

5 THE HOUSE OF WISDOM 146

6 DESCENT TO THE PIT 182

7 THE WAYS OF AN EAGLE 227

8 THE BURDEN OF GLORY 264

Bibliography 309

Index 313

THE DESERT AND THE STARS

In his loneliness and fixedness
He yearneth towards the journeying moon
And the stars that still sojourn
Yet still move onward;
And everywhere the blue sky belongs to them,
And is their appointed rest,
And their native country and their own natural homes,
Which they enter unannounced, as lords that are certainly expected,
And there is a silent joy at their arrival.

From *The Ancient Mariner*

❊

I

❊

THE WEB OF YOUTH

One day at the end of February, 1935, a small, well-formed man posed for his photograph astride a bicycle, one foot on the pedals, one hand balancing against the brick wall of a building. The winter sunlight made him half close his eyes, but he was smiling faintly, and the lock of thick fair hair which fell over his forehead fitted well the general informality of his dress: gray flannel suit, plaid muffler, and, as a matter of course, no hat.

He was forty-six, going on to forty-seven, though he seemed much younger; and he might easily have passed for a skilled factory hand or a garage mechanic starting off on a bicycling holiday but for the impressive mold of the head and the driving strength of his jaw. It was in fact T. E. Lawrence leaving the Air Force at Bridlington after more than ten years' service, preparing to travel south by bicycle and enter what appeared to be a new life. Yet it was not a beginning but the end of a life that had seemed a pilgrimage from lightness into dark; for in less than three months after leaving Bridlington he would be dead.

Because at one point in the forty-six years he had reached a strange and disproportionate fame, the world claimed him, history disputed him, critics damned him, and he was driven to work out his salvation in a solitary exile of spirit which was partly the result of all this, partly the effect of his own complex impulses. The story was not a simple one.

It began early one morning in the summer of 1888 when there was born to Sarah and Thomas Lawrence a second son whom they called Thomas Edward. The house at Tremadoc in Caernarvonshire where he was born stood in the midst of a garden where the August flowers bowed their heads to the wind, and over which islands of Atlantic cumulus moved in shadowing phalanxes. To the south of Tremadoc the waters of a bay shimmered; and to the north the green foothills rose slowly up to the craggy peak of Snowdon. A sign marks the house now as the birthplace of "Lawrence of Arabia," but the accident of his birth in Wales—neither of his parents was Welsh—affected him only to the extent that he became eligible later on to sit for a Welsh Exhibition at Jesus College, Oxford.

It was an undramatic year so far as the march of historical events was concerned. In April Matthew Arnold had died, and as the season advanced, many parts of the country were flooded under the heavy rains of a dismally wet summer. On the political scene, a special commission appointed to inquire into the sensational charges against Mr. Parnell and other Irish Members of Parliament held its first tense meeting in September; there was occasional aspersive comment inside Parliament and out over the inadequate state of the country's defenses—the Eastern Question, which in one form or another seems always to plague European statesmen, had flared up again. But one looks in vain for any augury that the child born on August 16 in that year was to be in any way unusual. Yet August 16, significantly or not, was the same day on which a hundred and nineteen years earlier the Corsican, Napoleon Bonaparte, had been born.

From the beginning it is said Thomas Edward Lawrence was a strong, well-developed and active child who quickly learned to stand and then to walk unaided. When he was little more than a year old, his parents deserted Tremadoc for Kirkudbright on the Solway Firth, and Wales knew young Thomas Edward no more until he returned in boyhood to explore its castles. By the time the family left Scotland he was nearly three and had mastered the English alphabet, rudiment of the literature he was to know and love so well, from overhearing the lessons of his brother, who was three years older. At five he had learned to read and write with no small degree of fluency, but he was not then or afterward regarded as being in any way precocious.

The family, which now included three sons, moved briefly to the Isle of Man and then to Jersey; from there in 1891 they went to Dinard in Saint-Malo. Here the children acquired a governess and a little later went to school to learn French. Here also, we are told, they took private lessons in gymnastics which Edward Lawrence, or Ned as he came to be known to his family, greatly enjoyed. Three years later the Lawrences were back in England again, living at Langley on the edge of the New Forest, where the two older brothers began to lay the foundations of a classical education with Latin lessons.

Among the stories related of Edward Lawrence in his infancy to reveal the distinctive and early evidence of his unique personality is one which clearly suggests the endurance and courage that later were to stamp all his actions. At two, following his father without his knowledge, he climbed up a steep ladder into a loft, never pausing until he had reached the top and safety in the arms of an astonished parent. During the family's sojourn in the New Forest this prodigiousness on Ned's part became even more marked. "No tree was too high for him to climb," his mother said, adding that she never knew him to fall.[1] He was strong and tall then for his age, fair-complexioned and imperturbably adventurous; he possessed an unusual degree of mental alertness, a nearly infallible memory, and he was a natural leader of all his brothers' games and romps. They were romps indeed: flying gambols around the room by way of beds and chests of drawers without once touching the floor; and a game of propulsion in which the beds were moved across the room by the muscular exertion of small bodies straining forward and then backward in a strenuous weaving

---

[1] A. W. Lawrence, ed., *T. E. Lawrence by His Friends* (New York, Doubleday, Doran, 1937).

exercise. It was at Langley that Ned learned to ride and to swim, and if he lacked enthusiasm for the equestrian art, he reveled in aquatics.

This gypsy life of the growing family came to an end in 1896 when the parents moved to Oxford to be near a suitable school for their small sons, who now numbered four, and settled in Polstead Road, in the northern suburbs that were part of the city's late Victorian expansion. There at Oxford, which Quiller-Couch called "the City of my young desire," Edward Lawrence was to grow in knowledge, in grace, and in wisdom.

A child seldom sets down on paper his thoughts and reflections; reminiscence comes later and is inevitably colored by subsequent events. But Edward Lawrence never tried in his writings to recall his childhood or boyhood imaginings, and so they can be known only by inference. That there was in the mature man a profound—it was more a malaise of the spirit than of the mind—and at times crippling negativism and diffidence is undeniable, but from all the available evidence, it appears more likely to have had its roots in adolescence rather than in childhood experience.

"We had a very happy childhood which was never marred by a single quarrel," said Dr. M. R. Lawrence, the eldest of the brothers, and to search in the childhood of Edward Lawrence for the seeds of his later maladjustment is unrewarding. There were of course some shadows; the family of mother and father and four—ultimately five—dependent sons had to practice rather stringent economies, stringent that is for people in their social circumstances, in order to live within their means, and there was one deep shadow, though it was not allowed to blight the happiness of the children. The parents had come together for love, and out of love remained constant; and the brothers were a contented, carefree, affectionate brood, unusually devoted one to another and proudly self-sufficient within the limits of their little society. Perhaps this self-sufficiency militated against the four elder boys somewhat, especially since with the coming of war their ranks were to be sadly decimated. Yet along with this carefully inculcated independence, they were taught to be kind, gentle-mannered, soft-spoken, and deferential—the younger toward the elder—and they were given a thorough grounding in Christian principles and practice. Quite early they were taught to read and to cherish the Bible, both as divine revelation and as literature, and they were all of them keen and able Bible students. (In young manhood Edward Lawrence was to carry around with him a pocket Greek Testament in which he was fond of reading.) These were the latter days of Edwardian England before Christianity had lost its hold on the country and while Bible-reading was considered a proper occupation for children and adults alike; and Victorian piety—not all of it cant and hypocrisy—was still strong before World War I swept it away with the peace and security of which it seemed a part.

Later the boys were to come under the influence and guidance of the popular Canon Christopher of St. Aldates; and while he was still a schoolboy, Edward Lawrence taught a Sunday-school class of small boys at St. Aldates, though it meant a walk of five miles each Sunday there and back. This is a side of him too often ignored, especially in view of his later antagonism toward all formal or institutional religion; but this early religious training set its stamp on him, as it did on his brothers. His faith, like the rest of his personality, was to suffer acute permutations in later life; it was severely strained by his adult experience and inevitably worked on by the great and stark—but to him appealing—monolithic systems of the East to which he was exposed. And it was inevitably diluted by his ruthless questing for an absolute standard which could be held not by faith but by intellectual discernment. Pure faith in any case is easier of achievement for those of simpler attitudes, and the logical sequence for complex minds is an orderly progression from agnosticism into mysticism, a course Edward Lawrence could not or would not contemplate.

One of their schoolmasters, the Reverend Ernest W. Cox, remembered the brothers in a pleasing little vignette as they bicycled to school, Indian file, the eldest in front, the youngest behind, wearing neat, identical blue-and-white-striped jerseys. They attended the City of Oxford High School for Boys where they were well taught by capable masters, and where they impressed and astonished a contemporary, T. W. Chaundy, a school friend of Edward Lawrence, by the regularity of their appearance: each boy as soon as he was old enough to go to school, in a seemingly inexhaustible supply, until he wondered how many sons the Lawrences possessed. They did not go to a more fashionable school for the obvious reason that their father could not afford to send them to one. It was not a vital deprivation; gentility the family possessed in a marked degree, but the snobbishness that sorts out schools and labels environments was alien to them. Thomas Lawrence's own background was not so rigidly conventional that he should seek to foist conventionality off on his sons as a prized virtue.

He was born in County Meath, Ireland, as Thomas Robert Chapman, the younger son of an Anglo-Irish family of varied strains genealogically allied to Sir Walter Raleigh, a collateral ancestor, and had changed his name by deed poll to Lawrence upon leaving Ireland—as his son was later to change his name from Lawrence to Shaw. The change of name in both instances was significant—the casting off of an old identity. Thomas Robert Chapman had left a wife and family of four daughters in Ireland to come to England with the woman he loved and who was to bear him five sons. "Lawrence" was apparently a name chosen at random, as his second son was to choose "Ross" and later "Shaw" for his incognito. He had pursued a normal classical education, followed up with a dilettantish interest in agriculture and a period of travel, if not in the grand manner, certainly in the spirit of grandness. Faced with the problem of rearing a large family on an income of three hundred pounds a year which he did not deign to increase by any sort of remunerative work, he retrenched socially and cut down on those gentlemanly pursuits, shooting, yacht-racing, mountain-climbing, which had formerly occupied him.

Posterity has left only a scant picture of him as a tall, comely man who was grave, instinctively shy, and, in the defensive manner of the shy, sometimes brusque. But all impressions agree that he was completely the aristocrat, refined but not scholarly, a true sportsman and a gentleman. He was all of this and a great deal more. A man who surrenders name, position, and fortune for love is usually a man endowed by nature with more than a mild capacity for passionate feeling, however deeply hidden the impulse is. Cool-blooded men nearly always prefer compromise to discomfort where their hearts and their well-being are both involved. But the contrast between him and his wife was a startling one. "Observers noticed a difference in social attitude between the courtly but abrupt and large father, and the laborious mother. The father shot, fished, rode, sailed with the certainty of birthright experience. He never touched a book or wrote a cheque." [2] Toward his sons Thomas Robert Lawrence cherished a quiet, undemonstrative affection, encouraging them as much as possible to share in his own sporting enthusiasms, and in Oxford at the turn of the century he set himself to live without complaint the somewhat tame suburban life imposed on him by circumstances. He indulged in photography, another of his hobbies, took his young sons down to Port Meadow in season to watch or to sail boats, and, an ardent cyclist, bicycled with them when they were old enough to endure long jaunts without fatigue.

From his father Edward Lawrence seems to have inherited the characteristically Hibernian charm which he could exhibit when he chose, for among all the strains—Irish, Hebridean, Scandinavian, Dutch—which between them he and Sarah Lawrence passed on to their sons, the Irish seemed destined to exert the strongest influence on their second son. In later life friends of Edward Lawrence thought they detected an unmistakable Irish lilt in his soft-spoken English voice, but that might only have been a reversion to type after his years in the air force. Certainly his humor seemed often more Irish than English, and an unobtrusive but genuine Irish feeling and sympathy pervaded his childhood home, since Thomas Lawrence bore within him an exile's longing for his native fields which never left him. That and the unconscious, sad pride of a man who has burned his bridges behind him, has forsaken the familiar way for the unknown and the more awkward. These are states not easily communicated, but the spirit that engenders them is, and this spirit he certainly transmitted to his second son.

---

[2] So wrote B. H. Liddell Hart, with the approval of Lawrence, in *Colonel Lawrence, The Man Behind the Legend* (New York, Dodd, Mead, 1934).

He was also to bequeath to him a taste for adventure, a competence with firearms and cameras, and a fondness for boats as well as an instinctive understanding of their management. But if one seeks for dominant influences in the developing psyche of young Edward Lawrence, it is in his mother rather than his father that these influences must be sought. It was from her that the most significant part of his heritage came, for in her originated those traits which, undergoing their natural mutations in his separate entity, gave him his formidable will, his intellectual catholicity, his strict conscience, his resilient body—strong for all its brittle bones—his capacity for enduring hardship and pain, and his undeniable asceticism. Their physical resemblance was very marked indeed, and her effect on him and upon all her sons was incalculable. As in young womanhood she had been a nursery governess, she undertook with confidence her childrens' first lessons, and it was her opinions and standards which were inculcated into their minds and shaped their attitudes from their earliest perceptions.

Three of her sons were born within short intervals of each other, but except for a nurse during their infancy she performed all the necessary duties for them herself. It should not be supposed that the domestic tasks to which she applied herself with so much energy blunted her perceptions and intelligence; far from it. It was she who guided and encouraged them in all their pursuits with eager, untiring devotion; her lively intelligence helped to set them going on their appointed paths, and their letters to her show how much she shared in their pursuits and interests, though she may not have been able actively to participate in them.

In her devotion to her sons, Sarah Lawrence might easily have overreached reason and made them excessively dependent on her, but this unhappy course she was able, as many a mother of sons is not, to eschew. But that she lived in them and for them wholly, comforting herself by pride in their comeliness, their intelligence, their achievements, is undeniable; and she longed always for that unguarded love and confidence which is proper and natural for boys to give their mother, but which grown men shrink from giving except to a woman not their mother. And hers being a morally strong and deeply pious nature, who can doubt that she imposed the pattern of her strength, her piety, her strict, and, in the circumstances, troubled conscience on her sons? It may well be that, as Geoffrey Faber believed was the case with John Henry Newman, Edward Lawrence grew up with a cleavage between intellect and emotions on the one hand, and the body with its sensual experience on the other—a wholly unnatural and dangerous cleavage. Her sons were given complete freedom to go where they would, with parental consent and approval of course. During the school holidays when they were older, it was the practice for each boy to be given a small sum of money to spend on whatever planned expedition he chose: alone if he desired to be alone, with a friend or with one of his brothers if he preferred. The only stipulation attached was that each boy should arrange his journey so as to insure that, however far he traveled, he would have sufficient time and money, barring accidents, to return home without an extra allotment of either being granted; and there is no reason to believe that any of them ever exceeded their limit. It was the same when as young men they traveled abroad; always in the recital of their adventures are assurances to their parents of their practical economies, their determination not to go above their allowance. In the light of a later fashion of regarding parental largess as rightfully unlimited, their dutiful and willing frugality seems all the more ingratiating. As each young wanderer returned to the nest, he appeared for breakfast next morning as eager and full of his adventures as a young Sinbad. No better way of encouraging self-reliance could have been found.

Theirs was a family knit together by the closest ties of affection. As each young son was born, he was enfolded and protected not only by the love of his parents but by the joyful allegiance of his brothers. By the time Arnold, the youngest of the five, was born in 1900, Ned, then a sturdy boy of twelve, was prepared to lavish on him all his own strong but tender solicitude. "May I take him out?" he would ask his mother, and three years later, at fifteen, when his youngest brother shrank back, afraid of the carved figures in the Ashmolean Museum, he revealed a remarkable psychological insight when he carved a face on a stone in the garden and gave the frightened little boy a hammer to smash it and prove to himself that faces of stone were not real and therefore not to be feared.

The pastimes of boys growing up in this period before World War I seem odd by modern standards: The brothers learned to sew—a practical accomplishment for boys who are learning to become self-sufficient—by making flags from bunting; they learned carpentry and indulged their boyish passion for collecting in novel ways. The pastimes and pleasures of the Lawrence boys during their formative years served to form them into the young men they ultimately became: manly, sensitive, generous-hearted, possessing a grace of demeanor and charm of character that is not often equaled today. Nevertheless, these small boys, so closely linked by blood and upbringing, exhibited a fascinating variability of temperament.

Bob, the eldest, was thoughtful and conscientious, not priggish, but aware quite early of his responsibilities as the eldest of the group and the need for showing a good example to his younger brothers.

From the beginning Will, sixteen months younger than Ned, was brilliant and impetuous, with his sanguine desires often running ahead of his immediate capacity for fulfillment.

As for Frank, his was a practical, down-to-earth, yet deeply religious nature, unclouded and straightforward—"a dear boy; lovable and greatly loved; one whose happiness and radiant smile remain an enduring and ever helpful memory," said Canon Cox.[3]

And there was Ned, the deep one, whose unfathomable thoughts and resolutions set him apart as a boy to be listened to, not because he was older or even stronger, but because even then his persuasive powers were becoming irresistible. He was dependable, too, for all his secret dreaming. "Ned was always the one to mend any object or find out what was wrong with the electric light," said his older brother, adding that Will never waited to hear half the directions before darting off, and that even his own errands were often fruitless. Ned, on the contrary, never returned from any errand without bringing back exactly what was needed—or something better. Always he was the

---

[3] *T. E. Lawrence by His Friends.*

bringer of order into whatever chaotic scene he introduced himself; the bearer of a quiet joy which, without fully comprehending it, his family and later his friends, were able to share. Silence or conversation were equally rewarding in his presence, but there was an undeniable spell in his words. He was to become not only consummate master of the language he spoke, but master too of his ideas.

When Edward Lawrence was nine or ten, his strong affinity for history began to assert itself, and it is possible from this time on to sense how his devotion to it blossomed and unfolded. Commencing with small things, Roman coins and bits of pottery begged from workmen excavating among the foundations of old Oxford in order to make room for the new, and passing to ambitious rubbings of knights and bishops taken from the brasses in the many churches around Oxford, his interest led him at last to medieval sculpture and military architecture and, by the time he was sixteen, to a study of siege engines and the science of war. In the course of time his historical knowledge became quite formidable, enabling him to demolish utterly in argument those rash enough to cross with him on any controversial issue. History was the balance in which later he weighed his own actions as well as the actions of the kings, soldiers, and politicians into whose lives his peculiar destiny was to thrust him, and judged them in their own and older historical contexts. He was scarcely eight when on a steamer excursion on which his parents had taken the children to view the Fleet at Spithead, he was discovered below in the saloon reading Macaulay's *Introduction to English History*. Water and ships held their own fascination, but each book was a kingdom waiting to be explored, and reading was too imperative a pleasure to be resisted. "His memory was remarkable," said his mother. "Any book he took up he seemed to read at a glance, but he knew it all as I soon found out." [4] This is an interesting commentary in view of the later and extraordinary claims made for his erudition and reading ability. Robert Graves was to say,

[4] *T. E. Lawrence by His Friends.*

with Lawrence's approval, that he had read every book in the library of the Oxford Union—the best part of fifty thousand volumes, probably. This is certainly an exaggeration, or an oversight which needs to be qualified and corrected. Even a boy of catholic tastes who reads avidly and quickly reads only the books which interest him; but it is surely pedantic to take seriously the statement that he read six books a day for six years, and then to be outraged because this does not add up to fifty thousand. The chances are it was never intended to be taken seriously; the operative word in Robert Graves' sentence is "probably."

His rummaging about in and around Oxford for bits of pottery, and his arrangement of that pottery, was soon to bring him to the attention of D. G. Hogarth, author, archaeologist, and orientalist, at that time and for many years afterward Keeper of the Ashmolean Museum. In later life Edward Lawrence was to describe Hogarth as "the man to whom I owe everything I had since I was seventeen"—the age at which he found himself. Certainly it was Hogarth's recognition of his abilities that set his feet on that fateful path which led from history to archaeology into soldiering and politics and all that devolved from them. Meanwhile, the Lawrence family continued its inconspicuous residence at 2, Polstead Road, just off the Woodstock Road, where several curious factors combined to set them apart from their neighbors: their seeming social superiority which was kept by their kindliness and intelligence from degenerating into snobbery, and their near-isolation, for they seemed to have few friends and almost no relatives. Most of their neighbors knew them only slightly, for they never attempted to establish even the tenuous social contact usual in English suburban dwellers. There is one instance of Ned's presence being remembered at a children's party where he took part in a charade as the "tail" of a dragon. Generally, however, the boys were jealously guarded from association with other families and taught to rely wholly on themselves for fellowship and conviviality. Quite apart from these peculiarities, the Lawrences were conspicuous for the overwhelmingly masculine character of their household, and it is at this point that one of the most provocative aspects of temperament, not only in Edward Lawrence but in Sarah Lawrence, becomes apparent.

"He was brought up to do without female society and the habit has remained with him," wrote Robert Graves in *Lawrence and the Arabian Adventure.* Compare with this the remark Sarah Lawrence is supposed to have made to Graves: "We could never be bothered with girls in our house," and not only are they a most interesting corollary but they constitute a clue—though only one—to Edward Lawrence's later coldness toward women.

"She was a woman of decision and quiet power," wrote Robert Graves of Sarah Lawrence, and so she was and is the remarkable mother of a remarkable son.[5] Her impatience with her own sex was in part the natural impatience of a woman formed in a strongly independent mold. The more common feminine failings, obsession with dress and trivialities, shallowness of mind, and frowardness she repudiated with all her mind. And she may well at some time have suffered personally from the barbed stings of feminine malice. She was Evangelical in practice but Calvinist by temperament and upbringing. Dissemblement was alien to her. The more difficult then the position in which she found herself in this marriage which was not formalized, since there had not been nor could be a divorce.

That all women are not frivolous and empty-headed nor all girls silly she most certainly knew, but her attitude did not encourage the invasion of her household by any girl or woman. Naturally, there were women visitors to the house on Polstead Road: the children's old nurse, Florence Messham, tested and loyal friends of the family, but scarcely any of her sons' generation. One lone girl, the sister of a school friend, seems to have penetrated the wall of sheltered intimacy of those early days sufficiently to be able to recall the cycling trips she made with Edward Lawrence and her brother. For the rest, there were matrons, the wives of teachers and friends, but no girl visitors to Polstead Road.

The late Victorian house in North Oxford was not pretentious; it

---

[5] At the time of writing she was ninety-three.

was frankly simple in a manner that, today, would be condemned out of hand as bourgeois. There was no attempt at elegance, and indeed, for a family of five boys to be happy in a relatively small house, elegance was a luxury which had to be sacrificed like so many other luxuries. On the walls of the drawing room hung reproductions of Holman Hunt's "The Light of the World" and Noël Paton's "The Man with the Muckrake," and everywhere in the house the furnishings were plain, solid, and comfortable with occasional lightening touches of pre-Raphaelite artfulness and the more carefully prized handiwork of a family trained to use its hands. There is a photograph dated about 1897 which portrays the four brothers in a stereotype but charming fraternal pose: Bob the elder standing, already grave and dignified; Ned and Will, whose later beauty was so arresting, dressed in identical sailor suits; and Frank, nicknamed "Chimp" by his brothers, who most resembled Ned in features, seated in their midst wearing Highland dress. Here is the child which fathered the man, easily recognizable by his wide, high forehead, the fullness around the eyes, the sculptured mouth and well-formed chin; and all his latent verve and power are there concealed under a child's frank and disarming gaze.

As a brother and as a son Ned was gentle and considerate, and toward Arnold, who followed him into archaeology, he showed a most tender solicitude. Dr. M. R. Lawrence has told how his brother purposely left a Scriptural examination paper incomplete in order to forfeit the prize which might then with more propriety fall to him as eldest, and how disappointed Ned was when, after all, he won it himself. They were all exceptional, but he was in a sense their exemplar, the "eagle among eagles" as Sir Ernest Barker later described him, and there is no mistaking the tone of quiet authority in a letter written when he was eighteen to his near-twin, Will:

". . . what is it you are going to dig up? Your letter bristles with inconsistencies. You think it is a Roman or a Celtic camp (the two things are absolutely opposed to each other) and then you proceed to say it is a mound on some rising ground." [*Letters*, No. 3.]

And a few years later: "What is a nympholept? It sounds like a sort of newt: don't use these words: your letter on the whole needs a chastening of Bunyan and perhaps Addison. Don't reply and say they are not alike." [*Letters*, No. 31.] These are typical examples of an elder brother's privileged criticism, through which however an affectionate leg-pulling clearly shines.

At thirteen Edward Lawrence began a series of strenuous bicycle tours alone around England in pursuit of his favorite hobbies: architecture and brass-rubbing. The walls of his room at home were by now papered with the results of former quests, a dramatically splendid décor, especially by firelight when he could lie surrounded by a great black frieze of knights and bishops flickering and dancing in a perpetual *auto-da-fé* in which they burned but were never consumed. In Waterperry Church, Oxford, where the brasses were found to be quite inaccessible behind a barrier of forbidding pews, Ned, described as already ruthless by his school friend T. W. Chaundy, who shared the adventure with him, broke through the barrier of pews with an alarming crash of splintering wood and his own soft, triumphant laughter. It was historical enthusiasm not sacrilege, however; he was far too devoted and conscientious a student for vandalism.

These cycling expeditions soon made him master of the complex and superimposed architectural periods of England, their forms and impediments, and before long he was developing strong and instinctive preferences. The Romanesque with its solidity of line, its rounded simplicity and grace of arch, seemed particularly germane to his temperament, though he was able fully to appreciate and be enthusiastic over the Gothic. These perambulations and the vociferous reading that complemented them were quite apart from his formal education at school. There he construed Caesar and abandoned himself to an intense but not overly enthusiastic study of higher mathematics which was to last until, at seventeen, his greater love of history supplanted it once and for all. However, "Any conception of him as a solitary, moody schoolboy shunning the company of his fellows is wide of the mark," said another of his schoolfellows, explaining that he was far too whimsical, too novel, in his hobbies ever to be unpopular. For one thing, he possessed a three-speed geared bicycle, newly invented, the first among his contemporaries to own one. On this specially built Morris machine with its low-slung handle bars he raced along with a natural zest for speed which only his later and powerful motorcycles could fully satisfy.

Perhaps where he most clearly departed from the common attitudes of boys was in his total lack of interest in the natural sciences. Not for him a boy's curiosity over wild life, an enthusiasm for bird-watching or collecting live specimens. His observations of animals, such as they were, when undertaken were for the benefit of his younger brother, Arnold. Of topography and rock strata he possessed an adequate knowledge, as any reader of *The Seven Pillars of Wisdom* will remember; but knowledge of them did not constitute a desire to understand their separate components from a scientific or a historical viewpoint. It was the same with other natural objects; trees were merely a part of the landscape, beautiful perhaps but not important; cliffs and mountains were there only to be climbed; rivers and streams to be sailed on, swum across, or forded. About their individual and teaming life he felt no curiosity and read in them no telling allegory. He swam, cycled, canoed, climbed, with unabating vigor, and, when small, took part enthusiastically with his brothers in cross-country paper chases. But the mystery and the fullness of creation never enticed him.

Most small boys play at soldiers at some stage of their development, and Ned was no exception; only he played the common military games quite differently from most boys, giving full scope to all his unusual imaginative faculties. "When we were small and shared a large bedroom," said Dr. M. R. Lawrence, "he used to tell a story of adventure and successful defence of a tower against numerous foes." [6] The heroes of this fantasy were three furry dolls, Fuz, Pompey, and Pete, belonging to the younger brothers, and this intrepid trio were set to defend their tower in an amazing nightly rigmarole of alarms and excursions all recounted in rhyming prose by their inventor. There is more than a passing similarity in this to the web spun by the Brontë children in their Haworth vicarage around Branwell's wooden

[6] *T. E. Lawrence by His Friends.*

soldiers which was to lend color and vigor to their later creative efforts. So the pattern is often set quite early. In those games where the assault of an imaginary castle, the storming of an impregnable rock, was the object, Ned was ever a strong and victorious leader. Any enterprise fortunate enough to have him as prime mover and organizer was certain of success then as later: He could not fail. And any boy paired off with him for his own special pursuits found himself treasuring long afterward an experience rich in a pleasure not quite definable and in adventure pervaded with the originality of a unique mind which gave it zest—the satisfaction of a goal essayed and won.

Oxford, living memorial to the past and guardian of the future, was to prove an ideal forcing ground for a temperament as sanguine and as sensitive as Edward Lawrence's, and the turn of the century an ideal time in which to live as a child—a time such as no child since has been privileged to enjoy. The new and magic century which was ushered in with steam, combustion engines, electric power, and telegraphs to give it impetus, with the first tentative flight through space in heavier-than-air machines already achieved, promised marvels to come that none could foresee, none limit. For those who lived in its promise, the prospect seemed dazzling: it offered an opportunity to exist in the most exciting of presents and yet possess the past more fully and comprehensively than any other generation had possessed it, while looking forward to a still more splendid future. This was the promise of the twentieth century, before a first and then a second world war blunted the vision. Edward Lawrence had already laid hands on the past; the present was a thing of moment, to be lived through unconsciously as children live in time, reckoning only in terms of school holidays, while the future, happily, lay hidden from him.

When Edward Lawrence was sixteen there occurred one of those odd accidents with far-reaching effects which was to contribute not a little to his growing self-consciousness. In a hand-to-hand scuffle one day with a school bully whom he eventually overcame and pulled to the ground, he broke his leg just above the ankle. This event is of particular interest, partly because it is claimed that the accident was responsible for retarding his physical growth which, up to then, had been normal, and partly because it is the earliest example of his stoicism under pain.

The accident occurred during the noon break, and he went in afterward to a mathematics class and worked for two hours until his suffering became unbearable. Not until then did he own up to his disability and one of his brothers was delegated to wheel him home on his bicycle. A broken bone may be a trifle, or it may be an event of great moment, psychologically speaking, in the intimate and subtle consanguinity of mind and body. If it did retard his growth, then its share in the development of his personality may well have been out of all proportion to its importance as an incidental event. What is clear is that sixteen was the age that began tentatively Edward Lawrence's inward recoiling from himself; it was then that the pattern was set and the whole mechanism of defenses and compensations began to operate.

An enforced absence from school resulted, affording him the pleasure of indulging his passion for reading through the day far into the night, stretched out on a mattress which served him both as hearth rug and bed. On this mattress before the fire where his mother, finding him asleep with a book still in his hand would cover him over with a blanket and then quietly withdraw, he embarked on the course of self-imposed military study which he described later to Captain Liddell Hart as "the usual schoolboy stuff." Creasy, Henderson, Mahan, Napier, and Coxe were his mentors; from them he went on to technical treatises on castle-building and the equally intricate art of castle destruction by way of the experts, the Greeks Procopius, Demetrius, Poliorcetes, and others. And while nursing his broken leg, he appears also to have dipped heavily into works of chivalry, establishing within himself that wholly romantic bias which motivated his later actions.

In afteryears he set little value on his formal schooling, describing it as "usually an irrelevant and time-wasting nuisance which I hated and contemned." And in his notes on life in the Royal Air Force, he speaks of the return, during his recruit's training, to the school fear of punishment for default which had haunted him between the ages of eight and eighteen and to which university came as a blessed relief. But this may well have been hindsight reflection. His mother has said he was always very happy while at school where most certainly a facile brain spared him the more onerous drudgery of inculcated education.

The broken bone healed, he returned to school and quickly caught up with the work of his schoolfellows, but one result of the weakened ankle was to strengthen his determination to take no part in organized sports. Other boys might be active on the cricket pitch or the football field; he would never join them except under compulsion, though he sometimes came to watch or to criticize—not the game but their movements accordingly as they fitted or did not fit into the classical Greek ideal of athletic perfection. It was not fear of being unable to excel that kept him out of games, but dislike of the enforced competition which sets two boys or two teams one against the other and which at best seemed to him purposeless rivalry, and at worst pernicious contest. In this attitude toward sports he was joined by Bob and Will Lawrence, so that it seemed almost a matter of family honor until first Frank and then Arnold broke with the tradition. To Ned, Frank's deflection seemed almost a betrayal of an ideal; with Arnold, so much younger, his attitude was tolerant and he was able to exhibit an interest, half-serious, half-amused, in his young brother's exploits. But even Arnold Lawrence confessed himself infected by this anti-games sentiment of his older brothers to the extent of feeling embarrassed whenever Ned inquired of him how well he had run a race or played a game.

The truth is that games and the team spirit could not interest Edward Lawrence. He was a boy of intense individuality, possessing absorbing hobbies which took him out of doors and kept him reasonably active, and he felt himself wholly independent of competitive sports which, in his view, did nothing to nourish the mind even if they developed the body. And where he chose to excel, Edward Lawrence could and did show as much and often more prowess than the ordinary athletic boy. He climbed hills, scrambled over ruins, explored streams, and cycled with a robust energy that was difficult for his contemporaries to match. On various occasions, with his brothers and with friends, he traversed by boat or canoe all the waterways encompassing Oxford, and one Easter holiday he and Will Lawrence paddled up the Cherwell from Oxford to Banbury in three days, tying up their canoe and returning home by train to sleep each night.

The pursuit of a mathematics scholarship came to an end when he was nearly eighteen, leaving him with a useless and top-heavy knowledge of higher mathematics about which he sometimes complained. And history which replaced it as his principal study made another more subtle alteration in his mode of existence. The modest, three-storied, semidetached house on Polstead Road had long been strained by the size of the family which occupied it, and now, to provide their second son with the quiet necessary for concentrated study, his parents had built for him at the bottom of the garden—where it remains still—a two-room bungalow with a fire grate, electric light, and a telephone connection to the house. The walls of this sanctum he hung with soundproof sheeting, gathering about him his books and the few objects which claimed his devotion, and here he lived and worked somewhat apart from the rest of the family throughout his university career. So there commenced subtly, and certainly not with any conscious intention, his spiritual segregation: the withdrawing, "like the intact course of a snowflake" as he was later to describe it, from the common levels of human intercourse—a trend he was subsequently to deplore and try desperately to remedy.

There is enshrined in myth and folklore the forewarning that the best of life's gifts often bear within themselves their own curse. In its more fanciful forms, it is the uninvited spirit, chagrined at being slighted in the birthday festivities of a favorite child, who retaliates by imposing a condition which renders all the fair gifts of more benevolent spirits null and void. In its modern and historic versions, so much that is pure and good of intent is proved to be marred and negated by a cross-grained talent for accomplishing evil. This ill-starred and ancient malevolence seems to have presided at the birth of Edward Lawrence. He was endowed with an abundance of the natural graces: intelligence, strength of body, perception of beauty, versatility of mind, and yet all these rare faculties were condemned to be fretted away by the caustic action of his ingrained self-distrust. Never did the

Old Woman of the Dark Kingdom exact a more cruel revenge in all her long years of turning princes into swans or pricking the fingers of princesses with her poisoned needles.

A child is seldom conscious of himself as an entity apart from his surroundings. Introspection belongs to youth and to maturity, when it should properly pass over into reflection. At this period of his youth Edward Lawrence seems to have begun to look consciously into himself, and what he saw did not wholly please him. For one thing, he seems not to have liked his physical envelope. It should not be supposed that this was any vain hankering after good looks in the conventional sense and for their own sake, but there may have developed in him through his reading an ideal of classical or heroic beauty which moved him [7] and to which he was devoted. What is certain is that he was dissatisfied most of all with his small stature, a physical imperfection that plagued him the more in later years and which he was driven on occasion to condemn and at other times vehemently to defend. "I cursed my littleness," he wrote of a crucial moment in *The Seven Pillars*. (Earlier in his history he had referred to himself almost contemptuously as a "little man in silk.") This littleness of which he complained was not excessive, however, nor as ludicrous as some enthusiasts for his uniqueness have claimed. He was between five-feet-five and six, and finely proportioned, which is better than Bonaparte's stunted five-feet-three and the similar scale of the diminutive hero of Trafalgar.

"Too much body and too little head," was a favorite, often caustic stricture of his against stature combined with ineffectualness, as he felt it later in certain army officers; and tall friends who knew his views were made self-conscious by the thought that he might silently be applying the stricture to themselves. But if he was small, he was very strong—"a pocket-sized Hercules" was how he later described himself in young manhood—able to cycle over a hundred miles a day without strain, notwithstanding that for three years in youth he adopted a meatless diet of milk, eggs, cereals, fruit, and vegetables,

[7] As revealed in his brother Will perhaps, and later on in Dahoum, the boy who helped him at Carchemish.

and while living at home never drank tea or coffee. In the first flower of young manhood before the war ravaged his strength, his weight was nearly one hundred and fifty-five pounds, distributed solidly through shoulders, back, and chest, as in the body of a prizefighter, giving him with his heavy jaw and long head a slightly top-heavy appearance. This top-heaviness however was most beautifully compensated for by the economy and grace of his movements. Contemporaries who met him during his university years found themselves confronted by a short, stocky, yet seemingly slight young man who looked out at them shyly from deep-set and light blue eyes lodged under their thatch of thick fair hair. He walked with rapid, springing steps, looking directly in front of him and never recognizing even intimate friends if he passed them on the street, a curious aberration which he claimed to share with his father. Yet at times there seemed a latent power in his movements, a hidden vigor less physical than mental which was brought into play at will: like an eagle at rest unfolding its wings and revealing the hidden propensity for flight.

From this incipient aversion to his physical appearance, it was only a step to distrust of his mental attitudes. The suspicion that he was somehow perversely different from others, cast in an awkward mold, seems to have come upon him early. And he reacted, not by bending all his efforts to overcome the handicap, if indeed it was a handicap, but by emphasizing it, by adopting a deliberate eccentricity of behavior: walking his bicycle downhill and riding it up; jumping fully clothed into the river in the depths of winter; and in his undergraduate days walking about the quadrangle at night while others slept; and then lying in a bath of hot water until dawn. It was as though he had determined to increase the imagined gulf between himself and others instead of lessening it by these considered attempts to justify it.

The broken leg was the first of many smashed bones his patient body had to endure. It did not stop him, when healed, from going on ever longer and more arduous explorations. When England and Wales had yielded up to him their archaeological and architectural treasures, France knew him next as a dusty vision, reddened by sun and exertion, racing wildly through Normandy and Brittany; a mad cycling streak which ruffled the geraniums in the window boxes and made the villagers cross themselves for fear or relief at his passing. As he had sought out and studied every twelfth-century castle in England and Wales, so now he sought out those of France, spurred on by his devotion to Richard Coeur-de-Lion. Armed with Violett-le-Duc's *Dictionnaire Raisonné* he recreated for himself Richard's massive sieges and for the three summers of 1906, 1907, and 1908, cycled strenuously along the French roads and byways, once in the company of his friend and schoolfellow, "Scroggs" (C. F. C. Beeson, who was to go in for forestry), sometimes with his father, but more often alone. In August of 1906 he and Beeson met at Saint-Malo, each furnished with a waterproof cape, an American cloth-covered basket on the rear of their bicycles to hold their sparse belongings (those of Ned including a silk shirt made by his mother for lightness and compactness), and a spare pair of boots slung over the handle bars. Over the Côtes du Nord and Finisterre they raced in search of cathedrals and obscure fragments of fortifications: Léhon, Montafilant, Tonquedec, names that breathed history and a romantic flavor. "Lawrence's main preoccupation was with the minds of the designers of these defensive works and the extent to which history had tested their intentions," wrote C. F. C. Beeson afterwards.[8] He was to amaze his friend "Scroggs" on this journey by climbing down thirty feet of crumbling wall after getting stuck in a tower. The collection of Lawrence's letters, edited by David Garnett and published in 1938, begin with this period of questing, as do the later-published *Home Letters of T. E. Lawrence and His Brothers.*

"My ride to Fougères was very pleasant: part of it lay through woods where it was deliciously cool; (it was the hottest day of the year, I never felt such heat before). There is great difficulty in getting a decent drink in France: milk is not obtainable anywhere and eau de Seltz only occasionally. The result is that one gets very thirsty and the only fruits are plums and pears, their apples are uneatable: I have not had a good one yet. I upset myself with too many plums on Wednes-

[8] *T. E. Lawrence by His Friends.*

day, effects visible today." [*Letters*, No. 4.] So he wrote his mother in that August of 1906, evoking an incredible image of a young man in Epicurean France concerned only with fruit and soda water.

A serious student of history now, he made expeditions to Rocroi, Crécy, and Agincourt, and occasionally stepped out of his medieval milieu in order to have a curious look at newer battlefields. At Malplaquet, Sedan, and Valmy, the field of Marlborough, he refought for himself and his own satisfaction the wars of later history as a variation from his usual occupation with castle sieges. To each of these youthful excursions he brought a definite problem to be solved—it might be determining how Coeur-de-Lion got his death wound at Chaluset-Chalus—or a point of view to be confirmed, and about every facet of his chosen subject he held very definite opinions not always in accord with the accepted authorities.

What was it he sought on castle walls in the hot sun where the wild rose and clematis tressed over the stone to cover already ancient wounds; while his feet carefully paced out the distance between broken machicolations? His mind certainly was busy reconstructing the battles of Edward, Black Prince, and Richard Plantagenet, but beyond them he saw a vision, half-history, half-fantasy, in which youths—mere boys sometimes—embraced great causes and disposed of national destinies with results that far outweighed their years. Harry of Monmouth at sixteen, camping with his army hard by Shrewsbury, was already at Agincourt a king and a seasoned soldier though still in his twenties; and the Black Prince at twenty-five had Crécy and Poitiers to his credit. But for all this enthusiasm for siege engines, armor, and hand weapons, there was in Edward Lawrence no real love of soldiering; he would never have made a good soldier. His envy of youthful conquerers, though sweet, was no more than his own longing after heroics which he sometimes admitted to himself shamefacedly and then put aside. Yet when he had put it aside, he found within himself still an obstinate spur to action which he could neither deny nor subdue.

"Young man, be careful what you want, for you will surely get it!" said Emerson with shrewd discernment of the truth that passion of desire breeds its own fulfillment. Lawrence was later to confess to Liddell Hart that as a boy he had dreamed of doing "great things," of combining the active and the contemplative life, but had learned it was impossible to achieve both. Yet there was an even more romantic, more fanciful side to Edward Lawrence's questing, an aspect wholly sympathetic with his favorite Morrisonian heroes: Walter searching for The Wood Beyond the World, Ralph setting out to discover The Well at the World's End. It was in the dedicated spirit of the Sangreal —the hope of the incalculable reward which is beyond all earthly prizes. And his hunger for the transcendental quest never quite deserted him.

Chateau Gaillard—Richard's "Saucy" Castle—Fougères in France, and Caerphilly in Wales were his favorite castles. "Here I am at my last Welsh Castle and I think, in most respects, my best," he wrote his mother from Caerphilly in 1907. [*Letters*, No. 6.] But military architecture did not absorb him to the exclusion of all else; beauty too claimed its tribute from him.

"Here I am at last about to spend a night at the Mont. The dream of years fulfilled," he wrote Sarah Lawrence later in 1907. [*Letters*, No. 8.] Mont Saint-Michel, named for the archangel who, Henry Adams assured, loved the heights: the phosphorescent water lapping at its foot; the muted starlight, and later, the rising moon which blanched garments, buildings, flowers, into a ghostly neutrality, crumbling a wall here, magnifying a spire there, silhouetted against a limpid silver sky—incredibly visible yet hardly real, above all deeply at peace.

And nature which "is but a name for an effect, whose cause is God": "Nature contains that spirit and power which we can witness but not weigh, inwardly conceive but not comprehend, love but not limit, imagine but neither define nor describe. Nature is incomprehensible, fleeting, and yet immortal, and a love for it and its impressions are both ineradicable." [*Letters*, No. 5.] Here is Edward Lawrence stating analytically what Cowper had defined allegorically, and here is a mind ripe, when the time should come, for the stark, inimitable beauty of the desert scene, so relentlessly cruel, but yet so memorably profound that the taste, sight, smell, and sound of it—the silence that splits the ear—never left his unconscious mind. But the guilelessness of the schoolboy is there too. "People here say that I am much thinner than Bob, but stronger and have a better accent. Still Bob's fatness is much better than my muscle in their eyes except for Mme. Chaigon who got a shock when she saw my 'biceps' while bathing. She thinks I am Hercules." [*Letters*, No. 5.] His energy, too, was a source of amazement to their French friends at Dinard: "*Deuxcent cinquante kilometres, Ah la-la, qui est merveilleux!*" [*Letters*, No. 8.] This is an indication of a happier relationship with the French than any he was able later to achieve.

At school, as afterward at university, Edward Lawrence's performance was not regarded as exceptional, though he was recognized as a first-class student who had paid his way with scholarships since the age of twelve. "It was not until the end of his time at school that it came to be recognized that he was remarkably unconventional when, for instance, he would work out a problem in algebra in a way that would not have occurred to a mathematician," said his youngest brother, Arnold Lawrence.[9] He matriculated in 1907 and though his place in the Senior Finals was high, when he sat for a history scholarship at St. John's College, he failed to get it. This should not be cause for surprise however. It is generally conceded that the standards at Oxford, like all other standards, have suffered in the decades since 1914, and what was then considered a sufficiently high criterion of excellence would probably now be beyond the scope of most present-day candidates for scholarships and exhibitions. A little later he sat for an exhibition at Jesus College and in this he was successful.

Edward Lawrence had lived out his boyhood in the shadow of the university, and now in October, 1907, he entered it as an undergraduate; but somewhere between school and his entering Jesus College came the interlude of his odd and mysterious service as a young private in the Royal Artillery about which so little is known. "In his

[9] *T. E. Lawrence by His Friends.*

teens he took a sudden turn for military experience at the urge of some private difficulty," was how, later, he persuaded Liddell Hart to explain it, but behind the tersity of phrase lay an adventure into the depths which lasted until his father bought him out. Where or for how long a period he served is not really known, but it seems most unlikely that this early military service lasted for the six or nine months that have been claimed. A more reasonable assumption is that it lasted only a few weeks—a short enough time for it to be covered up by an explainable absence, even to his brothers who seem to have been unaware of it. And in running away from home to satisfy this agonizing youthful urge, he remained the ever-dutiful son who sent his anxious parents a postcard telling them where he was so that their distress at his disappearance should not be aggravated by his silence.

A boy who runs away from a home as happy, seemingly, as the one on Polstead Road is driven by a strong motive, but over and above the motive is this sudden, sharp revelation of a boy provoked by personal crisis into a curious self-abnegation which moved him to act then in precisely the same manner that in later years, as a man, he would act in the face of a more severe crisis. Adolescence is always a difficult, impulsive state, inclined to moodiness, and to a boy no longer a child but on the verge of manhood, the realities, or what he perceives as realities in the erstwhile shadowed world of adult living, loom up before him terrifyingly. His parents, their relationship one with another, are often the most complex issue in all the excruciating tangle which confronts him. Edward Lawrence looked with this new and painful awareness of adolescence upon what had been and would again become the sanctuary of his home, and his world foundered. There is no real evidence that knowledge of his own and his brothers' illegitimacy came before the age of seventeen, and everything points to the coincidence of that discovery with his bolting into military service, however it may have come about.[10]

A sensitive boy would be easily hurt by the impugnment of that

---

[10] His statement to Mrs. Shaw in 1927 that he knew of his illegitimacy before the age of ten seems another instance of his covering a trail, and highly improbable.

which he had been brought up to honor and revere. The parents set a pattern of devotion which many a less fortunate husband and wife might envy, yet the fact remains, their union was irregular. The children of such a union are, frankly, deemed bastards, and sophisticated society smirks over the word. The effect on Edward Lawrence of this discovery was profound; it added to the romantic urge for heroic conduct—the dream of the Sangreal—the seed of ambition, the desire for honor and distinction: the redemption of the blood from its taint.

Then, too, the parents who were patterns of conjugal affection were patterns of respectability in clerical, scholarly Oxford, and that may also have hurt on a more superficial level and brought about his later revolt against respectability. However it was, momentarily he lost his balance, as he was to lose it again later on; and it was one of the earliest signs that there were in him, for all his Irish humor, his whimsicality, shadowed depths, and a violence of feeling ready to erupt in moments of severe stress. It was, too, his first encounter with a society where animalism and brutality hold full sway. Coming straight from his parents' sober, affectionate, and cultured home and the clean fellowship of his brothers, the shock of it on his mind and nerves must have been raw indeed.

Before 1914 the British Army, with no statutory conscription, was not the army of citizen-soldiers it has since become, but, in peacetime at any rate, was the backwash of society, the last refuge of social misfits and ne'er-do-wells who could be safely hidden away, kept under strict surveillance and bullied into some semblance of respect for order and discipline which their betters acquired in public schools. The old barbarity to be sure was gone, but the rough and tumble remained, and Friday and Saturday nights were not uncommonly given up to whoring and drunken brawls the account of which would be presented and paid in full with Monday's charge sheets. The Royal Air Force and even the Royal Armoured Corps barracks at Bovington, when he entered them later, were for all their harshness mild by comparison.

The crisis passed, leaving its invisible scars; Ned took up the threads of his family life where they had become snarled. He came back to his home unobtrusively, as though he had only been absent on a more than usually long bicycle tour. Outwardly there was no change except, perhaps, the switchover from mathematics to history and the building of his garden house. The building of the garden house has been peculiarly exaggerated into a sign of friction between Lawrence and his parents, but there is no evidence of such friction. His letters written to them afterward are the letters of an affectionate son anxious for and integrated with his family. He returned from the Royal Artillery a boy shocked and hurt, and the privacy of the garden house was a welcome one, but there is no reason to doubt his own and his mother's word that it was built to insure him uninterrupted quiet for reading and study. But neither is there reason to doubt that this was a turning point in his life, the warp in the fabric of being: the idyl of childhood was shattered.

It is not easy to visualize the Oxford of pre-1914; it is too close to the present, not sufficiently worked on by the transmuting action of time with its cumulative accretions, its rubbing away of trivialities. But it is reasonable to claim that it was a quieter, less populous Oxford. Motor transport had not yet encroached upon it. The first encroachment, the first influx of industry upon its borders, occurred in 1912 when Morris Motors built their first works at Cowley. Around the university, the medieval atmosphere of infinite calm and unhurried scholarship lingered in a last twilit glow; the college staircases were not crowded with students doubled up and quadrupled as they were later to be, and, except perhaps during Eights Week, there was no jostling on the streets. This is not to say that things were better then than they are now, for Oxford preserves its own singular charm in spite of encroachments and crowding, but it does emphasize the violent revolution that took place between 1914 and 1920—the beginning of the interwar period and of our own particular era in which the past was swept away and the new mechanical and scientific age entered upon for better or worse.

Traditions at the senior universities are slow to change. There were at Oxford then as now certain forms, some perfunctory, some *de rigueur*, with which undergraduates were expected to comply. Edward Lawrence complied with none of them. He took no part in the life of his college, living at home under a special dispensation by which his mother undertook to see that he was under the parental roof by midnight—a restriction which did not prevent him from going out again after midnight, if he was so inclined. He had rooms in Jesus College, since the rule required that an undergraduate must be in residence for part of his university career, but he was hardly ever to be found in them. Except for the odd assortment of books neatly stacked on his table, they showed little or no signs of his presence. And the one weekly meal which statute demanded be partaken in the college hall, he sat throughout, benignly charading, passing plates and dishes around amiably, but eating nothing at all himself. One wonders what the High Table thought of his eccentric behavior if they noticed it. To the athletic "mandarins" who according to custom called on him early, he was a source of exasperation and puzzlement. Here was a strong, healthy, vigorous young man who ought to have rowed, bowled, or batted, or defended a goal post, or hit balls over a net with distinction, but who would do none of these things. Less to prove his athletic competence than to amuse himself, he became a proficient roof-climber, though usually these aerial escapades had an ulterior motive—photography or the close examination of a piece of otherwise inaccessible carving.

And he popularized until they were banned by the authorities the subterranean expeditions along the ancient Trill Mill stream from The Friars to Folly Bridge. The voyagers sailed with a candle in the bows of their canoe, an acetylene lamp on the stern—to test which would be extinguished first in the foul air—and a pistol to awaken the echoes under St. Aldate's Church. And it is clear the captain of these daring but frivolous adventures derived more than half his pleasure from teasing his companions as they steered themselves by hands through the sewer lying prone in their canoe. What if this confounded stream of his did *not* come out into the open? In the darkness his wicked smile and the reply: "At any rate, there is no room to turn back!"

While at university, Edward Lawrence ventured upon another of those curious military exercises which he later described as negligible, by joining the Oxford Officers Training Corps, to the disapproval of intellectuals who felt that it showed a lack of that singleness of mind which makes for the real scholar, and betrayed his regrettable love of antics. The Oxford O.T.C. learned to march, to drill in squads, to mark up creditable scores on the rifle range, and in summer camp at Tidworth Pennings, to deploy and maneuver and dress their tents in a neat row. Meanwhile Edward Lawrence, who presumably had learned to do some of these things during his period in the Royal Artillery, had embarked upon his own course of training for what was to come.

Here is an impression of him at this time contributed by a friend:

> He came into my rooms in College . . . and began to fire a revolver, blank cartridge fortunately, out of the windows into the Turl. I was left in doubt whether he was play-acting; but one glance at his eyes left no doubt at all that he told the truth when he said that he had been working for 45 hours at a stretch without food to test his powers of endurance.[11]

Those eyes blazing with exhaustion might be terrible to behold, but he had tested his will and hardened it. Occasionally he would stretch out his fast periods for three days to see how long he could go without food and still remain master of his physical and mental faculties; and invariably he fasted at Christmas to show his disapproval of the more vulgar custom of feasting. There was an even more stringent protest implicit in this insistence on fasting on the Feast of the Incarnation. To be carnate was to him not a privilege; rather it was the result of some awful autochthonous catastrophe in which the spirit and the flesh became inextricably and damnably confused. Birth for him was inseparable from a sense of shame, and it may well have been this shame which made him determined not to pander to the cravings of the flesh for food or rest or comfort.

This was his own peculiar sense of original sin with which his brother Arnold Lawrence felt he was endowed, and which, conjoined to his later conviction of culpability in the misuse of power, was to undo him. But this is to look too far ahead. These were only occa-

[11] E. F. Hall in *T. E. Lawrence by His Friends.*

sional and mild forms of the malady that was to attack him, not at this time too frequent nor too severe. There was far too much to be discovered, too much to be absorbed, to allow introspection to cloud his vision for long; and there was his carefully nurtured and concealed ambition fostered by reading, unfolding, and developing in the hot sun while he paced out the length of a castle wall: his secret and heroic dream of power and self-fulfillment.

If the medieval was the dominant influence in Edward Lawrence's early life, William Morris with his contrived forms of the medieval, and Charles Doughty with his biblical rhythms and Nordic syntax, lent an accompanying stimulation to the influence. William Morris had strived to superimpose the fourteenth century upon the nineteenth, swept away by an enthusiasm which envisaged a return to simplicity—that was not simple at all but complex; to the homely, useful art-crafts and household skills now fallen into decline, and a fervent dedication to the rights of man as embodied in Socialist principles with their promise to redress the evils wrought by the Industrial Revolution upon the defenseless poor. Edward Lawrence was not interested in socialism. In young manhood he fell in naturally with his father's Tory sympathies, while maturity found him distrusting all politics and political creeds, for he saw through their unavoidable frauds. But William Morris's pseudo-medievalism with its emphasis on individual craftsmanship, as opposed to the mass-produced horrors which were beginning to flood the civilized world, made a direct appeal to him. He was never really taken in by it, but it illumined his own dream of a life apart from accepted forms, in a house which was to be medieval in spirit and Roman in comfort with heated floors and an abundance of hot baths.

Doughty was a different matter. Edward Lawrence had read the *Travels in Arabia Deserta* many times by now, and there is no doubt that, in spite of its harsh judgments on the Arabs, it had stirred in him a desire to know and to live with the Bedouin, had planted the seed which was to quicken, once he saw the Levant for himself, and set the standard for his own book about his life with the Arabs when he came to write it. Then as later he read widely and read much poetry. Especially he was moved by the mystical poetry of Christina Rossetti. Vyvyan Richards, his vigorous-minded friend, son of an American mother from whom he had inherited the adventure, the boldness of spirit, the uninhibited enthusiasm of the New World, has related how Lawrence pressed him insistently to read her "Martyr" poem which includes the lines:

> Now I am tired, too tired to strive or smile;
> I sit alone, my mouth is in the dust:
> Look Thou upon me, Lord, for I am vile.

"But I have read it three times already and it leaves me cold," Richards protested. "Oh, read it a dozen, fifteen times and then see," Lawrence urged.[12] His letters of this period were sprinkled with Greek quotations and with lines of poetry which adorned them as pendants and bracelets adorn a statue. Books indeed were the substance on which his spirit was nourished, and reading was a passion he could share with his mother.

"You know, I think, the joy of getting into a strange country in a book," he wrote her in his last summer of exploring France in 1910. "At home when I have shut my door and the town is in bed—and I know that nothing, not even the dawn, can disturb me in my curtains: only the slow crumbling of the coals in the fire: they get so red and throw such a splendid glimmering on the Hypnos [13] and the brasswork . . . why does one not like things if there are other people about? Why cannot one make one's books live except in the night after hours of straining, and you know they have to be your own books and you have to read them more than once." And he adds: "Father won't know all this." [*Letters*, No. 21.] Father was not a man of books and therefore could not know.

Friendship with Edward Lawrence was a new and exciting experience for those who came upon him at Oxford, though few of them recognized his genius. When he made such extraordinary remarks as: Civilization came to an end in 1500 A.D. with the invention of gun-

---

[12] Vyvyan Richards, *Portrait of T. E. Lawrence* (London, Jonathan Cape, 1936).

[13] A bronze statuette of Sleep he had picked up in Italy.

powder and cheap printing, they were dazzled, and they were easily lured into cooperation with his favorite scheme to set up a hand-printing press in a disused windmill or an abandoned lighthouse. With Vyvyan Richards he planned a Morrisonian hall which they were both to build and inhabit at Pole Hill in Epping Forest where William Morris had played at knights in his childhood. Many were the hours they both spent with blowtorches and pitch fashioning utilitarian ornaments of beaten copper, and in doing wood-carving and burnt poker work. In this phase of his creativeness he copied in brass the lantern from Hunt's "The Light of the World" and fitted it with electricity, and throughout his life he liked to use his hands to make things, having, said Arnold Lawrence, the craftsman's appreciation of sound workmanship irrespective of aesthetic appeal.

With Vyvyan Richards, Lawrence seems to have been quite at his ease. It was not so with all his friends. Friendship to be complete and mutually fruitful demands an intimacy of thought, a comparing of experiences, a revealing of self to others; and the difficulty always is to be able to call a halt to confession when it is undesirable to lift the veil any higher. To side-step this dilemma Edward Lawrence developed a teasing and tantalizing, almost feminine, technique of confusing his friends by alternately exposing and withdrawing himself and by revealing wholly different facets of personality to different friends. This is largely responsible for the confused impressions his friends often gained of him. "People can't put me into three words because I am various and have no single characteristic," he told Robert Graves. That this should be so was partly his own doing. If friends tried to know him more intimately, he slipped out of their grasp and fled. And if they turned reluctantly but resignedly away, giving him up as a bad job, he was back again, apologetic and most ingratiating, as perhaps only the Irish can be. Yet to be with him seemed a privilege, and C. F. C. Beeson many years after recalled with pleasure his last complete day of comradeship with his friend during the Christmas of 1908.

They had set out across an Oxford unfamiliar in its shroud of snow to the top of Cumnor Hurst west of the city. Blowing snow, deep drifts, ice-covered streams, a camouflaged landscape, were a challenge Edward Lawrence could not resist. At his instigation the return walk was made across country on a compass bearing which, but for the intervention of Folly Bridge, would have precipitated them straight into the River Thames.

"I was all boldness—as who was not in after years, English or Arab with Lawrence in reserve," wrote Vyvyan Richards, describing how they journeyed together into the Cotswolds to look for the William Morris house at Broad Campden. And the seemingly shy young man who inspired such confidence would step forth smiling, ready to disarm any possible antagonist, with force if necessary, but by a subtle skill and the matching of wits if he had his choice.

By now the four older Lawrence boys had grown into an exemplary and charming group of young men with a younger brother in their midst to guide and cherish. Bob, dignified and comely like his father and imbued with a high sense of spiritual values, was at St. John's College pursuing a medical degree. Will, the beauty of whose regular features was redeemed from the awe of classical perfection by the sweetness and firmness of their mold, went up to St. John's in 1909 and later on taught history at St. Stephen's College, New Delhi. And Frank who, said his brother Ned, "with us stands for law, order, and the British Constitution" [*Letters*, No. 57], followed Ned into Jesus College in 1913 as a mathematics Exhibitioner in preparation for a career as an army engineer. "But for him the society would have taken fire long ago, or wings," wrote Ned in 1912.

They lived together in a most amicable and loyal fellowship, but by now there was an obvious sympathy, an obvious pairing off among them: Ned with Will who shared his taste for history and literature; Bob with Frank to whom he was linked by mutual understanding and a common missionary zeal. There was an atmosphere of abstemiousness as well as piety in the home in which they had grown to manhood, with its devotion to temperate habits—none of the boys as young men smoked or drank, and to gamble or indulge in other frivolous pursuits would never have occurred to any of them. Ned taking a mouthful of brandy by mistake spat it out; Frank as a young subaltern took the beer his men had obtained illegally, paid them for it, and poured it out on the ground. Yet they should not be thought of as crankily pious, indulging in a deplorable, humorless, straight-laced denial to others of what they themselves did not crave, which practice so discredits abstemiousness and robs it of all virtue.

In the summer of 1908, Ned was off to France again, and this time he penetrated deep into Provence, riding down the Rhone Valley toward the Mediterranean coast while subsisting exclusively on bread, milk, and fruit. In late July he came to Arles and for the first time felt all the lure of a southern land. The narrow streets were shaded by flat-roofed, pastel-tinted houses with their closely shuttered windows; the air throbbed and scintillated in the intense light and deep shadow of a subtropical sun; and walls were garlanded by thick veils of wisteria and bougainvillaea which trailed over their pink and white surfaces. Attendants were sweeping the amphitheater clean in readiness for Sunday's bullfight, but he passed it over with scarcely a glance and went quickly on to his goal: the lovely Romanesque cloisters of St. Trophime.

"*The* thing in Arles is the cloister of St. Trophimus: it is absolutely unimaginably fine with its sculptures and its proportion: all other architecture is very nearly dirt beside this Provençal Romanesque, when the scale is small (Provence has never done anything big in anything at all)." [*Letters*, No. 10.]

From Arles he rode to Les Baux: "A queer little ruined and dying town upon an 'olive-sandaled' mountain." Here on the hillside, where the only other sign of life was an eagle on a hill opposite, he saw suddenly off in the distance, glittering in the heat-haze, a sapphire shell of light. With an exultation such as he had never before experienced, he recognized it: the Mediterranean Sea gleaming through a break in the haze, laden with the odors, the spices, the tumultuous eventualities of the East, whose crystal waves lapped up to the shores of Greece, bathed the rocks of Cyprus, shimmered and broke upon the sand bars on the Syrian coast in the sight of which the Frankish knights, armed *cap-à-pie*, had ridden under the scorching sun roasting in their armor. Smyrna, Constantinople, Alexandria, Tyre and Sidon, Beirut and Damascus—these were names to conjure with, to dream upon. He looked; he saw its gleam, felt its ancient lure settle upon him and knew he would never be at rest again until he had crossed its blue expanse and beheld its antique glories.

At Aigues-Mortes, where St. Louis embarked on his Crusade, Edward Lawrence explored the fortifications of Philip the Bold. An air of damp decay and pestilence—like that which had once brooded over the water of the Étang de la Ville close by—seemed to haunt the dead streets and the canals that joined Aigues-Mortes umbilically with the sea. By night, beyond the margin of the town, the noctifluorescent marsh lights flickered until the dawn fog, rolling in from the coast, obscured them. And by night the chirping of crickets and the song of the thousands of frogs in the canals replaced the rasping daytime chorus of the cicadas and kept light sleepers awake wrapping towels around their heads to discourage the mosquitoes, alert to the invisible but audible scurrying of cockroaches on the floor below. At Aigues-Mortes, Edward Lawrence was badly bitten by mosquitoes that doubtless relished his fresh northern blood, and the result was an attack of malaria from which he was to suffer intermittently ever after. But there were compensations.

"I bathed today in the sea, the great sea, the greatest in the world; you can imagine my feelings," he wrote his mother from Aigues-Mortes. [*Letters*, No. 10.] Being nocturnal by inclination, he roamed about the town at night, after ten—the best part of the day he told his friend "Scroggs," adding in parenthetical humor: "my father is Irish you know, so I'm allowed these little things." [*Letters*, No. 12.] From Aigues-Mortes he rode to Nîmes, to Agde, Béziers, Narbonne, Carcassonne, and on to Cordes where time seemed to have stood still.

The castles of England, Wales, and now France were exhausted. There remained the Crusaders' castles of the East. He had already made up his mind that military architecture should be the theme of his graduating thesis, if he produced one, and through Doughty's *Arabia Deserta* he had come to know and to long for contact with the

Arab lands. (Already he was showing an interest in and knowledge of Turkish politics.) At the instigation of his patron, D. G. Hogarth, he wrote Charles Doughty of his intention to visit Syria and Palestine on foot, and the old man replied discouragingly:

> I have not been further north in Syria than latitude 34. In July and August the heat is very severe, and day and night even at the altitude of Damascus it is a land of squalor where a European can find evil refreshment. Long daily marches on foot a prudent man who knows the country would consider out of the question.

This was in 1909, when handbooks of Syria and Palestine were filled with cautions about the selection of dragomans and camels, the necessity of obtaining proper permits, and the advisability of European gentlemen wishing to travel in the Levant arming themselves with a good pistol from which on no account were they to be parted day or night. Edward Lawrence was not prudent; in spite of Mr. Doughty's gloomy picture and Professor Hogarth's misgivings, he went to Syria on foot in the heat of the summer, having first taken a few lessons in coloquial Arabic from the Reverend N. Odeh, a Syrian clergyman then residing in Oxford. He did, however, carry a Mauser pistol in addition to his camera, tripod, some spare socks, a clean shirt, and an extra pair of boots. No European gentleman could have traveled lighter.

He sailed from England in June, 1909, in a P. & O. steamer and, arriving at Beirut, went almost immediately by foot to Sidon (Saida), glory of the Phoenicians on the Lebanese coast, a distance of about thirty miles winding through mulberry plantations and olive groves. Now he made his first acquaintance with Arab food: *leben*, the Syrian yoghurt; *burghul*, boiled wheat; bread, "as thin as ordinary brown paper, tough and pliable, almost leathery when fresh"; *haleeb* (warmed fresh milk with sugar); prickly pears. ". . . by the way this diet is only my lunacy, and the native habit: no other European would think of it," he told his mother. [*Letters*, No. 13.] Sometimes he was able to get figs or grapes or watermelons, but if not, bread moistened with water from a spring or from his water bottle was his midday meal. The evening meal served in a Syrian village house on a large straw dish was only a little more lavish. Bedtime was at nine o'clock and the Arab families with whom he stayed were up again at sunrise—about four-thirty—which fitted in with his own plans to be up and well on the road before the worst heat. Dressing, he said, consisted of smoothing one's hair and moistening the hands and face with water from a spouted pitcher; a simple toilet.

From Syria he went southward into Palestine, to Baniyas (Caesarea Philippi), Safad, Capernaum, Lake Hula, Gennesaret, Tiberias, walking through fields of thistles; from thence he journeyed to Nazareth, the Plain of Esdraelon (or Jezreel), Mount Carmel, Athlit (Atlit), Haifa, Acre, Tyre, Sidon again, and back to Beirut. For a Bible student it was a peculiar pleasure to be journeying in the world of the New Testament to places so hallowed by a presence whose name has drawn worship. And for those who think of Lawrence as a confirmed and stubborn Arabist, it is worth while recalling his earliest reactions to Palestine:

> . . . it is such a comfort to *know* that the country was not a bit like this in the time of Our Lord. The Renaissance painters were right who drew him and his disciples feasting in a pillard hall, or sunning themselves on marble staircases: everywhere one finds remains of splendid Roman roads and houses and public buildings, and Galilee was the most Romanized province of Palestine. Also the country was well-peopled and well-watered artificially . . . Palestine was a decent country then, and could so easily be made so again. The sooner the Jews farm it all the better: their colonies are bright spots in a desert. [*Letters*, No. 13.]

Later he was to recall: "What was lovely about Galilee, in Palestine, was that green grass grew in Gennesaret right into the very (sweet) water." [*Letters*, No. 315.]

Next he tramped northward to Tripoli and Latakia, crossing and recrossing the hills between the coast and Antioch. From Antioch he went east to Aleppo, northeast to Urfa and Haran, and then south again down to Damascus. In all he visited fifty castles in four months, the steep walls of some of which he scaled bare-footed for a surer grip on the stones, and took a series of photographs, which are a fine achievement by any modern photographic standards, to illustrate the thesis that was the result of all this journeying. Margab where the women of Latakia still climbed the rocky slope to fill their water jars from the old cistern built by the Crusaders; the proud Crac de Chevaliers; Sahjun, the beautiful ruin—all knew his searching hands and feet, his inquiring and analytical mind.

Once in a lonely place he was set upon by a Turkoman who beat him badly, stole his watch, his money, the Mauser pistol which the thief was fortunately unable to fire, and a collection of Hittite seals he had just acquired. As a grim memento of this encounter, the map belonging to H. Pirie-Gordon which he had borrowed for the journey was returned spattered with his blood. The watch, a copper-cased one and therefore of less value than his assailant thought, and the other articles were eventually recovered. Only his camera stolen from a carriage in Mesopotamia was left behind. Hospitality he sought with missionaries, or in the villages through which he passed, living on Arab food and becoming, he said, "Arab in habits." Except for Palestine he did not find it so much a land of squalor, though squalor there undoubtedly was, and although he was plagued with fleas and sudden bouts of fever, he survived, having tramped eleven hundred miles [14] in all, averaging twenty miles a day.

He was late in returning. The chrysanthemums in the garden at Polstead Road bloomed; the ash trees drooped under their weight of new berries. Already there was a dryness, a hint of dissolution in the air, and the sun making little arabesques out of drying twigs seemed indifferent to the autumn opulence: the harvest was already gathered. Michaelmas term at Oxford commenced but there was still no sign of Edward Lawrence. He wrote from Aleppo to the principal of Jesus College, Sir John Rhys, explaining his delay:

> I have had a most delightful tour (the details naturally won't interest you) on foot and alone all the time, so that I have perhaps, living as an Arab with the Arabs, got a better insight into the daily life of the people than those who travel with caravan and dragomen . . . My excuse for outstaying my leave must be that I have had the delay of four attacks of

[14] M. R. Lawrence, ed., *The Home Letters of T. E. Lawrence and His Brothers* (New York, Macmillan, 1954), p. 108.

> malaria when I had only reckoned on two; even now I am exceedingly sorry to leave the two Castles in the Moabite deserts unvisited. I would go to them certainly, only that last week I was robbed and rather smashed up. [*Letters*, No. 17.]

Then all at once he was back, nearly as empty-handed as he had set out. But he had secured what was for him conclusive proof of his theory: that the art of castle-building, far from being an importation from the East via the Crusaders, was taken by them to the East and there transplanted in the Holy Lands. And he had brought back with him some jars of crushed murex used in the making of Tyrian purple, to stain the vellum of the books he intended to print.

He was sunburned, worn thin by privation, but finely tempered as steel, and behind his pale and flashing eyes the inner enigma had deepened.

2

THE GARDEN OF PARADISE

The winter of 1910–11 in the Levant was the severest within memory of seventy-five years. Snow covered the peaks of the Lebanon with deep drifts, and there was no certain passage through them. Traffic on the narrow-gauge railway from Beirut to Aleppo was suspended, and there seemed no possibility of traveling from Jebeil (ancient Byblos) in Lebanon to Jerablus on the Euphrates littoral. Nevertheless, Edward Lawrence was determined to go—on foot if necessary.

He had spent nearly two months, from Christmas Eve to mid-February, at the American Protestant mission school in Jebeil being coached in Arabic by a most gentle Arab Christian woman, Fareedah al Akle. "I am on a divan (anglice—an American bentwood chair) inhaling Haschich (a tannery next door but five) and dreaming of odalisques (who were upper housemaids) and bulbuls," he wrote to a friend in January. [*Letters*, No. 26.] The voyage out to Syria on a Messagerie Maritime steamer, which stopped for a week in Constantinople for engine repairs, was a fruitful one, enabling him to admire the Golden Horn, to explore St. Sophia and the marvels of Suleiman the Magnificent, all at his leisure.

At the Jebeil mission he beguiled the ladies, Miss al Akle, Miss Holmes, and Mrs. Rieder, with his gentleness and good manners, his ability as handyman; and he passed the time there with his Arabic and Assyrian studies, with letter-writing and an attempt, unsuccessful, to "bag" the tail of a jackal for Arnie his youngest brother. Hogarth was expected in February, and on February 18 Edward Lawrence was in Beirut impatiently awaiting his arrival. By February 22 Hogarth, Lawrence, and Gregori, the Cypriote foreman of the Carchemish digs, were assembled in Beirut.

Another severe snowstorm had buried the line between Beirut and Aleppo and put it out of action again. They would have walked over the mountains but that Gregori's sixty years forbade such an exercise, and so the three of them took ship to Haifa, where they went up Mount Carmel to visit the monastery and then boarded a train for Damascus. Traveling by way of Nazareth and the Yarmuk Valley, they touched the great *Darb al-Hajj*—the Pilgrims' Way—and looked out upon the Hills of Moab still wreathed in their winter snow. At Der'a, the rail junction which was to play so fateful a part in Lawrence's life, the sun was warm and benign, belying the severity of the waning winter. Nothing in the calm sunlit scene, mercifully, foretold of the morbid horror to come. He entered and passed through it with no premonition of the havoc that was to be wreaked on him there.

From Damascus the three travelers came circuitously to Aleppo and, from thence, joined now by R. Campbell Thompson, Hogarth's deputy, and a retinue of baggage horses and camels, to Jerablus, to Carchemish, fortress city of the Khatti empire which for three years was to be the scene of Edward Lawrence's greatest happiness, the vision of his dearest dream.

Lawrence had read for the History Schools at Oxford, taking a First with Honours, though much of his actual reading had been in the field of Provençal poetry and the *Chansons des Gestes* rather than the prescribed books which he had read long since in any case. He had thought to continue reading for a higher degree on medieval pottery, but D. G. Hogarth, who had kept a close watch on him ever since his Oxford City schooldays when he arranged some of the pottery cases in the Ashmolean Museum, persuaded him to abandon the idea.

Men follow the path of their choice largely because it is their choice, because they are impelled along it by their desire, and it is desire which sets into motion the chain of fortuitous events that help to bring about its realization. The Greek civilization would probably have attracted Edward Lawrence if his sympathies had not already been elsewhere engaged. On the way out to the Levant in December, 1910, he passed through Greece and wrote back his subdued but clearly devoted impressions of the Parthenon, ending with the remarks:

> There will never be a great book on Athens unless it is one by an enemy: no one who knew it could resist its spell except by a violent attack upon its spirit, and who can attack it now of artists, when Tolstoy is dead? He, and he alone, could have uprooted Greek culture from the world. [*Letters*, No. 23.]

The Crusades interested him, and in 1911 he was projecting what he was pleased to call a "monumental" book on the subject. Crusaders' castles he had already dealt with in his Oxford thesis; it was Crusader strategy and its impact upon history, military and political, which he now proposed to propound, and some idea of his thought on this may be drawn from the letter written in January from Jebeil to his friend L. H. Green who for a time was another interested party to the book-printing project. His summary there of the problems posed by uncertain allies and difficult terrain—problems common to the Crusades and the Arab Campaign—is concise and authoritative:

> The whole history of the Crusades was a struggle for the possession of these castles (the defensive points of the Damascus and Homs gaps); the Arabs were never dispossessed of Aleppo, or of Hamah, or of Homs, or of Damascus, and so they had all possible routes open to them; they had unlimited resources to draw upon, as soon as the Mesopotamians had recovered Urfa (Edessa), which the Crusaders could not hold on account of its restricted position (Euphrates 10 feet deep, 150 yards wide, very rapid, and often flooded, much difficult hill thence to Seruj, and even

nearer Edessa) and the shiftiness of the Greek Armenian population, who were allies, at times, but fighting men not at all: more harm than good usually. [*Letters*, No. 26.]

As for the Crusaders themselves, they made little or no appeal to him, though for the descendants of those who stayed behind in the Holy Lands and whose mentality and way of life was metamorphosed by the land and people they had come to conquer, he felt a certain affinity. But it was essentially the Arabs, more particularly the Bedouin with their backward glancing to a vanished age of chivalry, who awakened a deep responsive impulse in him. It is not possible wholly to account for this sympathy—which was not an objective, inquiring sympathy but an upsurge of feeling so strong as to demand his complete identification with it. There was his devotion to a medieval past and his wistful envy of the uncomplex, uncompromising way of life which climate and poverty imposed upon the Arabs, and these were strong elements in his sympathy; but behind them was his own peculiar bias to austerity, and his effervescent romanticism which was its complement.

"You guessed right that the Arab appealed to my imagination. It is the old, old civilization which has refined itself clear of household gods, and half the trappings which ours hastens to assume," he was to write in 1918. [*Letters*, No. 103.] Yet there remains the inexplicable element ever present in any strong appeal of a particular place and people: a hidden, mystical lure in the unconscious that urges and goads the active mind and body on toward its fulfillment in and through them. In this half-deliberate, half-fateful choice of Edward Lawrence, Hogarth was the instrument. Through his offices Lawrence was awarded a senior demyship at Magdalen College and one hundred pounds a year for four years in order to join the British Museum's expedition to dig up Carchemish on the Euphrates. And he came to Syria not as a stranger but as a "lord expected" into his natural home, his native land.

Jerablus, at the site of Carchemish, southern outpost of the Khatti empire, lies near the 37th parallel in northern Syria on the west bank of the fabled river which separates it from the country now known as Iraq, but which before World War I was more familiarly called by its Greek name, Mesopotamia—the land between two rivers. The excavation of Carchemish was begun as early as 1878 under the orientalist George Smith, but the lack of a satisfactory agreement with the Ottoman government prevented any serious work being done until after 1908 when Hogarth first prospected the site. By the time the work on the great mound was resumed in that March of 1911, the Syrian sun had gained in power though the days were cool as yet and the evenings chill; and in the beneficence of that sun Edward Lawrence basked like a cat and prepared to unfold all his faculties of mind and spirit in a climate which was both mentally and physically propitious.

"Today we are moving great stones," he wrote to his mother in April; "the remains of walls and houses are buried about two-thirds of their height in fairly clean earth, but the upper few feet are filled with rubble and small rocks, with the ashlar masonry and concrete of the late Roman town." [*Letters*, No. 27.] It went hard against the grain to destroy these Roman ruins which had so long withstood the onslaught of time and weather, and yet since what they sought lay beneath them, the remains of Roman "Europus" had to be sacrificed after being carefully recorded and photographed and its artifacts removed. It was a bright, level landscape in which the archaeologists worked—except for the great mound which rose a hundred feet steeply from the river; a rock-strewn plain tumbled with stones, scored by wind and sun which lapped up to them like an ocean tide, splashed over them and broke into ripples along their eroded surface. And through the plain ran the tawny river, one of the four streams of Paradise. With the Tigris and the Nile it had spawned the whole rich galaxy of civilizations which give the biblical East its special significance; and with the Tigris, flowing parallel to it, the Euphrates ran down to the Shatt al Arab and the Persian Gulf. In April its waters were still turbulent, augmented by the melted snows that drained off the Taurus Mountains. On the landward side the acropolis fell away into sand dunes with a thin copse of poplars lying at the right hand of a stony pathway; and beyond, a field of bamboo stalks flourished near a little meadow which was made fertile in the spring by an old mill stream that ran through it and emptied into the river. Across the river were visible the fields and orchards of the village of Zormara, poised against the delicate green and lavender hills of Mesopotamia: and above it all spread an eggshell sky plumed and fringed with cirrus clouds.

After midday in the spring, sudden gales blew up out of the north and whipped the dust into clouds and spinning funnels that choked and blinded as they approached, obliterating the river from view and halting the work on the mound. But by evening it was always calm again. Scarlet anemones grew in the cracks of old pavements; lizards ran along the crumbling walls and vanished behind gnarled olive trees and dusty oleanders. And the iguanas which lived in caves amid funereal urns slid over the rocky ground like miniature dragons. It was a place of legend where the triumph of warrior, the pomp of kings, the sweated labor of slaves, had procured a splendor seeming immortal, but doomed to be smited and leveled by Nebuchadnezzar into oblivion beneath the dust of centuries. Into this place of legend, into this demi-paradise of sun and water and fallen stones, Edward Lawrence had entered as into a promised heritage.

Hogarth and his deputy, R. Campbell Thompson, were the leaders of the British Museum's excavations, and to his young protégé Hogarth gave charge of the pottery work in which he had shown himself adept, the photography at which he was an expert, and the keeping of some of the archaeological records. For the rest, his mechanical skill soon turned him into "odd-job" man:

> My faculty of making and repairing things has recently demonstrated how to make paint (black and red for marking antiques), how to render light-tight a dark slide, how to make a camera-obscura, how to reworm a screw (difficult this without a die), how to refit a plane-table, and replace winding mechanism on a paraffin lamp. Also I have devised a derrick and a complicated system of human-power jacks (out of poplar poles, and rope and Arabs) which has succeeded in setting an Ishtar on her legs again. [*Letters*, No. 27.]

Later he was to learn how to use explosives for blasting a way into the more inaccessible sections of the mound—a knowledge which was later to prove useful. Above all, he made it his special duty to look after the Arab and Kurdish diggers, keeping them amused, while at the same time he studied their dialects and idiosyncrasies. After 1912 he and (Sir) C. Leonard Woolley, who replaced Campbell Thompson, were to settle blood feuds among the diggers, arrange marriages, arbitrate in family quarrels, dispense a rough-and-ready but effective justice—as when they locked two fractious leaders of a feud in the expedition house's dark room for two hours until heat and fleas had reduced them to the friendly level of fellows in misfortune—and behave generally like the bearded patriarchs they were not. For these many and varied duties Edward Lawrence was paid fifteen shillings a day during the digging season, which ran from March to June, paused through July and August for the harvesting of the barley and liquorice crops, and then continued from September to November before the winter floods brought the excavations to a standstill. It was an apprenticeship, a time of waiting and learning, of perfecting the instrument and technique which later were to be put to good account. And no more suitable ground than Carchemish, lavish in history and al fresco adventure, could have been found for the apprenticeship.

The expedition was served by two foremen, Gregori the Cypriote and the Sheik Hamoudi, a local man nearly always referred to in letters by his formal title, the *Hoja* (chief foreman) who for five years had been an outlaw hunted down by Turkish *gendarmerie*. The domestic needs of the archaeologists were cared for by Haj Wahid, an irascible, almost Rostandian, character with a love of fine clothes, *raki*, and the manly art of combat; he bristled with firearms even when he presided over his pots. When trying out a new dish, said Woolley, he would sling a rifle over his shoulder to give him confidence.[1] Most beguiling figure in the Carchemish scene was the young Sheik Ahmed, better known as Dahoum,[2] who commenced his service with the archae-

[1] *Dead Towns and Living Men* (New York, Oxford University Press, 1929).

[2] Meaning the Dark One, a quaint Arab sobriquet, for he was actually quite fair.

ologists as waterboy and worked himself up to the privileged position of houseboy and personal assistant to Edward Lawrence. And Ottoman law stipulated there should be present at the excavations at all times an Imperial Commissaire representing the interests of the Turkish government, and a few local *gendarmes* to act as guards. Ultimately the life of this polyglot English, Arab, Greek, Kurdish, and Turkish community was as rich in comic incidents as an *opéra bouffe*.

"I am the only one who gets any sleep at night," he wrote his mother in that March of 1911. "Mr. Hogarth is always getting up to chase cats, or rats or birds or mice or dogs; everything comes in and out of the window holes." [*Letters*, No. 27.] And again in May to Hogarth: "The Muktar carried off his cousin on his saddle-bow from amid the shrieking women at the spring last week." [*Letters*, No. 29.] One night when Lawrence and Campbell Thompson were sleeping they were awakened by a loud rustling as a huge white flapping apparition came in through a hole in the roof of the local liquorice magnate's house which they were occupying. Both archaeologists jumped out of bed and grabbed the same revolver which they were simultaneously trying to fire when they discovered that it was only a newspaper which they had pushed into the roof to keep out the nightly invasion of rodents and felines and feathered vertebrates. Eventually a large solidly built expedition house at Carchemish replaced the makeshift of borrowed house and tents and made the nights somewhat less adventurous.

A mile removed from the mound, it was not merely a reasonably habitable abode but almost luxurious by the normal standards of accommodations for archaeologists in the field. And as many of its amenities were due to the ingenuity and taste of the youngest member of the expedition, it is interesting to compare it with his later efforts to provide for his well-being in his own cottage at Clouds Hill.[3] Forbidden by the Turkish authorities on pain of prosecution to erect a building containing more than one room, the archaeologists confounded their antagonists by constructing a long, U-shaped structure and then inserting partitions afterward to provide themselves with a

[3] See Chapter VIII, pp. 284–285.

living room, a sitting room, three bedrooms equipped "with English beds, washstands and furniture," [4] storage rooms for pottery and the smaller sculptures, a dark room for developing photographs, and a bathroom, all in the teeth of Oriental bureaucracy and obstruction.

The house was approached through a courtyard where each week the archaeologists sat at a table to pay the diggers their wages from a carved Syrian chest—a cross, said Robert Graves later, between a circus and a lucky grab. Inside the house, the living room was hung with prayer rugs, furnished with bookshelves and flower vases, a table covered with a fine piece of Syrian embroidery, an alcove for statuary, and a hanging lamp over the table which was flanked by two black and white armchairs made in Aleppo to Edward Lawrence's design—the William Morris motif again. The adjoining sitting room where the archaeologists received visiting headmen, itinerant missionaries, and Turkish officials, was floored with a fifth-century Roman pavement which had been discovered nearby and retrieved by the archaeologists who painstakingly relaid it in the mud floor of their house to prevent any further deterioration from weather. The walls of the bathroom Edward Lawrence originally proposed to cover with Roman glass melted down by a blowtorch, but the project was unfulfilled and the bathroom seems to have remained the "bare cell with a round tin bath on the cement floor" which Will Lawrence found on his visit. Guests at Carchemish being served their after-dinner coffee in curiously shaped, black, dull-glazed handleless cups were startled to learn that they were already four thousand years old when retrieved from the great mound. Turkish coffee in Hittite cups was the sort of caprice Lawrence especially relished.

The days at Carchemish passed as in a dream, but it was a dream which was shaping itself gradually into a portentous reality; and the young *Franzi* archaeologist meanwhile was gaining in knowledge and honor.

> Today I cured a man of compound scorpion-bite by a few drops of ammonia [he wrote his mother]; for that I have a fame above Thompson's as a hakim: and as a majician who can conjure devils into water from my

[4] W. G. (Will) Lawrence in *T. E. Lawrence by His Friends.*

mixing a seidlitz-powder for the Haj in the kitchen before visitors. [*Letters*, No. 32.]

Gales and thunderstorms made adventurous the late spring days, but mostly during the digging seasons the weather was fine and not too hot, though the sun overhead at noon was a white incandescence. Each morning against a lapis-lazuli sky a flock of glossy ibis flew down the river to Jerablus, and each evening returned to their nesting place in the walls of the Birijik castle twenty miles upstream—a living link with the past, for their likeness was embodied in the mosaic design of the Roman pavement in the expedition house. In the late afternoon the warm wind shimmered through the poplars and then, blowing in stronger force just before sundown, it set the dust eddies whirling in a last capricious gale. A subdued and ruddy light then caught the landscape in its luminous net, so that it hung suspended over eternity: apocryphal and altogether fabulous, until darkness blotted it out at last.

Hogarth meanwhile came and went between England and Syria, keeping an eye on the progress of the work he had started but prevented by his other duties from remaining long at Carchemish. He was wise and kindly with a sharp, refreshing humor, able fully to appreciate the unusual qualities of his young protégé even though prone to storm with Olympian wrath when he found himself—as often happened—the victim of one of Lawrence's practical jokes. He was moderately tall, squarely built, with a short, neat Edwardian beard which made him appear genuinely patriarchal in contrast to his two young, clean-shaven assistants. He was Edward Lawrence's senior by twenty-six years and had already behind him a distinguished career of exploration in Asia Minor, Cyprus, Egypt, and Crete. Lawrence wrote of him years later: "D. G. Hogarth to whom I owe every good job (except the R.A.F.) I've ever had in my life." [5]

And, too, life at Carchemish was considerably enlivened by a constant coming and going of Turks and Arabs to and from the village of Jerablus, and later by skirmishes with the German engineers who

[5] *T. E. Lawrence to His Biographers.* Robert Graves (New York, Doubleday, Doran, 1938).

were engaged in building that part of the "Berlin to Baghdad" railway which passed through Jerablus and crossed the river into Mesopotamia. Edward Lawrence spent much of his time with the diggers, and with Hamoudi's help organized them into two rival groups to speed the labor of excavation: "pickmen pitted against basketmen, or the entire gang against the wagon boys, until with 200 men running and yelling, half a day's output would be accomplished in an hour; and Lawrence would lead the yells."[6] He also instituted the custom of firing a *feu de joie* with revolvers whenever a particularly good find was unearthed and on which it was certain that the finder would be rewarded with a special bonus. Surrounded by apocryphal lions, ritual bulls, sacred birds, and high priests in procession, there can be no doubt that Lawrence felt himself in his true element as he looked on at the diggers chanting in rhythm: "*Yallah! Issa!*" and straining on the ropes that hauled to light a great slab of carved basalt belonging to the Processional Wall.

At Carchemish he soon adopted a curious dress which became for him standard wear in the field: a soft finely woven shirt open to the waist, white shorts—rare before World War I—bound at the waist with a multicolored woven Kurdish belt, whose red tassels bunched over the left hip proclaimed emphatically, in accordance with local custom, his bachelorhood. "It was the belt, not the shorts which marked the young blood," he was to tell Robert Graves in 1927.[7] Brown boots nailed for durability, old O.T.C. puttees, and a Magdalen College blazer completed his dress. "Young man, we don't play cricket here," he was told by (Sir) Flinders Petrie in 1912 when he appeared in this garb at the great man's camp at Kafr Ammar near Cairo. But at night the boots and the puttees gave way to gray wool socks and red Arabic slippers; his thick, fine, fair hair, tousled by wind, and worn far too long was then most carefully groomed. And on winter evenings it was his habit to sit by the fire reading Homer or Doughty, wearing a white and gold embroidered Arab waistcoat over his shirt, and over that if it was really cold, a weighty (sixty pounds) Arab cloak woven of gold and silver thread. In such a garb, absorbed

[6] C. L. Woolley in *T. E. Lawrence by His Friends.*
[7] *T. E. Lawrence to His Biographers.*

in the *Arabia Deserta*, he seemed to Mrs. Fontana, the wife of the British Consul at Aleppo, a fitting subject for pen or brush, but she was never able successfully to portray him.

"You must not think of Ned as leading an uncivilized existence," wrote Will Lawrence to his mother after a visit to Carchemish in 1913.[8] "When I saw him last as the train left the station he was wearing white flannels, socks and red slippers, with a white Magdalen blazer, and was talking to the governor of Biridjik in a lordly fashion."

He was not as yet a fully qualified archaeologist, though he was learning to decipher bilingual inscriptions with fluency and skill; it is doubtful whether he ever desired to become one. Being tabbed, put into a pigeonhole of any kind, was distasteful to him, and he was ever dubious about assuming professional status. "I fought very hard, at Oxford and after going down, to avoid being labelled: but the insurance people have nailed me down, now," he was to write his friend Vyvyan Richards in 1913. [*Letters*, No. 65.] As for worldly success: "I fear Father is right about our careers," he wrote in May, 1911.[9] "But this idealistic disregard of the good things of the world has its bright side. And to say that he had five sons, none making any money would be a glorious boast." It was an attitude that remained with him. And yet there was for him an irresistible lure in this role of historian: for the historian holds in his hands the strands of human destiny, and is able to coordinate in his mind the impulses which prompt men to become heroes or clowns, saints or sycophants. And there was an added seduction in the functions of the archaeologist whose labors evolve for him a synthesis of human destiny. In one sweeping comprehension the archaeologist can encompass the cycles of growth and decay in ancient cultures until history is reduced for him to a single perspective that embraces all cultures. Old civilizations so touched by mind and hand alike become dynamic in the present, are perceived as surging tributaries emptying into the swollen river of human life—so brief in individual experience yet so infinite in promise. The archaeologist too is able to discern myth patterned on inexplicable event becoming sublimated into creature worship of a deity: stone shaped

[8] *The Home Letters*, p. 447.
[9] *Ibid.*, p. 160.

to typify a state of mind, to perpetuate an ideal of beauty, of courage, of fear or bestiality, and to perceive behind all, integrating all, the great imponderable of human existence which some call God.

There is a heady power in the thought of possessing so much, and at the same time a solemn curb. For the historian's vision of the future can be no greater than his survey of the past teaches him to believe is probable. He may dream, but ultimately he must deal with tangibles, must reckon with all the influences, social and economic, which bring about greatness or decline. And there is one formidable temptation which may assail him: the urge to take a hand in history himself, to be not content merely to piece together shattered civilizations, but to experience a compulsion to use this knowledge of men and the genesis of nations so to direct some part of the contemporary record that it will stir mightily under the impress of his own deeds. Fortunately, perhaps, not many historians feel such an urge. Edward Lawrence did; and this was his secret spur, the hidden craving nourished by book learning and an inner vision which, at some point in Oxford or in Syria, grafted itself to the Arab cause—since the Arabs were the only peoples left to be freed; the only peoples, that is, who appealed to him historically and emotionally.

"I had dreamed, at the City School in Oxford, of hustling into form, while I lived the new Asia which time was inexorably bringing upon us," he wrote at the conclusion of his war history. This was an audacious dream for a schoolboy; but the Arab was the pivot on which his dream was to turn slowly into reality, and Carchemish and the country adjacent to Carchemish in which he wandered, was the book where he read the lessons he had yet to learn. Foremost among them was an understanding, as the days passed, of the tenuous hold which the then-moribund Ottoman Empire kept on her Eastern sanjaks: the fragility of a ruling caste which any sudden crisis would shatter and set into motion the new ascendant fervor of nationalism.

The year 1911 was the year of King George V's Coronation and the archaeologists celebrated the event by releasing a great fire balloon over the river from Carchemish, inadvertently terrifying the entire population of Jerablus. The spring digging season came to an end, and before parting company Campbell Thompson and Lawrence went off to dig for a few days at Tell Ahmar, the Til Barsip of ancient times, prized river ford of the great Assyrian warrior-king, Shalmaneser II.

"I am off to Harran, Urfa, Biredjik, etc. from Tell Ahmar," Lawrence wrote to Hogarth his patron in June. [*Letters*, No. 34.] The ostensible purpose of this journey was to collect material for his history of the Crusades, which unfortunately never got itself written, and of this summer journey of 1911 he kept a diary record which was published in a limited edition after his death and later included in the miscellany, *Oriental Assembly*.

He started on July 12 from Tell Ahmar, about fifteen miles south of the village of Jerablus, and from the beginning it was an ill-starred journey. From Tell Ahmar he set out for Ras el Ain and then tramped across a dusty plain overgrown with wild liquorice shrubs, veering northeast toward Urfa, his destination. Already he had begun to feel feverish. By the time he arrived at Urfa an abscessed wisdom tooth was causing him much pain and discomfort, to get relief from which, on the fourth night, he drank quantities of iced rose-leaf sherbet—a truly exotic remedy for toothache! The added complication of blistered and festering feet followed a few days later, but still he went on, measuring and photographing ruined fortresses, traveling on compass bearings when the route was uncertain, and keeping up the terse daily record of his travels.

> Day very hot: drank five bottles of water between 6 and 2.30 . . . soles of feet very tired.

> Tooth much better; swelling going down: feet sore. Got off about 4.30 (A.M.) and passed over rough hills till 7.30. No water.

> Washed shirt ii and wrote this account. Biridjik about 1½ hours away. Ate my other halfpennyworth of bread: feet very sore, but otherwise very pleased with the day.

In archaeological analysis and occasionally in topographical description the account was more expansive; generally, however, brevity prevailed. Whenever he paused in his work of surveying and photography he was aware of the great silence that enveloped him: a stillness that he valued highly as an interruption in the everlasting onrush of living. Only it was not a total silence: the wind sang over the ruins and its cadences rose and fell against the rhythmic pulsing of his blood. Here were no distractions; it was possible for him to strip his soul naked and see how he had grown since the last time he had looked into himself. Fear and a certain arrogance were in him, both interdependent and growing out of the same root. The arrogance was partly the complement of his youthfulness, partly of his fear; and the fear was essentially fear of himself and his potentialities, when he stopped long enough to think about them. At Carchemish, with the workmen and with his adversaries, he tasted for the first time the heady wine of his power over other men, and it was undeniably a sweet taste. But fear had an obverse side. There was that personal and intimate denouement into which he had fallen before entering the university and from which only his natural resilience of spirit and the sympathy of his family had snatched him. At twenty-three the memory of it was not oppressive, and yet it was ever present; it would not be stifled; and within the framework of his ambition it was the prick that goaded him on to stir the waters of history by his own effort and so bring honor to his name. The diary, however, says nothing of these things.

When there seemed no wind at all over the Mesopotamian plain, the dust-devils still rose up in fantastic spirals, whirling across and away along the ground. The mirage vibrated tremulously, shattered into unrecognizable fragments and then reassembled again before his eyes. There were nights spent on rooftops with local headmen and their kinsmen, talking on into the early hours of many topics, especially government in England and marriage. And on one occasion, at Harran, he wrote: "the sheikh ended by going to sleep with his head on my knee!" So popular was he at Harran and so welcome his company that he was offered two wives of good quality by the sheik if only he would stay and make his home with them. (In the patriarchal East where a boy of twelve was deemed old enough to fight and a man of sixteen old enough to marry, his persistence in celibacy seemed surprising and perverse.) And there were nights spent in local khans being plagued by sand flies which swarmed over from the neighboring mulberry trees, and being kept awake by the wail of Arab music drifting up from nearby cafés.

Jacob's Well was passed, and then on to Birijik on July 21, where briefly he joined up with some of the men from the Carchemish dig. Two days later he was off northward again to Rum Kala'at, through an orchard valley and a village of picture-postcard prettiness. Here he enjoyed a passage of arms with the muktar who demanded of him a permit which he refused to produce. "He threatened to imprison me, and I turned and twisted him into knots," is the laconic diary entry, which ends wryly: "Ended by his kissing my hand in tears and promising never to be naughty again." But whether it was moral or physical persuasion he used, or both, he does not say.

At Kiachtan, well into the Turkish-speaking north, he found a village "full of running water and the wind-noise rustling up and down the trees—like Blake's 'innumerable dance of leaves.' " Refreshed by an evening meal of *burghul* and, for once, meat, beans, stewed apricots, and bread of "inferior quality," he slept soundly on the roof from 9 P.M. to dawn under a gorgeous white and purple quilt.

The road to Rum Kala'at led along the west bank of the Euphrates, through pistachio groves, and then up a sheer cliff skirting a cave village, from thence descending to the river bank again. The Kala'at was enormous—"a town rather than a fortress"—with a ninety-foot wall and escarpment, five double gates each defended by its own tower and by a deep rock moat: "a perfectly appalling thing—it cut off a mountain from a mountain along a col like the coupe at Sark." [*Letters*, No. 36.]

The blisters on his feet healed, but his right instep collapsed, weakened by the broken leg of seven years ago. Even so, on July 26, he wrote: ". . . there is plenty of reserve force to draw upon yet." By the end of the month however, when he returned to Jerablus, he had developed a bad case of dysentery and lay on his back alone on the Carchemish kala'at nearly an entire day, fainting whenever he tried to sit up or exert himself. For a week afterward he lay ill in Hamoudi's house in the village, surrounded by his few possessions—a comfort in his weakness—visited and consoled by Dahoum who had lamented his long absence, and able to take only arrowroot and milk for nourishment. Then, having resolved to be prudent at last and return to England, he started out with Dahoum's help: by horse to Tell Ahmar, by horse and wagon to Aleppo. In Aleppo while the final arrangements for his departure were being made, the diary records his strong distaste for the Levantine population of the Syrian cities. "In the evening felt a little better, and got down to dinner all right: there summoned up enough irritation to tell my vis-à-vis he was a pig. Tremendous uproar of Levantines (little man a Greek Jew), eight or ten of them shrieking together and dancing about. I was the only person at the table who went on eating." It should be clearly understood that it was the Levantine, not the Jew which earned his disapproval.

He made a rapid detour by train, traveling third-class to Damascus in order to pick up a shirt of chain mail he had promised to Charles Ffoulkes, later keeper of armories in the Tower of London; then on August 9, still unfit, he started out for Beirut. On August 12, after a quick visit to Miss Holmes, his American friend at the Jebeil mission school, he sailed for England with a high fever.

What is remarkable about this summer odyssey—aside from the persistence with which it was pursued until he was virtually in a state of collapse—is its unwitting divulgence through the diary record of those special and peculiar traits that were to be fully revealed in all their later adumbrations in his war history. The estimating of his length of pace—two feet seven inches after the first hour of walking and two feet nine and one-half inches in the last hour during one sustained tramp of twenty-seven miles—shows his curious self-conscious assessment of his efforts. And there is his treatment of the muktar at Shard'at so cursorily and provocatively described; but there are also the confidence and friendliness which, generally, he was able to inspire in the poor illiterate Arab and Kurdish peasants among whose villages he came and went; the preciseness with which he describes each progressive symptom of his physical collapse, not with morbid interest in their development, but with the cool objectivity of an engineer reporting on the performance of a machine under testing. He was in fact testing out his powers of endurance and noting with satisfaction or the contrary the capacity of his body to stand up under imposed strains. And the record so maintained seems to have been a literary exercise, the raw material for an expanded work which he appears to have contemplated publishing under the title, *Seal-hunting in Mesopotamia.*

At home once more in Oxford he wrote to his friend Vyvyan Richards: "Don't imagine I am ill: merely a hopeless weakness that sits me down after a hundred yards is done on foot, and also I cannot go upstairs save crab-wise." [*Letters*, No. 40.] Dysentery was complicated by an attack of malaria which had been brought on by it, and the one complaint could not be cured until the other abated sufficiently—"a giddy round that seems to have no opening" was how he described it. The doctors were adamant that he must wait at least three months before returning to Syria, but upon Hogarth's happy announcement of another digging season at Carchemish, he was back within two months.

The reunion at Jerablus with Haj Wahid, Hamoudi, and Dahoum was a festal night, the climax of his sudden dramatic appearance in December which stopped the work on the German railway, since all the workmen, ex-Carchemish, downed tools and set off in a wild frenzy of delight to welcome him. As for the Germans: they drank *raki* all night, said the Arabs; sat in their tents by day and did no work; they could not swim; they made bargains which they had no intention of keeping, and, "Oh God, the pigs, they eat crabs—and tortoises!" Edward Lawrence held court among the Arabs at Carchemish that night of his return like a young prince, and like a young prince—of their own, not alien blood—he was held in affection by them.

It was still too early however for the spring digging season at Carchemish, and at the instigation of Hogarth who wanted him to experience other archaeological methods than their own, Lawrence went off for a few weeks to dig in Egypt under (Sir) Flinders Petrie. The work at Kafr Ammar provided ample scope for his own particular brand of humorous comment: "A Petrie dig is a thing with a flavour of its own: tinned kidneys mingle with mummy-corpses and amulets in the soup: my bed is all gritty with prehistoric alabaster jars of unique types—and my feet at night keep the bread-box from the rats." [*Letters*, No. 47.] In the sudden cold of desert evenings the archaeologists wrapped themselves in predynastic funereal linen for warmth and walked back to camp exuding a strong scent of embalming spices. Flinders Petrie was the life-sized, full-blown eccentric scholar with a voice like a speaking trumpet and a mane and beard of white, wild hair, who stormed about the Egyptian desert like an ancient prophet scorning officials, flies, and sand alike. He would pop willy-nilly into the tea of his assistants the exact number of lumps of sugar he took in his own, regardless of their taste, and with Presbyterian thoroughness would set all visitors to his camp to rethreading bead collars or washing pots, so that there should be no idle hands among them. Edward Lawrence impudently made fun of him to his face, but he respected him and recognized him for the great man he was. For his own part, Petrie thought enough of the young man in shorts—once he had got over the first shock of his appearance—to recommend him as the most suitable archaeologist to undertake excavations in Bahrain on the Persian Gulf.

There followed a few more weeks in Aleppo seeing after the crating of pottery, seals, and sculptures—mostly collected and assembled by himself—for shipment to Hogarth at the Ashmolean Museum. Then back to Carchemish for the building of the expedition house and the beginning of an association with (Sir) C. Leonard Woolley—renowned for his subsequent excavations of Ur of the Chaldees—who came to

Carchemish as senior archaeologist in February, 1912. It was the beginning too of real difficulties between the English and the German camps. A wooden railway bridge already spanned the Euphrates. It was soon to be followed by a steel structure about a quarter of a mile south of the excavations, and if the Germans had had their way, one end of the steel bridge would have been anchored to the mound—the only natural promontory in the vicinity. It was this constant threat to the digging site which was the chief cause of antagonism between the English and German camps.

Fifty feet below the great mound, trenches were now dug through Arab, Armenian, Byzantine, Roman, and Greek strata down to the later levels of the Hittite period: the fort of Sargon the Assyrian who had conquered the Khatti kingdom in 717 B.C. Below this the older Hittite stratification went back to about 2000 B.C., but the vestiges of the fortress-city of Sargon spread out far beyond the river acropolis which was its key defense, preserved by strength of arms and a constant vigil against invasion. The court of the temple, the royal palace, the processional wall along which the chariots had dashed, lay at the foot of the mound. Still farther removed were the walls which encompassed the city and defended it from chance marauders, with strong gates inset at nearly exactly the four cardinal points. It was these tumbled remains scattered over the southwest steppe, barren and treeless and falling back from the littoral, which gave the Carchemish scene its wild and stony appearance.

In the evening a dust-laden, blue-violet dusk fell over the excavations; there was scarcely any twilight, only this crepuscular instant before nightfall. In the star-decked and luminous dark that followed, the dust of day was laid in the diminishing of the northerly wind. All about the expedition house it lay, and, like a sheet upon an unfinished carving, it covered the mound where all labor ceased at sundown. The mound was at rest then, close by the tawny river and devoid of its daytime babble of voices: a hushed ruin flanked by crumbling walls, crouched lions, and grimacing gods. As the moon rose, the frogs croaked in the little stream that embroidered the land with a thread of fertility; the bats took wing, an owl hooted, a jackal bayed. To the young archaeologist laying out the night on the acropolis and watching the shreds of cloud swim sensuously across the moon, it was the most gratifying landscape ever, river and steppe; the most perfect life he could hope to live—now and for always.

3

THE LOTUS EATER

Of all the persons who move through the Carchemish scene there is perhaps none more ingratiating than Dahoum, the young Sheik Ahmed. He was at this time, says Sir Leonard Woolley[1] "a boy of about fifteen, not particularly intelligent . . . but beautifully built and remarkably handsome." Opinions on Dahoum's intelligence differ but not on his comeliness. His photographs show him to be not tall but strongly fashioned, with a mobile, sensitive face and finely shaped hands and feet. He was an accomplished horseman, a fair shot with a rifle, a good swimmer, and a very adaptable youth generally. His young master taught him to read and to take photographs and, in the off-season for digging, indulged a penchant for sculpture by carving naked figures of him out of the local limestone. Above all, he gave him of that same warm but undemonstrative affection he had for his brothers. This is important for the understanding of their relationship, for this and later friendships have been cited to support the popular theory of Lawrence's homosexuality. Even by the Arabs, said Sir Leonard Woolley, the friendship of Dahoum and Lawrence

[1] *T. E. Lawrence by His Friends.*

was regarded with a mildly scandalized air, but, he continues: "He (Lawrence) had a remarkably clean mind. He was tolerant, thanks to his classical reading, and Greek homosexuality interested him, but in a detached way, and the interest was not morbid." [2] And, too, he liked to shock. The delight of outraging respectability or jarring solid complacency remained constant with him to the end of his life. He knew, of course, what the local people were saying about him and Dahoum, just as he was aware of what was said about him later when he had become a public figure, and it pleased both his sense of whimsy and his contempt for conventionality to do nothing whatever to dispel the rumors.

Miss al Akle of the Jebeil mission school once asked the boy Dahoum why he and the others—for there were others—loved Lawrence and was told:

> Who can help loving him? He is our brother, our friend and leader. He is one of us; there is nothing we can do he cannot do, and he even excels us in doing it. . . . we love him because he loves us and we would lay down our lives for him.[3]

This is nearer the sentiment of the New Testament than that of the Satyricon, yet sophisticates will have their say and find even in the New Testament food for their sick appetites. Certainly there was in Edward Lawrence's attitude toward the problem of sex a bias which invites inquiry, but following the obvious line does not always lead to an accurate solution. With Dahoum, Lawrence swam, canoed, and trekked off into the Syrian desert on the trail of some notable ruin which, more often than not, turned out to be the vestiges of a Roman outpost. It was on one of these excursions that Dahoum showed him the rarest, most fragrant perfume in all the world: the pure, unscented wind of the desert. Between digging seasons, when the other archaeologists returned to England, Lawrence went off adventuring with the *Hoja*, Hamoudi, and the boy Dahoum. Together they harvested in the Syrian fields, ran camels for hire, traveled by canoe down the Euphrates, slept in the beehive-hutted villages where he passed him-

[2] *Ibid.*

[3] *Ibid.*

self off sometimes as a Turk, sometimes as a Circassian. And once he found himself, with Dahoum, flung into prison as a deserter by an overzealous recruiting sergeant anxious to meet his quota for the Anatolian draft. There is every reason to suppose that Dahoum's death, when it occurred in 1918, was a real and grievous loss to him.

Woolley had arrived; the expedition house was completed, and difficulties with the German railway engineers were daily exacerbated. "Very hard to make the railway people love me," Lawrence wrote to Hogarth in February of 1912. "They think English people are spoiling their line: and by being turned out of the Kala'at they have lost that mid-stream rock to build their bridge on at Carchemish." [*Letters*, No. 48.] Most of the antagonism centered around Contzen, the chief engineer, son of a Cologne chemist, by nature a surly, Teutonic bully with a thick skull, an unpleasant manner, and an insatiable thirst. But relations with the Germans were not always uncongenial, though the fact that they were rival employers of labor, proponents of radically different systems of dealing with that labor, and competitors for the land on which they worked at their separate projects naturally made for friction. Even so, one or two of the engineers were regular visitors to the English camp, and on a more propitious occasion, Contzen's successor was saved from the consequences of his folly and the wrath of an angry crowd of Kurdish workmen by the intervention of Edward Lawrence who stopped the tumult with a "trick" of raising his hands slowly and clasping them behind his head—a gesture certain to attract attention if only by arousing curiosity. It was, he said, an effort "to bring the local noise into relation with the light-year distance of the lesser nebulae," [4] a fanciful notion to be accepted or rejected as taste inclines.

The other trouble-maker at Carchemish was the *kaimmakam* [5] of Birijik, a wily Oriental supernumerary, full of dissemblement and false dignity, whose machinations were a considerable annoyance to the archaeologists until they had taught him the wisdom of noninterference in their affairs. In one dispute involving title to the Car-

[4] *T. E. Lawrence to His Biographers*. Robert Graves.

[5] Turkish governor of a subprovince.

chemish site, he peremptorily summoned Edward Lawrence to trial under the Sher'ia courts—a wholly illegal procedure, since the Sher'ia courts were religious tribunals authorized to hand down judgment to Moslems only under Koranic Law. The two archaeologists were prepared to humor the local authorities to the extent of appearing in court to protest the irregularity of the proceedings; then the *kaimmakam's* intriguing hand revealed itself. Immediately and dramatically they both drew revolvers, a gesture which underwrote their earnestness and cleared the court, cowed the presiding vali, and persuaded the now-amiable *kaimmakam* to surrender all their legal documents which the court, acting on his instructions, had impounded.

This and other incidents related by Sir Leonard Woolley in his book, *Dead Towns and Living Men*, have about them a "Boy's Own" flavor, the evocation of a highly colored, faintly incredulous world of escapade where the author is not above a wink of eye and an occasional stretching of truth. "This is a Woolley yarn," said Lawrence of the story of his threat to Contzen after the flogging of a houseboy by one of the German engineers. In the Woolley version of the story, Lawrence had gone down to the German camp and informed Contzen with ominous quiet that he would himself take the engineer responsible for the flogging into the village and there, in front of whatever gathering of spectators cared to assemble, flog him unless he made an immediate apology to the Arab houseboy. The apology was made. In the later version recounted by Robert Graves with Lawrence's approval, Contzen was told merely that his engineer would be taken into the village and *made* to apologize. This repudiation of the Woolley yarns should not obscure the fact that Sir Leonard Woolley was at Carchemish with Lawrence and knew more about him in that period of his life than any of his later friends could know. And while it is true that Lawrence was not given to swashbuckling braggadocio then or later, he was, even in youth, able to impose his will on others when he desired. He was also capable of making quite dramatic threats and of carrying them out if circumstances warranted. "When I fight it's with everything anyhow and everywhere," he was to tell Lady Scott years later, jocularly but not wholly without some truth.

He did not like the German Contzen or his methods: "The back of his neck was too thick. It lapped over his collar," he told Robert Graves; and there can be no doubt he was sufficiently aroused over the unjust punishment inflicted on their Arab houseboy, whether Dahoum or not is not clear, to threaten a retribution which, whatever its nature, was not to be taken lightly, even by Contzen.[6]

The truth is there was in the Near East at this time more than a suggestion of the American Wild West; indeed, life at Carchemish often took on the semblance of an Oriental game of Cowboys and Indians with the diggers, the foreman-sheik, the house servants, the German engineers, the English archaeologists, and the Turkish officials all joining in. And no one enjoyed these high-jinks more than Edward Lawrence. Through them, and through his ingenuity as camp engineer, doctor, teacher, and first-class "trouble-shooter," his reputation was spread far beyond the confines of Jerablus. In December, 1911, he wrote Hogarth: "There is a new oath in the village—*b'is-sait el khowaja* [7]—by the aid of myself: so I have thrust down the prophet from his place. I shall grow a beard." [*Letters*, No. 44.] By this time too he was a crack shot with a revolver from persistent practice at Carchemish where he used tiny match boxes as targets and aimed to shatter them from thirty paces. This was an ability which could not fail to be respected in the Near East where sharpshooting was greatly admired. In one early adventure in 1909 he had wounded in the hand an assailant who tried to shoot him while bathing, and then bandaged the injured member for him and sent him off with a good kick in the rear to teach him prudence. But it was not only as a marksman—and he was never a "trigger man" then or at any time—that he was becoming adept. His faculty for presenting contradictory facets of personality to his observers began, at Carchemish, strikingly to reveal itself.

C. W. Ceram in *Gods, Graves and Scholars* has related how, in 1911, a Syrian guest at the house of Mrs. Fontana, wife of the British Consul at Aleppo, remarked of the two young English archaeologists:

---

[6] *T. E. Lawrence to His Biographers.* Robert Graves.

[7] "By the Man," meaning Lawrence.

"What an unhappy contrast *le jeune* Laurens makes with M. Woolley who is such a man of the world and a *parfait gentilhomme!*" Mrs. Fontana on the other hand, says Ceram, was so carried away by Lawrence's later reputation that in afteryears she professed a stronger interest in him of the two. Perhaps she did find him, artistically, the more interesting of the two; but she was not at first drawn to him. When they met in 1911 he looked considerably younger than his twenty-three years, but something uncouth in his manner, she says, contrasting with a donnish precision of speech, chilled her.[8] Certainly, Woolley, a serious young man of thirty-one engaged to be married, correct in topee, collar, and tie, Norfolk jacket, breeches, and leggings, was more representative of what a field archaeologist ought to be than his younger colleague who went about bare-legged, hatless, long-haired (his hair was too long, he said, when it got in his mouth while eating), and was altogether harum-scarum: more "street-arab" than Arab, as he would jokingly point out. Yet on second glance there was something most arresting in the younger man—that is, when he was at his ease and not made awkward by the wrong company and the shyness he had inherited, with differing effects, from his father. Behind this shyness there was clearly a masterful pride in achievement which later was to exasperate some of his superiors; and his own genuine attempts to stifle it were to develop in him a curiously inverted vanity which deprecated his actions most savagely, even while defending what he recognized as their undeniable achievement. At Carchemish the pattern was less rigid, and the shyness operative only on a social plane. Even then he was capable of letting fall an occasional bombshell in polite society. Mrs. Fontana related how once, when she was wearily reciting to a disaffected gathering at the Consulate her difficulties with the Syrian climate which made her feel dull and listless, her young friend suddenly interposed from across the room, "You should contemplate your naval, Mrs. Fontana."

His strong features: the heavy jaw balancing a long, straight nose and massive forehead over deep-set, pale, and brilliant eyes, formed a plastic screen on which he could project a variety of images—the

[8] *T. E. Lawrence by His Friends.*

grinning, Irish boy; the romantic dreamer of Oxford; the resourceful leader with the tyrant will—tyrannical toward self, not others—with all the ruthlessness of which he was capable clearly trapped in the up-curled corners of his wide mouth. All these images appeared and reappeared in a startling iridescence of personality; and he could, when he chose, withdraw them all so that the screen was empty. It was then that the strength seemed momentarily to degenerate into coarseness of feature. Failing to make any headway with him, Mrs. Fontana took to lending him books. "Lawrence would stroll into the Consulate," she said, "his boots thick with mud or dust according to the season, his hair hanging below his ears (but for all that giving an impression of neatness and grace inherent in him)—deposit the books gently and say . . . 'May I have some more?' "[9]

Later Mrs. Fontana grew to like him, if only for the kindness he showed her and her children whenever they came to visit the Carchemish digs. She was one of an exclusive little band of women, including his old nurse, Florence Messham, Miss al Akle, and, later, the wife of his commanding officer at Cattewater, Plymouth, to have spent long periods alone with him. At Carchemish, not so much from courage as from implicit confidence in his ability, she used to go with him in his Canadian canoe on the Euphrates, braving the unpredictable currents in order to cross over to a little island in mid-stream which in spring bloomed with anemones, cyclamen, cornflowers, and jonquils.

This tenderness and compassion of Lawrence for the very young, for the weak, and for the defenseless seemed to augur well for a later tenderness toward women. But women who displayed too sudden a curiosity about him repelled him, even when less forward than the Kurdish girls near Rum Kala'at who tore the clothes off his back to see his white skin, arousing his hot embarrassment as well as his indignation. When after nearly eight years' almost continuous sojourn in the East, in a society even more uncompromisingly masculine than that of his early youth, he became discomforted in the presence of European women with their wide license to provoke him, he might

[9] *Ibid.*

wryly have felt that the ideal state was for women to keep to women's quarters and be content to be visited there when occasion required: seclusion, the classic Oriental solution to the problem of sex differential.

"Then across the Channel and away like mad to Marseilles, Gibraltar, Genoa, any port from which we can sail to a Mahometan country where men are protected from women," says John Tanner to Straker in *Man and Superman.* To the extent that the Mohammedan countries were notably men's countries, little exposed to petticoat influence, Edward Lawrence would have perhaps agreed, though that was not his reason for going to them.

Like most young Englishmen of the upper and middle classes, Lawrence was slow to grow into awareness of the full implication of his manhood. Purity of mind and the demands of his intellectual preoccupations tended to postpone in him, if not to arrest completely, the curiosity a young man normally feels about sex generally and about women in particular; and the life of the family circle in which he had grown up had certainly not stimulated it. Isolation from feminine contact in youth, together with an avid reading into books of chivalry, may well have fostered in him an unconscious idealization of women: a kneeling to an image in his shield which his self-distrust was to set forever beyond his reach. This was the opinion of Robert Graves, who thought that Lawrence was unable rationally to accept the existence of women and so relegated them to a romantic, wholly remote plane of being. It seems at least probable; but if there was a secret image, what was it like? A boy's first impression of women, and his most important one if he has no sisters, must of necessity come from his mother, and in Sarah Lawrence there was presented to him a cogent feminine ideal difficult to equal. She had shown herself a devoted wife and mother, untiring, intelligent, perceptive, militant in her faith, a woman endowed with her own sense of mystery and independence of spirit which he shared with her. "There's nothing accountable in our crew, Mother least of all" [*Letters*, No. 186.] he was to write to a friend in 1922, and no one reading the letters written to her can fail to be impressed by their revelation of the esteem and affection in which he held her. Not that they contain any effusive sentiments; neither of them was sentimental by nature, and their feelings were lodged far beneath the surface of their remarks, too deep to be betrayed by mere words. Only once in a cry of pain over the death in battle of her fourth son Frank did she betray her feelings and draw from him an unhappy and agonized rebuke: "You *will* never understand any of us after we are grown up a little. *Don't* you ever feel that we love you without our telling you so?"[10] Yet there was a hidden discord, or at least a note of discord, between them. They were both strong-willed, and he seems at some point to have protested the imposed pattern. Protested, but not rebelled; a rebellious son would have cast out all the precepts and counsels. Edward Lawrence remained abstemious and ascetic, hating the flesh but repudiating the piety which three of his brothers, none more beautifully and successfully than Will Lawrence, accepted.

Apart from this unconscious feminine ideal, if indeed it existed, there was in him an intense, almost passionate exaltation of masculinity for the sake of those things which men can do which women cannot: the fellowship they are able to enjoy with one another around a campfire, in war, in adventure which only the odd woman here and there seems capable of achieving. Nothing excluded him from women so much as the feeling that, constitutionally and temperamentally, a woman was unable to share in his exploits, partake of his experience —and therefore to understand his sensations—or in any way meet him on his own ground. It was this attitude which made him deprecate women writers as being less significant than men, since no matter how bright the fire of their genius burned, they could not hope to achieve that breadth of vision which greater opportunity and freedom, hence more varied experience, gave to men. What woman could have written *War and Peace* or *Moby Dick*, he would demand. As time passed he was to become even more censorious of women writers until in 1924 he could say: "All the women who ever wrote original stuff could have been strangled at birth, and the history of English literature (and my book-shelves) would be unchanged." [*Letters*, No.

[10] *The Home Letters*, p. 304.

238.] Istar, the Lady of Heaven, under whose aegis he worked at Carchemish, could not command his worship, however much she sued. But there were a few exceptions to his strictures: Gertrude Bell on the intellectual level, and on the emotional, Christina Rossetti and perhaps Violet Clifton nee Beauclerk, the author of *Book of Talbot*, a strange, diffuse biography, half-travel and exploration, half-confession of a woman exultant in her love for and subjection to her husband. Later, after some thirty proposals from women, all of them strangers, who were willing apparently to submit to unknown lechery at his hands for the opportunity of boasting that they had given themselves to a public hero, the fine shell of his romanticism cracked. But that is to look too far ahead; at Carchemish Edward Lawrence, young, romantic, audacious, daring, felt only remotely if at all the dark stirrings of his dilemma of spirit, not least of which was that war of attrition to be waged against sex in any form as being the ultimate degradation imposed by our half-animal nature.

By this time he was in a fair way to becoming what he later described as "a travelled, archaeological sort of man, with geography and a pen as his two standbys." [*Letters*, No. 329.] Yet he was still very much a member of his family circle, for all his separation from it, fulminating against the Ottoman post which delayed interminably his mail from home and held up his own letters to his family, arousing their worst fears: "Sorry my people bothered you," he wrote Hogarth early in 1912; "they have got absurd ideas that people may disappear quietly in the East. I can't persuade them everybody knows thereof five minutes after the disappearing." [*Letters*, No. 50.] It was the golden age of his life with family ties still intact and before the stigma of events which, in his view, were to set him apart forever from the achieving of normal happiness. In June of 1912 there were serious outbreaks of cholera and smallpox in Aleppo, and the temperature rose as high as one hundred and twenty degrees on some days. To his youngest brother, Arnold, then aged twelve, he confided humorously some of his extracurricular activities.

> First of all, I had malaria—a short spell of the usual two-day sort. Mrs. Haj Wahid got a new baby and turned very ill. Haj's boy fell down and broke his head to pieces and had to be tied up; Haj himself went drinking and collapsed with internal troubles of sorts. So I brought in Dahoum to help Haj's mother in the kitchen, and he ungratefully produced malignant malaria (autumno-aestival) and raved his head off for three days until he nearly died. I had to sit on his chest half one night to keep him in bed. [*Letters*, No. 54.]

As for the summer heat in Aleppo, it was too hot even for crocodiles!

> They line the canals you know, and swallow the water as it comes down from the river: everything in Aleppo loves water. Even the hippopotami sit all day on the kerb with their feet cooling in the gutters, and when sunset comes they boom for very joy, till all the valley is giddy with the sound.

This is the sort of fantastic nonsense young boys rejoice in when it is written by absent and admired elder brothers. It was something for which Lawrence had a distinct flare and which make his letters to children such a delight to read.

"For some reason, Mr. Hogarth is very anxious to make me learn Arabic," he had written jocularly in May, announcing his intention of spending another summer in Syria. His teacher this time was to be Dahoum, and the summer was to be spent partly at Jerablus, partly in and around Jebeil in the Lebanon where he wore Arab dress to keep himself unobtrusive, and flourished on *leban*, bread, and fruit like the four children of Judah who waxed fairer and fatter than the children of the king on their diet of lentils and water. When he had a mind for adventure, Dahoum was always ready and they would set off together seeking the hospitality of friendly headmen, a roof or a mud-floored guest room where after ceremonial coffee and talk, they wrapped themselves in their cloaks and put their folded headcloths under their heads by way of precaution—seldom successful—against their host's domestic vermin. ("These quilts are of course far too hot for a European to stand, since they are stuffed with wool and feathers and fleas—in equal quantities, I fancy" [*Letters*, No. 13.], he had written to his mother in 1909 describing the bedding provided in more lowly Syrian houses.) August of 1912 was the month of the great fast of Ramadan, and when it ended early in September, Lawrence and Dahoum were back at Carchemish eagerly awaiting the beginning of the autumn digging season.

On the Id al-Fitr, Arabs and Kurds moved in gaudy conclaves in and out of the courtyard, firing revolvers and bringing him portions of the village feast: sheets of unleavened bread wrapped around parched corn, grapes, and cucumbers. Beyond the courtyard was a babel of voices rising and falling in the late summer air as ninety-odd men devoured a sheep on the threshold. Off in the dusty blue haze, graying feathers of smoke curled up from the village fires and the glow of their light stained the dusk with rose and orange-gold. All about him tumbled a confusion of festal garments: the dress of The Seven Kings with its brilliantly striped caftan, vivid surcoat, black and silver headcloth, and woven belts with tassels in thirteen colors. And amid all their restless activities, the shouted greetings to which he made the proper responses, the jests which he answered with counter-jest, the sharp report of revolver shooting, he seemed an apotheosis of tranquility: beatific as the image of a sun god, moving and gesturing little, but focusing his alert blue eyes here, then there, losing no detail of his surroundings, no aspect of their aesthetic and emotional significance.

The great Night of Deliverance wore on, marking the end of the season of repentance, when a man might eat and drink in the sure knowledge that the next day, when it came, would bring no obligation during daylight hours for an abstinence more rigid than any imposed by Christian canons. In a greater sense it was for Edward Lawrence a culmination, a reaching to the very apex of his desires; more complete gratification than this he felt he need never seek. The hedonist in him was wholly satisfied. It was like living a legend far removed in time from the present, and though, a true child of his age, he was devoted to the machine and its potentialities, there was a beneficence in the past which ever lured him. Even the plan to print books—always a recurrent project—and live in a Morrisonian hall with open rafters, hanging lamps, and a refectory table, could make no claim against the idyllic existence that was now his. He was well, contented; they had books, pistachio nuts, six if not seven kinds of soap. They ate a lot, slept a lot, talked a lot, he said; they rose with the dawn, tramped with the sun and the moon for their lamp and the spray of the wind in their hair. He read much Meleager, some Meredith, Rossetti, and Shakespeare. Could anyone show a better existence?

In December of the following year he was to write Vyvyan Richards, his Oxford partner in the erstwhile printing scheme:

> I have got to like this place very much: and the people here—five or six of them, and the whole manner of living pleases me. We have 200 men to play with, anyhow we like as long as the excavations go on . . . then there are the digs with dozens of wonderful things to find . . . and hosts of beautiful things in the villages and towns to fill ones house with. Not to mention seal-hunting in the country round about, and the Euphrates to rest in when one is over-hot. It is a place where one eats lotus nearly every day, and you know that feeling is bad for ones desire to do something worth looking at. [*Letters*, No. 65.]

It was an apologetic letter written to explain why, when he was last in England, he had not come to see Richards and talk over the printing press idea on which his friend had lavished time and some money: and it ended on a somewhat embarrassed note: "It is rather a miserable come down. I haven't any money; can I offer you a carpet?"

Work on the digs commenced at five each morning and continued until sunset with only brief pauses for meals. Occasionally dinner at the consulate in Aleppo broke the monotony of expedition cookery, but even with Haj's catering, the archaeologists fared quite well. The railway meanwhile brought mendicants, merchants, missionaries, marriage brokers, prophets, and dancing girls to their doorstep. The missionaries, mostly American Presbyterians, were welcomed for their own sake but strongly discouraged from proselytizing among the workmen. Arab and Kurdish notables came also, as well as British officials and fellow archaeologists: Baron von Oppenheim who stopped there in September, 1912, and Gertrude Bell who first visited Carchemish the year previously. Miss Bell's visit in 1911, when she was guested by Campbell Thompson and Edward Lawrence, was a notable and delicious battle of intellects: the masculine with the feminine. For she had just come from the German digs at Kalaat Shirgat in Mesopotamia, full of enthusiasm for Teutonic efficiency. Campbell Thompson's ideas were prehistoric, she said, "and so we had to squash her with a display of erudition," wrote Campbell Thompson's assistant.

> She was taken (in 5 minutes) over Byzantine, Crusader, Roman, Hittite and French architecture . . . and over Greek folk-lore, Assyrian architecture, and Mesopotamian Ethnology (by Thompson); prehistoric pottery and telephoto lenses, bronze age metal technique, Meredith, Anatole France and the Octobrists . . . : the Young Turk Movement, the construct state in Arabic, the price of riding camels, Assyrian burial-customs, and German methods of excavation with the Baghdad railway (Thompson). This was a kind of hors d'oeuvre: and when it was over (she was getting more respectful) we settled down each to seven or eight subjects and questioned her upon them. [*Letters*, No. 30.]

Miss Bell may be excused for being more than ready for tea after all this. Not least, Will Lawrence passed through Jerablus and paused there on his way to India in 1913.

> I went north through a really hot day-long train journey, far hotter than the Red Sea, with a wind one shrank from, hotter than air, to Aleppo where my Bedawi brother met me. He showed me Aleppo well, taking me on calls to houses in the Moslem quarter, so bigotted still that he's the only European who knows it owing to his habit of going in Arab clothes.

So wrote Will Lawrence in October, 1913,[11] and one must make due allowance for the enthusiasm of a younger brother. Edward Lawrence was certainly not the only European who knew the then-strict Moslem quarter of Aleppo; Hogarth knew it equally well, and in going about inconspicuously in Arab dress, Lawrence was only following his patron and exemplar who, in his own youth, had done likewise. Moreover, the magic word *antika* was the password to many levels of Near East

[11] *T. E. Lawrence by His Friends.*

society, and Lawrence who both knew what he wanted and knew the just price that should be paid for it, was a respected buyer. He was a familiar figure in the *suks* of Aleppo and Damascus and had many contacts among Syrian townsmen as well as with the river peasantry.

At Carchemish, Will Lawrence swam, practiced pistol shooting, and looked over his brother's and Woolley's excavations with a critical eye. From this visit and the letters he wrote describing it come the earliest impressions of his brother as a political conspirator, correct in essentials though wrong in detail. One of the best friends of Lawrence and Woolley, a Kurdish chieftain, Busrawi Agha, had taken part in the Kurdish uprising and massacres of 1909, and his brother Ned, Will Lawrence claimed, was on the spot in disguise at the time. Not only that, but he had plotted with the Kurds for the sack of Aleppo during the first Balkan War of 1912, should the fight go against the Turks. This latter claim appears to be reasonably true, for Edward Lawrence had arranged to smuggle rifles into the British Consulate in Aleppo in case of trouble, a knowledge and anticipation of which he obviously possessed. But the massacres had taken place before Lawrence had even visited the Levant, and his brother merely confused the two events.

"I had been going up and down the Semitic East before the war, learning the manners of the villagers and tribesmen and citizens of Syria and Mesopotamia," he wrote in his war history, and the first five chapters reveal how well he had mastered their ethos and the complex cross-work pattern of political conflicts then being woven. In the first Balkan War of 1912 Russia, with the connivance and aid of Greece and the Southern Slavs nominally subject to Ottoman rule, had attacked and defeated Turkey. In 1913 the victors of the first Balkan War, disagreeing over the spoils of battle, precipitated the second Balkan War which broke out in June and from which Serbia emerged with an increase of territory, population, and confidence. The first Balkan War had seen Turkey, now nearly at the end of her role as "the Sick Man of Europe," keeping a most precarious foothold in Europe through the exercise of authority in Constantinople, Adrianople, Janina, and the Albanian Scutari. Adrianople fell to the

Bulgarians and Janina to the Greeks in March of 1913; Scutari fell to Montenegro in the same year, narrowing the foothold still further. Meanwhile, in Turkey itself Enver Bey's *coup d'état* and deposition of the Sultan Abdul Hamid in January had ushered in the victory of the Young Turk Movement with all its fair promises to the disaffected minorities within the Turkish Empire of which the Arabs were the largest and most important; and Arab jubilation ran high.

Under the Umayyad and 'Abbasid dynasties the Arabs, absorbing in immemorial fashion the cultures and living patterns of the peoples they conquered, touched greatness and achieved an ascendant power that was not only military but social and spiritual. For a time they had been guardians of that accumulation of human knowledge which had come down from the Greeks, but which, in Europe, was decimated by the invasions of Goths, Vandals, and all the other ravishers of the Dark Ages. That the time was ripe for a new era of Arab greatness was—and to some extent is still—the Arab enthusiasts' dream; and in the early part of the twentieth century the Young Turk Movement seemed the opportunity and the means of ushering it into being. Once in power, however, the Young Turks turned from universality to an insular policy of Turkey—which meant the whole of what remained of the empire—for the Turks; and with the growth of the Pan-Turanian movement, disillusion, anger, and frustration transformed the Arab and the Armenian social and cultural organizations into secret nationalist societies, pledged to the overthrow of Turkish rule whenever it should seem fortuitous.

In this early twentieth-century struggle of a people for freedom, in which doctors, merchants, lawyers, teachers, students, and Arab officers serving in the Turkish Army took part, American ideals of liberty and independence were to dominate through the influence of the mission schools and colleges established in the nineteenth century; and Arab nationalism may well be said to have been spawned on the campus of the American College at Beirut. Among the disaffected groups, townsmen, peasants, half-settled tribesmen, Edward Lawrence moved, observing and listening and sometimes offering his own opinions. It is not to be imagined that he went around at this time preaching sedition and revolt. He did not; such a course followed by a British subject temporarily resident in the Near East would have been highly embarrassing to his own government and would have unpardonably compromised those with whom he associated. But a man capable of great subtlety of behavior, who could shame an idling Carchemish workman with a single remark that showed clearly his knowledge of the most intimate details of the idler's domestic life, would not be hard put to express his sympathies indirectly. And his secret ambition goading him on would not permit him to forebear from doing so. He was by his own later admission deep in the councils of both Armenian revolutionaries and Kurdish rebels before 1914.

This was Syria, a land for which he had a love and a sentiment far exceeding that which he felt for its people. But always there were to be reckoned with, as Lawrence knew, those wide desert regions to the south in which the tribes moved, like wandering stars, in a lonely, almost rainless volcanic desert: wild, fierce, unpredictable men, neither touched nor tamed by their Turkish rulers. They were as distant in thought and custom from the Syrian townsmen in their semi-European clothes and tarbooshes, as they were from himself; and the only bond that could unite them—if indeed they could be united—was language and a common heritage. More practical, it was the nexus that could bind Christian and Moslem of the Fertile Crescent in a common effort and teach them to transcend their ancient enmity.

The heritage he knew in part and admired. What annoyed him most in the Arabs of the Euphrates littoral was their persistent: "*Wullah ma arif*"—"By God, I don't know!"—in answer to almost every question. What gratified him was their kindness to the stranger within their gate. In the 1911 diary he recorded: "After half an hour, I got up to go out, and was given a large handful of bread 'since it would be a shame to their houses if one departed empty.' These were Arabs." The gesture came, he knew, from the ancient traditions of the desert to the south which these poor Arabs had brought with them into the Fertile Crescent and which were rooted in the precariousness of life where hardship subdued men to charity. The Bedouin were the keepers of ancient traditions as they were the keepers of the purest strains of blood and language. And no one could think of revolt without reckoning with them.

Will Lawrence found his brother Ned strong and fit, though momentarily undergoing one of his periodic attacks of malaria. "Ned is on the roof in bed, whither he went about 8.30 P.M. to try and sleep off a touch of fever," he wrote.[12] In fact, Ned's bed was more often on the roof than inside the expedition house. Above the roof he could watch the constellations flicker and pale as the moon gained in brilliance, illuminating the little copse in the distance and lapping with silver tongues across the plain where Hittite and Egyptian had done battle for the city. That city, obliterated by Greece, by Rome, by Semitic waves rising fanatically out of Arabia, was slowly coming to life under the hands of the archaeologists. At right angles to the Processional Wall, a flight of stairs, now uncovered, rose from the public square of Carchemish to a terrace-palace whose upper sections, the archaeologists surmised, must have crowned the mound itself; and on either side of the staircase, basalt reliefs led up to a royal doorway flanked by crouched lions. All the ravishing of time and decay could not dim its majesty; it enshrined the full glory of Hittite power which had reached its ascendancy in 1350 B.C. and then declined.

The fever made Ned feel low, Will Lawrence said, but the next day the gift of a handsome carpet from a venerable Kurdish friend cheered him greatly. In Lawrence now were fully developed all the personal mores which were to be his peculiar identification: he walked with purposeful and rapid strides, his head thrust slightly forward; but it was a gait and a manner not without grace. He spoke in a low, precise voice, used short, lucid sentences and never fumbled for words; he employed few gestures, though he might well have used his hands to advantage, for they were finely shaped with wrists delicately turned for all their steel strength. And he was capable of sitting or standing

---

[12] *Ibid.*

perfectly still for long periods of time. His anger, even at twenty-four, was something to be avoided, not because it was blustering or vindictive, but because it was a slow, cold anger that cut deep as a knife. But he was quick to forgive; and he could be appeased, as the Carchemish diggers knew, by little acts of kindness, or by a gift of flowers from the garden of one Ahmed Effendi of Zomora whose roses across the Euphrates were often picked for the pleasure of Laurens Effendi. To some this may seem effete, but a man who endures heat and cold and pain with an almost sardonic disregard of their effects cannot be accused of softness.

Ever ready to effervesce was his puckish humour, the boyish delight in pranks which was to remain with him all of his life. Sir Leonard Woolley has related how, on one stormy night at Carchemish before the expedition house was finished, when he himself had retired early to his tent with a touch of fever, Lawrence cut a weathervane from a biscuit tin and mounted it atop of the tent pole where it screeched and rattled away all night long. For Hogarth his friend and patron, he rigged up a "boudoir" in one of the expedition house's bedrooms, winding yards of atrocious pink ribbon and tawdry lace around the room and cluttering up the dressing table with a pincushion and quantities of hairpins so that, as a married man, Hogarth should feel quite at home. Any attempt to assess Lawrence which fails to take into account his faculty for mischief must fall short and present too one-sided an aspect of him. Love of mischief is one of the keys to his character, and one which prevented him later in life from becoming a tragic figure.

Ned could not spend much of his time alone with his brother Will; the expedition house was kept busy playing host to a number of other guests including Captain (later Major Sir Hubert) Young of the Indian Army who was to serve with Lawrence during the last months of the Arab Campaign, and who was what H. H. Munro has called "elaborately British," totally unlike Edward Lawrence in temperament and inclination and yet able to recognize in the "little man at Carchemish" a unique entity of whom more would be heard one day. In his charge Will Lawrence was sent by his brother Ned, still indisposed with fever, on a visit to Busrawi Agha and the Mili Kurds: a wild gallop across the steppe followed by feasting and dancing all done in a setting reminiscent of the Tartar camp in *Prince Igor*. When they returned, Ned's fever was gone and he was well again; but even at its height, Will Lawrence said, no one would have known by looking at him that anything was wrong with his brother.

In that summer preceding Will Lawrence's visit to Carchemish, Edward Lawrence had returned to Oxford taking with him, as a reward for good behavior, the headmen Dahoum and Hamoudi who, with their long skirts to manage, learned somewhat imperfectly to ride ladies' bicycles in order to get themselves from one place to another. They were lodged in their young friend's garden house in Polstead Road, and for a month were the sensation of dignified Oxford where they raced on their bicycles round and round Carfax, precariously balanced, a rare spectacle for onlookers and a terror to the local police. They were something of a shock too to Lawrence's friends and acquaintances, as indeed he intended them to be; and his humor was richly rewarded by their impact upon urban and academic society. (They fell in love with the glazed white tiles in the gentlemen's lavatories and wanted to unscrew and take home to Syria with them the beautifully polished brass taps from which hot and cold water flowed in such abundance.)

The digging continued through the autumn of 1913, so rich in finds—bas-reliefs of lion hunts, processions of priests and priestesses bearing corn and fruit, winged monsters, gazelles, horrific demons, and pots of all kinds—that the British Museum promised funds for digging seasons over the next four or five years. Lawrence was content; and contentment being sometimes a difficult state to write about, his letters were sparse in comment and reflection. The redoubtable Haj continued to preside over the archaeological board, a little more adept than in earlier days when he had baked cakes "half custard, half rubber sponge" [*Letters*, No. 27.] and emptied a curry tin into the pilaff, threatening Campbell Thompson and Hogarth with liver cirrhosis. And Haj the father of two small daughters continued to curse a perverse fate which brought him no sons, drowning his disappointment in *raki* and envying the good fortune of Laurens Effendi's most esteemed father: "They think Father the most miraculously fortunate man—in fact they suspect him of female infanticide," Ned told his youngest brother. [*Letters*, No. 54.]

A steel skeleton spanned the Euphrates now as the Germans, working against time, hastened to complete their railway; and from the crest of the mound, dropping down sheer into the river, the youngest archaeologist had constructed a chute so that he and whoever cared to emulate him could slide naked into the river on a glorious water toboggan. The Canadian canoe fitted with an outboard motor made for greater mobility, water travel being to Lawrence infinitely preferable to horse travel, and its acquisition afforded him one of his greatest pleasures—that of tinkering with an engine. These were minor innovations which rendered an ideal life still more perfect.

The late autumn and early winter of 1913 found Lawrence and Woolley still at Carchemish finishing up the season's digging records, playing with a snow leopard which they kept that winter as a pet, and awaiting a new assignment. This when it came was ostensibly an archaeological survey of the Sinai Desert undertaken for the Palestine Exploration Fund. In reality it was the completion of a military survey begun by Lord Kitchener as a young officer, and the work was to be accomplished by Captain (later Colonel) F. S. Newcombe of the Royal Engineers with the two archaeologists as decoys. Archaeology was the screen behind which, without undue alarm to the Turks, a thorough mapping of the area was to be carried out. The project began in January with the gathering at Beersheba, Palestine, of the archaeologists, their army surveyor, tents, camels, and a few cameleers and servants, including Dahoum, who accompanied Lawrence. Newcombe, who had expected to be saddled with a pair of elderly, finicky scholars, was delighted with the youth and apparent vigor of his two companions. Lawrence, then twenty-five, looked no more than eighteen, he has said. In part it was the natural consequence of his fairness and his short stature; in part it was his boyishness and effervescence of spirit and, not least, what Sir Leonard Woolley felt was his essential immaturity.

By February they were in the Wilderness of Zin, camping in a valley sheltered from east winds by limestone and flint cliffs, lush with acacia groves, sweet-water springs, young corn, and spring flowers, but with "nothing to eat at all however, except the beans on which the camels feed, lentils, rice, potatoes, onions, Turkish delight, figs, raisins, eggs and marmalade, with bread. We are actually starving, you see!" he told a friend. [*Letters*, No. 68.] This was rather more lavish fare than he was accustomed to when on the march, which was why he jibed at it. After that splendid picnic the party split up: Woolley going east toward the Dead Sea, Lawrence traveling south toward the Red Sea, to join up a little later with Captain Newcombe in Aqaba. On this march however, as if to make up for the luxurious beginning, he lost his camels and Dahoum with them, and came on foot to Aqaba, to Arabia—for so it was then—for the first time, quite alone.

Aqaba was a wild escapade beginning with a row with the local *kaimmakam* who declared he knew nothing about them and their survey and capriciously forbade any mapping, photography, or archaeology within the area under his jurisdiction. But the *kaimmakam* had not taken the measure of one of his antagonists, at least. Lawrence took photographs and "archaeologized" with a bland and exasperating persistence, though Captain Newcombe, more prudent, refrained from carrying out any actual survey work. Then, learning of the existence of a promising ruin on Faraun Island in the Bay of Aqaba, Lawrence prepared to defy both the governor, his rudimentary police force, and the hungry sharks who were said to inhabit the waters of the bay. But in this second round the governor foiled him by forbidding the boatman to row him out to Faraun and by cutting him off when he attempted to row out himself. By then Dahoum with great joy had rejoined Laurens Effendi, and together during the siesta hour, they set off across the shark-infested bay floating on air-filled zinc water tanks borrowed from Newcombe with planks for paddles, and leaving the governor and his police to fulminate helplessly on the shore, unable to pursue them.

After all that, the island was not worth the effort. Lawrence had hoped to find an example of thirteenth-century Arab work, but the ruin disappointed him and the return voyage against the wind was a labor of hours which left both Dahoum and himself cold and exhausted at the end of it. There followed then a chase through the ravines of Mount Hor, as picturesque and exhilarating as a Wild West thriller, with a posse on camels unable to follow their quarry who, on foot and most strong and agile, were able to scramble like mountain goats among the overhanging rocks and so elude their pursuers. It was a boy's dream of adventure come true: the lusty chase and the equally lusty evasion through guile, endurance, and superior intelligence. To some extent, it was this same archetype adventure which he was to carry forward into the Arabian Campaign, motivated there by a man's vision, certainly crowned by a man's agony, but nonetheless characterized by this juvenile relish of high-jinks.

Eventually the police gave up the chase and Dahoum and Laurens Effendi were left alone on the top of Aaron's tomb. Darkness found them benighted on the mountain in bitter cold, with a fresh rain-water pool but no food. All night long they shivered in their sheep-skin coats. At dawn Laurens Effendi shot a partridge which they cooked over a brushwood fire—excellent-tasting but meager fare for two. In all, it was a most fortuitous escapade; as a result of it he discovered the two great crossroads through the hills into the Araba gorge which from time immemorial raiding Bedouin, and before them the tribes of Israel, had employed to enter the Sinai wilderness; and through them he passed northward up the great Wadi Araba defile. That day the errant camels turned up, scrawny from their long march, but he dismissed them and sent them on ahead to Wadi Musa.

Walking through Wadi Araba, fifteen miles or so beyond Aqaba, was like walking through a park with the flood beds ornamentally set out with scrub and tamarisk, all budding in a mist of spring green and interrupted now and then for variety by dignified little groves of acacia trees. But beyond Ain Ghadian the sandy floor became deep, loose, and treacherous, bare of vegetation except for colocynths and in the deeper sand layers, the ubiquitous tamarisks. It was for a

European then almost virgin territory: a deep, natural cleft in the earth's surface continuing the Jordan defile, bordered east and west by wild desert plateaus over which the wind sang its eternal soliloquy; and stretching up from the Gulf of Aqaba northward to the Dead Sea was the Wilderness of Zin. North of Ain Gharandel, the sand gave way to barren limestone, a long uphill slope which led to the watershed south of Jebel Harun in what is now the Kingdom of Jordan. And here the character of the valley altered still again. There were signs now of cultivation on the flanks of the bordering hills, and occasional traces of graves and cairns, silent witnesses to the persistent presence of man; and here Lawrence abandoned his exploration of the Wadi Araba defile, having acquired a knowledge and an understanding of its geographical formation and its strategic value that was to serve him well later on.

Skirting along the shoulder of Jebel Harun, Lawrence passed by way of Petra, the rose-tinted city of the Nabatians, into Wadi Musa, and from thence to Maan and the Hejaz railway which was to know him better in days to come. Petra was for him one of those supreme revelations—like the Cathedral at Reims, the Parthenon, and his first sight of the Mediterranean; but it was less for its ruins, which he considered second-rate, than for its exquisite coloring. "You will never know what Petra is like unless you come out here . . . Only be assured that till you have seen it you have not the glimmering of an idea how beautiful a place can be," he wrote to a friend afterward. [*Letters*, No. 69.] And so it had to be seen in all its wonder to be believed: the poetry of its carved rocks, a rich russet stone paling to rose with streaks of black and blue-green etched in the rose like veins in flesh, and all of it palpitating against the burning blue of the sky.

Near Petra two adventurous English ladies who had left behind the world of comfort and fashion to live in the wilderness encountered Lawrence camped with his men and camels, and deeming him a half-starved young compatriot in dire straits, lent him sufficient money to travel from Maan to Damascus on the Hejaz railway. So ended this southern odyssey, but not without a further brush with the Turkish police at Maan who illegally impounded the camels and were in turn impounded by Edward Lawrence, disarmed by him, and marched off in ignominy through the streets to their own police station. It was not the first nor the last time that his audacity triumphed over official belligerence. In Damascus he passed unnoticed, a dusty, travel-stained, fair-skinned native of polyglot Syria. "I had worn out all my clothes in Sinai, and turned up in Damascus dressed à l'Arabe," he wrote in April to Mrs. Rieder (formerly of the Jebeil mission school), explaining why he had not looked up mutual friends, including Miss al Akle. [*Letters*, No. 71.]

The spring season at Carchemish began as usual, and when it ended Lawrence and Woolley returned to England to write their report on Sinai for the Palestine Exploration Fund, as agreed. Lawrence never returned to Carchemish again; archaeology as a career was at an end, though he could not know it then. In June, 1914, when the shot was fired at Sarajevo, they were busily at work on their report and Europe's summer holiday exodus had barely begun. The people who were basking in Capri, enjoying the glories of Florence, Rome, Naples, and the Alps, were not greatly perturbed by the news of the assassination of Archduke Franz Ferdinand. Why should they have been? Who could have foreseen its far-reaching consequences then? At worst, it meant another Balkan war, and only in the foreign offices and chancelleries of Europe was a stir raised and the alarming implications perceived clearly enough to raise misgivings. Sir Edward Grey, who had not always guided the ship of state wisely, could later come to see in the dimming lights of Europe a dread omen, but only now, today, can we understand the awful havoc that was wrought that summer day at Sarajevo and recognize it for what it was: the belated end of the nineteenth century, and of an era of relative peace and security the like of which will not return, in our lifetime at least.

*

4

THE WILDERNESS

The genesis of the Arab Revolt is by now well known. After Turkey entered the war on the side of the Central Powers in October, 1914, Sherif Hussein of the Hejaz, a crotchety, devious-minded, but sincere Arab patriot, the traditional protector of holy Mecca, refused to proclaim the *Jihad* demanded of him by his Istanbul masters. In any case, the idea of a *Jihad* was patently absurd, since there were more infidels than Moslems fighting among the Central Powers; and the wily old Hejazi and his sons had different ideas. As early as February, 1915, they had been in communication with the British through the medium of the second son, the Emir Abdulla, and after protracted negotiations conducted in high Arabic which were to become the subject of dispute for long years after, the crimson standard of revolt was raised outside the holy city of Medina in June of 1916, upon assurances being given by the British that Arab independence if won would be honored.

War had come in August, 1914, and war had caught up Edward Lawrence, like so many others, and flung him in 1917 headlong into an Eastern enterprise which seemed especially ordered for him, and he for it. The boy was a man at last, and the dream nearly a reality. Lawrence came first on the Arabian scene in October, 1916, when he accompanied (Sir) Ronald Storrs, the Oriental Secretary, to Jidda after a tour of military intelligence work in Cairo. And he came to Cairo in December, 1914, as one of a hand-picked team of experts, originally under Colonel S. F. Newcombe after a spell of mapping work in the Geographical Section of the War Office where he completed the Sinai map for which, with Leonard Woolley, he had formed the archaeological front. There are reasons to doubt if he was ever properly commissioned in the army he was to serve as a most irregular soldier. All that happened apparently was that his chief in the War Office, Colonel (later Sir Coote) Hedley, to forestall criticism, hustled him without any formalities into uniform which he bought himself at the Army and Navy Stores; this after he had been in the War Office for a few months as a civilian.

When the standard of revolt was raised in Medina, Edward Lawrence was still in Cairo, working from 9 A.M. to 10 P.M. in the Military Intelligence Office and sleeping at the Grand Continental Hotel. And in Cairo then he cut quite a figure—a figure of impudence, whose undergraduate laxity and eccentricity both shocked and outraged regular army officers. This is not to say that he was a notorious figure; beyond the limited circle in which he moved he was unknown, but within that circle his presence was felt and often resented. It was not only hidebound prejudice that was offended. "Many men of sense and ability were repelled by the impudence, freakishness and frivolity he trailed so provocatively," wrote Sir Ernest Dowson, the Director General of the Survey of Egypt, later.[1] To balance the impudence and the freakishness, he showed a keenness for work and an ability that none, not even his severest critics, could deny, and in the Survey of Egypt where he assisted with the mapping work, his whimsicalities more often raised than irritated the drooping spirits of men who had been working too long at a stretch.

"Oh do let us have some hills. It would be such fun to have hills," he said when he was asked for his opinion on what ought to be done about the hills of Cilicia in the absence of a reliable knowledge of the topographical formation. And, said Sir Ernest Dowson, "the graphic

---

[1] *T. E. Lawrence by His Friends.*

creations, denudations and resurrections of these hills under Lawrence's wand and the draughtsman's brush were catastrophic."[2]

"Am in an office all day and every day, adding together scraps of information and writing geographies from memory of little details," he had written Hogarth in January, 1915. It was dull in theory, he said, but not so bad in action. Together with Newcombe, George (later Lord) Lloyd, Aubrey Herbert, and his old Carchemish colleague, Leonard Woolley—"the five musketeers" as they came to be called—he worked happily enough until internal divisions, prompted by professional jealousies which were rife in the General Staff in Cairo, made his position untenable. Later on the experts were banded together under Hogarth, Lawrence's patron and exemplar, who was mentor to them all, their father confessor and adviser, he said, "who brought us the parallels and lessons of history, and moderation and courage."[3] This was the beginning of the Arab Office to which Lawrence later addressed the secret dispatches that were to form the basis of his war history.

The experts served under the supervision and general command of Brigadier General Gilbert Clayton who was the Sudan Agent as well as head of Military and Political Intelligence in Egypt. Their amiable chief however was soon replaced by the commander-in-chief's (Sir Archibald Murray) own intelligence officer at Ismailia, Colonel Holdich, who in his earlier dealings with him had found Lieutenant Lawrence's cheek intolerable. And Lawrence, now a captain, was retained on his staff surprisingly, with the ultimate object—as he soon discovered—of keeping him as far removed from Arab affairs as possible. His sympathies were well known, but in this now unfavorable mental climate, the Arab Revolt was brushed aside as inconsequential and of little military value. Sir Henry McMahon, who had originally negotiated with Sherif Hussein in 1915, was eventually dismissed; official opinion set hard against giving the revolt any support in the form of British troops who could ill be spared in that year

---

[2] *Ibid.*

[3] *The Seven Pillars of Wisdom* (New York, Doubleday, Doran, 1935).

of carnage on the Western Front; and it was thought prudent to keep the brash young captain fully occupied on other projects.

To restrict his actions was one thing, to restrict his mind was another. In March, 1915, he had written a letter to his patron Hogarth which showed not only his grasp of the Arab situation but also that he had already made up his mind how to deal with that situation. "I want to pull them (the petty ruling powers in Arabia) together," he wrote, "and roll up Syria by way of the Hedjaz in the name of the Sherif. You know how big his repute is in Syria." [*Letters*, No. 82.] His plan, he said, was to rush up to Damascus "and biff the French out of all hope of Syria." It was a great game and one well worth playing, he thought. The fact that one pivot of this plan was the Idrisi of 'Asir whose value did not fulfill expectations does not destroy the essential prescience of the plan. Nor should its revelation of his opposition to French designs and ambitions, which is certainly open to criticism, be allowed to cloud the issue of his later achievement.

The two years he spent in Cairo were busy and on the whole happy ones. Because they were happy and because he was contented, apparently, with his static role in Military Intelligence among maps and codes, reports and handbooks, the fervor of his interest, his dream of Arab freedom, has been questioned. "Had the Arabs been a little more interested in the things of this world they would have been a nation by now," he wrote home in January, 1916. This is oversimplification, the impatience of youth to get on with the job. Edward Lawrence was not a soldier; as an ordinary military commander in the field he would not have been a success. Instinctively he knew that and waited, not consciously perhaps, for the revealed opportunity to play the lone hand which alone would permit his unique faculties to display themselves to advantage. And the fact is, had he been as eager as a greyhound to bolt off after an electric hare, he could not have maneuvered himself a place in the Arab Campaign before January, 1917.

Lawrence had gone out previously on secret missions from Cairo—to the Western Desert where the Senussi were training to fight the British, to Greece to treat with British agents there, and, in the spring of 1916, to Mesopotamia with Aubrey Herbert to try to bargain with the Turkish commander, Khalil Pasha, for the relief of British troops being besieged at Kut. In the autumn of 1916 the time seemed opportune for another secret mission, and he provoked the authorities into letting him go by persistently pointing out their shortcomings, both in intelligence work and literary style as reflected in official reports, until blind with fury, they were glad to be rid of him: to the Oriental Secretary, to the Red Sea, to Jidda or anywhere else in fact he chose to go. ("I was all claws and teeth, and had a devil," he wrote in his history.) He was aware that an "official shelf" was being prepared for him against his return from Arabia, but here he foiled his adversaries by arranging through General Clayton before he left for a transfer to the Arab Office where the atmosphere was more to his liking.

Once in Arabia he determined to see the revolt himself at close hand and to test its protagonists in the crucible of his mind. His observations were conclusive: Feisal was the obvious, the perfect choice for leader—a "veiled prophet" whom men would follow for his own sake; the Arabs could be organized to play their part in the defeat of Turkey if only a handful of British officers were sent into Arabia as advisers and tutors; to send whole armies of infidel troops into Arabia would be to court disaster. This latter opinion, coinciding as it did with official views in Cairo, won him instant acclaim after his return from his visit to the Sherifian armies—though his reasons for it were different from the official ones. He was unexpectedly back in favor now with the General Staff whose members had hitherto regarded him as a most impudent young interloper. (His appearance was against him; he looked scarcely twenty, an untidy, irresponsible boy.) And it was this sudden restoration to favor which brought about his return to Arabia against his will.

He returned to Arabia in January of 1917 to be British Liaison Officer attached to the Emir Feisal, and he came protesting that he was not the man for the job; that there were others more fitted than himself; that he was no soldier, only a book-learned student of the art of soldiering, and that he had far better be employed elsewhere.

The moment of destiny had come, and it is to his great credit that he shied away from it, knowing full well what his will was capable of once the reins holding it were loosened. His superiors thought differently, and once his protests were overruled, Edward Lawrence pried himself loose from his sedentary work and set about hardening himself for his new role. The ground work had long been laid: the testing of his physical endurance in Syria and Mesopotamia before the war; the long and practiced fasts from food and sleep; the perfected marksmanship with revolver and later rifle. The little exercises he now set himself in camel riding and walking upon hot stones to toughen the soles of his feet were by way of overlaying the gloss on a finished instrument. The neophite cameleer soon became an expert both at riding racing camels—on one occasion he was to average nearly a hundred miles a day for three days without stopping—and in judging them. Arab dress he had long accustomed himself to wear in Syria and Lebanon, and was soon at his ease in it again. And Arab dress, quite apart from its picturesqueness, is eminently practical in the desert climate for which it was designed, and greatly superior to the constrained Western trousers for sitting on the ground and for camel riding. The language with its subtleties and complexity of dialect (of which he was familiar only with that of Syria and Palestine), he never fully mastered, though his vocabulary, some twelve thousand words eventually, was better than some have claimed for all his unpredictable syntax; and his understanding of it was great indeed. As for soldiering, "with 2,000 years of examples behind us, we have no excuse when fighting for not fighting well," he told Captain Liddell Hart afterward.[4] To the Arab Campaign he brought all of his book knowledge, supplemented by that peculiar insight into the impulses and motives of other men that were his special genius. And he brought an enthusiasm which was only slowly dissipated by the friction of unwholesome events.

On February 12, 1917, Ned sat in the queer little Arab house in Wejh that served as headquarters and put down his thoughts on the

---

[4] *T. E. Lawrence to His Biographers* (New York, Doubleday, Doran, 1935).

Arab war in a letter for his parents. Because his development of those thoughts later in his war history has seemed to some contrived and omniscient, it is worth while to look at this simpler version which, in the hour of action and not its recapitulation, he passed on to his parents.[5]

> The Arab Movement is a curious thing. It is really very small and weak in its beginning, and anybody who had command of the sea could put an end to it in three or four days. It has however capacity for expansion—in the same degree—over a very wide area. It is as though you imagine a nation or agitation that may be very wide, but never very deep, since all the Arab countries are agricultural or pastoral, and all poor today, as a result of Turkish efforts in the past.
> On the other hand the Arab Movement is shallow, not because the Arabs do not care, but because they are few—and in their smallness of number (which is imposed by their poverty of country) lies a good deal of their strength, for they are perhaps the most elusive enemy an army ever had, and inhabit one of the most trying countries in the world for civilised warfare. So that on the whole you may write me down as a reasonable optimist. I hope the show may go as we wish, and that the Turkish flag may disappear from Arabia. It is indiscreet only to ask what Arabia is. It has an East and a West and a South Border—but where or what it is on the top no man knoweth. I fancy it is up to the Arabs to find out! Talk about Palestine or Syria or Mesopotamia is not opportune, when these three countries—with every chance—have made no effort towards freedom for themselves.[6]

In the months since the Revolt began, Arab efforts against the Turks in Medina had failed, armed Bedouin being a most unsuitable host to pitch against regular troops in entrenched positions. Disheartened, though Taif had fallen in September to the Emir Abdulla, the Arab forces before Medina began to melt away, and in the last months of 1916, the Revolt itself seemed to some like "the snow upon the desert's dusty face," lighting the hour but soon to pass away. Then the temper changed; the emphasis shifted, and there was born

[5] *The Home Letters*, p. 335.

[6] Notable Arab leaders in Syria however had already been imprisoned and tortured for their patriotism. See George Antonius, *The Arab Awakening* (New York, G. P. Putnam's Sons, 1938; rev. ed., 1946).

that idea—Lawrence's, or the concerted idea of Lawrence, Hogarth, and others in the Arab Bureau—of the Arabs as a mobile, striking force, dissolving and reassembling, with the gradual spread northward of the Revolt until it became an organized military action surging up to the gates of Damascus. Instead of beating futilely against the walls of Medina, Feisal, leading his army in the field, was persuaded to counter a Turkish advance on Mecca by a flanking movement on Wejh two hundred and thirty miles from Medina on the Red Sea coast. By so doing he would threaten Medina's communications with the north and prevent a Turkish advance on Mecca. Successfully on January 25, 1917, Wejh was occupied and at Wejh began the systematic training of Arab regulars, most of them recruited from prisoners captured in the Turkish levies; this in readiness for the northern operations which of necessity would require disciplined soldiers rather than untrained Bedouin marauders. Such was the general strategy.

With the Royal Navy controlling the Red Sea, Wejh was the base from which to make forays on the Hejaz railway, disrupting communications and preventing supplies from reaching the Turks in Medina; but the taking of Wejh marked the conclusion only of the first phase of the Arab Revolt. With Feisal in Wejh, the Emir Ali remaining before Medina lest the Turks there should think their way open, and the Emir Abdulla encamped in Wadi Ais harassing Turkish movements between Mudahrij and Medina, the Arab war was no longer a pious hope but a reality, though a side-show only of the main campaign in Palestine.

In March at Abdulla's camp in Wadi Ais, Lawrence collapsed with his old complaints, fever and dysentery aggravated by the Arabian climate, and lay alone in a tent for ten days. It was then, he said, that his mind cleared, his senses became acute, and the whole Arab situation—its tactics, its aims, its strengths, and its weaknesses—revealed itself to him. The account he wrote afterward of his cogitations has stretched credulity greatly, and the truth is no one thinks with such clarity and synthesis while the body gathers its hidden forces together to overcome pain or throw off sickness, and the mind sinks down into torpor or fevered fantasies. But it is possible between bouts of pain or sickness for sudden relief from physical distress to flood the mind with a new lucidity; and it is possible too for the mind to recollect afterward what in those moments seemed apt or illuminating. The illness passed; recovered but weak still, his thoughts cohered into a strategy: war of detachment, perfect "intelligence" so that planning could be made in certainty, and fervent preaching to order men's minds to the enterprise. Imperative for the success of the northward spread was the taking of Aqaba, ancient Elath where Solomon had launched his fleet of ships, where the gulf ran down blue to the Red Sea, and where he had outwitted the *kaimmakam* and his *gendamerie* three years before; and Aqaba was the next stage.

Who may take credit for planning the capture of Aqaba is not clear, and even by the most lax standard of historical exactitude the record is unsatisfactory. Lawrence was to claim that the plan was his; Lord Wavell supported that claim afterward in his history of the Palestine Campaigns which was based on the Official History. The French General Brémond on the other hand claimed that the plan was suggested to the Emir Feisal by himself and Colonel Newcombe; while George Antonius, the Arab historian, insisted with equal authority that Auda abu Tayi, paramount sheik of the Howeitat, recommended it to Feisal during their first meeting in Wejh. The student must take his choice. Aqaba at any rate was taken from the landward side on July 6th by Arab forces under Auda, the Sherif Nasir, and Lawrence, after an attack on bridges and railway in the area and a skirmish with the Turkish garrison of Abul-Ithl on the road between Maan and Aqaba. Stripped down to the bone, this is the course of the Arab Revolt up to the summer of 1917. It marked the ending of the second phase, and with General Allenby replacing Sir Archibald Murray as commander-in-chief and under him Edward Lawrence playing an ever freer and loner hand in fulfillment of his destiny, the third phase opened.

That war he fought from July, 1917, to October, 1918, was a war of movement—a masterly planned and executed guerrilla action in all that the term implies, and in a sense it has become a classic which all those engaging in similar actions find themselves bound to consider, the more so, perhaps, as their forerunner has set down his theories of warfare in superb language and bequeathed them to posterity for all would-be guerrilla leaders to read. "Our masters had been Lawrence and Wingate," wrote Julian Amery in *Sons of the Eagle*, a study in guerrilla warfare in Albania in 1943–45. But few if any guerrilla operations of World War II have equaled it in epic and romantic incidents. Each skirmish and foray was fought in the double dimension of body and spirit, more acutely individual, more devastating spiritually than that of most soldiers. In them he had to try to balance and synthesize almost inimicable elements: truth for himself, faithfulness to his countrymen who employed him, and justice for the Arabs who followed him. Upon this three-pronged dilemma, first his ideals and then his will were nearly shattered.

Yet there can be no doubt that in the beginning Lawrence relished the role he had adopted; it was Carchemish all over again, but drawn on a larger scale and with an added element of urgency, of imperative need in the face of the failure at Gallipoli and the frightful slaughter on the Western Front. And it was romantic adventure, of a kind that by instinct and training he was conditioned to enjoy. To ride with Feisal at the head of the great tribal army was an experience few modern leaders in war could enjoy; and none could draw from it so perfectly its historical analogies and sense its challenge to blood and imagination alike. It was the same when he sat in Feisal's great tent of state on Bokhara carpets, leaning against camel saddles, listening to and sometimes participating in war councils, in judgments and the subtle dialectics of Bedouin coffee talk. The free camaraderie of strong men, and between fights, the boisterous play of overgrown boys—even the darker moods of cruelty and violence—were part of the game. His early incognito as a Syrian officer deserted from the Turks, his later play-acting in his elaborate white silk and gold Arab dress, were the crowning extravagances. The temptation to "play to the gallery" was undoubtedly very great, especially if his onlookers were English and felt their dignity as Englishmen outraged by his masquerade.

When Colonel F. G. Peake, founder of the Transjordan Arab Legion (who was not outraged), saw him for the first time at Aqaba in 1918, he described him as:

> . . . a small man dressed in extremely good and expensive Bedouin clothes, a richly-braided and decorated goat's hair cloak over all, and on his head a wonderful silk kufaiyeh held in position by a gold agal. His feet were bare, and he had a gold Hejazi dagger in his belt, and in his hand he carried the usual almond-wood cane that every Bedouin camel driver uses.[7]

This dazzling apparition was such that Peake could only assume it to be some high Arab notable, perhaps even the Emir Feisal himself who was encamped at Aqaba, and he went forth to welcome him ceremoniously at the tent door. This was the sort of situation Lawrence most enjoyed. With that impulse for mischief never for long absent in his conduct, he let Peake offer him a profusion of Arabic courtesies and a chair, before he said in flawless English: "Well, Peake, so you have arrived at last."

That was one side of the counter. On the obverse was all the excruciating loneliness of the outlander cut off from his own kind; of the leader who must make decisions and assume responsibility for his actions and for the well-being and safety of his men without the benefit of consultation with higher authority. Lawrence had set himself to bring freedom to the Arabs, to catch at the new wind blowing across Asia and direct it to his own purpose. "Those who dream by night in the dusty recesses of their minds wake in the day to find that it was vanity: but the dreamers of the day are dangerous men, for they may act their dream with open eyes to make it possible," he was to write in the introductory chapter of his history which was suppressed in the early printings. This he did to make a new nation, he said, "to restore a lost influence, to give 20 millions of Semites the foundation on which to build an inspired dream-palace of their national thoughts." It was a proud aspiration. Because of his enthusiasm for their cause, he was able to employ the tide that

---

[7] Major C. S. Jarvis, *Arab Command* (London, Hutchinson, 1942).

compelled him to go among the Arabs and draw their undulations to his will in order to project his and their dream into reality. And therein lay the hazard of his endeavor and its threatened nemesis.

Lawrence was too good a historian to believe that history repeats itself exactly. The Arabs had been great; they might be great again, but it was not in their past glories but in their future potentialities that they must seek for their role in the new Asia; and his reason told him the new Asia would not be born without agony, and would, even after birth, have to struggle desperately to maintain itself in a world of political greed and concupiscence. It would moreover have to struggle against internal weaknesses: the debilitating effect of bridging the gap between medieval and feudal institutions and the more exacting standards of modern Western democracy; the frustration of temperaments impatient for progress, quickened in spirit, yet incapable of carrying their ideals over into the practical realm of action. And, he was to write in an article called "The Changing East" published in 1920, "We have to be prepared to see them doing things by methods quite unlike our own, and less well: but on principle it is better that they half-do it than that we do it perfectly for them." [8]

"No, I don't feel confident militarily," he told Lord Wavell in May 1923. "All the while we fought I felt like a conjurer trying an insufficiently rehearsed trick—surprised when it came out right. A succession of such chances gave me the feeling I was apt at the business: that's all." [*Letters*, No. 210.] But the aptness was a combination of intelligence, skill, imagination, and the audacity to attempt something new and untried. In October of 1917 when his youngest brother Arnold was thinking of his own part in the war and eager, boylike, to join Ned in Arabia, Lawrence outlined a course of training for him to follow.

> He should learn demolition work (explosives) practically, as the theory is very theoretic and does not always justify itself. However the effects of blasting gelatine and guncotton on stone and steel are worth working out, on paper as well as in the open. It is very easy. Fuse and electric firing.

---

[8] *The Round Table*, September, 1920; reprinted in A. W. Lawrence, ed., *Oriental Assembly* (New York, E. P. Dutton, 1940).

> He should also learn machine gun work, Vickers, Lewis and Hotchkiss, and if he has time get a working acquaintance with light Trench mortars, and guns. Of the latter we use field and mountain, and some fancy patterns. It is not worth while his trying to become a gunner, but if he spends a few days with a gunner, or near a battery, it will pay him to pick up how to set a fuse and train a gun. He should be able to ride a motor-cycle and drive a car:—we use Fords, Crossleys, and Rolls-Royces. If he can do some of the above, can write fluently in English, talk a little French, and shoot with revolver and rifle that will be useful enough. Bomb-throwing is a very handy thing. [And he ends wryly:] What a catalogue of talents! I wish I had them.[9]

He did have them, the whole catalogue, and this was assumed modesty.

It has been said with some justice that his war history, when he came eventually to write it, was slighting and neglectful of the efforts of other officers, British and French, in the Arab Campaign. He was however writing of his own peculiar role in the Arab war and his own perplexed state of mind. His history was not a history of consecutive parts fitted together in a comprehensive whole, but a history of hectic episodes, black despairs, and transcendent hopes and fears. As he was to acknowledge in his history and more frequently outside of it this slighting of other actors on the Arabian scene, it seems like flogging a dead horse always to be belaboring his negligence and duplicity in the matter.

> Have you read my account of the I.C.C. (Imperial Camel Corps) march? [he wrote Colonel R. B. Buxton in September, 1923]. Please say honestly what part of it, or of its tone, hurt your feelings. I was wrapped up in my burden in Arabia, and saw things only through its distorting prism: and so did third parties wrong. It wasn't meant: just the inevitable distraction of a commander whose spirit was at civil war within himself. [*Letters*, No. 219.]

Pinpointed on the map, reflected in a pool as still as glass except when the desert wind ruffled its surface, wrapped in its sheath of wind-torn palms, there rose the ruined fort: place of kings, outpost

[9] *The Home Letters*, p. 342.

of Roman legionaries, world of legend, island of the dead. In summer it was a hot, decaying paradise where the towers gaped under the blue flaming of the sky—the haunt of scorpions and salamanders. In winter a desolation more acute overtook it, for it was swept then by northeast winds and buffeted with driving rains. A pestilent dampness inflicted it, and a long and lingering melancholy which hovered like a hidden enemy in the gloomy passageways, waited upon the unwary, to swoop, to seize, to destroy. Like a banshee the wind blew notes of doom through the volcanic rock towers which echoed into the shivering quiet below, trembled there, and then departed until the next gust. This was Azrak, the desert fort, palace of ancient shepherd kings of the wilderness when the wilderness was kindlier there and a place of gardens.

In the autumn of 1917 there came to Azrak some of the Arab irregulars to a winter bivouac, and with them came Edward Lawrence, dubious leader of a now-dubious cause. At Azrak they were to wait for the ending of the rains while making sorties now and then for reconnaissance, or to startle the enemy, goading him into alertness when he had been lulled by their absence into a sense of false security. Nearly seventy miles to the northwest was Der'a, the junction of the railway, where a line branching off into Palestine was the source of supply to the Turkish Seventh and Eighth Armies; to the north were friendly Bedouin tribes and seminomadic peasants waiting only for a successful passage of arms that should remove from their hearts and heads the dread of reprisal.

There can be no doubt that Azrak with its pool, its whispering palms, its ruined towers, its memories of soldiers in other days, made a romantic appeal to the man who waited there like a robber chief in hiding with his men; but the enforced idleness was slow torture to his mind, in spite of the consolation of the *Aristophanes*, the *Morte D'Arthur*, and the *Oxford Book of English Verse* which were slipped into his saddlebag and carried with him always for hours of waiting like these.

Beyond the shelter of Azrak were the deserts of flint and lava and sand, seeded near the flood beds with pools which slowly turned from sapphire to ruby as the western sun touched them. In spring their brinks were garlanded with the tender green of camel-thorn and star-scattered with desert primulas. Here leaped the jerboa to sight, and rarer, the desert oryx; venomous snakes coiled secretly in the thickets, and over all the razor-backed mountains and their stony defiles loomed, harsh and without pity for the traveler. The blinding, white-hot flame of summer and the stifling sirocco it bred gave way in winter to bitter winds that blew off the snows of the rocky heights; there was bareness and cold then, an aching and bleak misery beset the traveler, without warmth, without succor. Against this background Lawrence moved in heat and cold throughout the eventful months of the Arab Campaign, tearing hands and feet on flint shards, suffering hunger and thirst, exultation and despair. Impossible to recount all the journeys made, all the raids undertaken against the enemy, all the deaths averted. In the end they ran together into one journey, one landscape, one victory, one death—in spirit, his own. Like the climate, he was pitiless, not sparing himself and yet not willfully expending the lives of others in reckless adventure. Exultation came from the thought of the nearness of his dream to realization; it did not come from the carnage he wrought among the enemy by his demolitions on the Hejaz railway; yet at times he seemed a whitened fury, an avenging angel, and in the heat of battle the taste of victory was sweet indeed, even on his lips.

But he had been impish too, when time and mood permitted, upsetting Arab and English dignities alike—as when he misbehaved at a tribal feast, shocking his companion, the gentle, well-bred Sherif Nasir. And he was compassionate, sparing lives that were his for the taking, straightening the twisted limbs of the Turkish dead on a field of battle. El Aurens, Lurens Bey, the Emir Dinamite, were the names by which he was variously called, while to the desert warrior Auda abu Tayi he was "the World's Imp"—Puck incarnate masquerading in Arab dress. For a man essentially nameless, his title was immaterial; he was not, however, a Prince of Mecca, even by courtesy. Photographs of this time show him a slim figure in fancy dress, all white and gold and scarlet, with the long trailing sleeves of

Bedouin nobility and bare, sandaled shapely feet; looking neither a soldier, an Arab, a prophet, nor even a recognizable guerrilla leader, but a young Englishman of scholarly bent, shy and sanguinary, with a flair for improbable adventure. Only in the mouth and chin can the strength of will be recognized, and as always, the pain lies well hidden behind the eyes.

The melancholy pleasure of Azrak was not his for long. In the wind and the rain, while the tribesmen and the six Haurani boys who formed the nucleus of his later bodyguard moved about him, all that had gone before rose up in Lawrence's mind and gnawed at it, fretting the ragged edge of his nerves. By taking Aqaba, he had been able to attach the Emir Feisal's army of Hejazi regulars to Allenby's right flank and win for himself a free hand; henceforth the Arab war would be fought in the larger strategy in which he conceived it, for the liberation of Syria and Palestine. For the irregulars it was a matter only of the employment of small raiding parties mounted on swift camels and stripped of everything that would hamper speed, engaging in the hit-and-run tactics of which his history was to give so meticulous an exposition.

"The whole art of war consists in a well-reasoned and extremely circumspect defensive followed by a rapid and audacious attack," said Napoleon. Defense in this case was mobility—the power to melt away beyond hills and gorges—and audacity of attack lay in the element of surprise, not in numbers. So much for the surface details, tidy and well ordered. Below them lay the morass of his doubts and fears, and it was there in the ferment of guilt and shame and anguish that his reasoning was trapped. As much as the history of an action, the book he was to write afterward was an elegiac recital of his anguish.

There were those who, listening to his preaching as he was pleased to call it, had given their lives in his service; there was the Turkish soldiery on the Hejaz railway blown to bits or fearfully mangled by the touch of his finger on a demolition key; and Dahoum struck down by typhus even while he was on his way to bear arms in the cause of his people under Laurens Effendi, his beloved friend. There was the harsh death and harsher punishment he was ever having to witness without his nerves either breaking or blunting; and there was the summary justice meted out by himself in default of a better arbiter, including even a capital sentence executed with loathing and despair to prevent the spread of blood feud and its marring of their effort—"the horror which would make civilized man shun justice like a plague if he had not the needy to serve him as hangmen for wages," he wrote of it.[10] It was not weakness that turned Lawrence's pride in his portion of the Arab Campaign into revulsion. He knew fear, as all men must know it, but in him fear was subordinated to will, and his recoil was a strong man's recoiling, and the more awesome for that. Rather it was the black and insidious belief that all who had listened to his persuasive voice, all who had been caught up in the orbit of his ardent, near-fanatic desire to free a subject people and bring luster to his own name, had been lured into unpardonable deception. This self-doubt was the wages of his achievement, as guilt was the reward of his boyish romanticism, and shame the recompense of his scholar's urge to plunge headlong into history instead of being content to record it. All of his dreams at Oxford and Carchemish had come to this. There was, however, another reason for his sense of defilement.

The burden of that effort Lawrence made during the months from January to November, 1917, had fallen chiefly upon his mind, but his body had not gone unscathed, for he had imposed upon it the most exacting tests, and without the finely tempered strength of his body, his exploits would have been impossible. This he fully acknowledged; it was that union of will and flesh which had accomplished his desires. Behind that union of will and flesh there had been a sense of wholeness, of consonance, despite the pre-eminent role of mind. This was so in 1911 in his tramp over northern Mesopotamia; it was so during the early part of the Arab Campaign. By autumn of 1917 that consonance was broken, and there in the southern gate tower which he occupied at Azrak, under a roof sealed off from the

---

[10] *The Seven Pillars of Wisdom.*

weather by a temporary layer of palm leaves and brushwood, Edward Lawrence held up the image of his strength and despised it.

Battle wounds freshly closed will ache in penetrating dampness, and Azrak in November, 1917, was a streaming citadel; but this was a minor hurt in the aggregate of punished flesh and of the mind's still greater agony. Unconsciousness came to him, slowly and reluctantly, he said, the stubborn mind stayed aggressively awake telling over its agonies until he longed for the black and blessed gulf into which at last he had fallen on that previous November night. For it is a loathsome thing for a man to be flogged into subjection and despair as he was on that night. It was even more loathsome to admit it. To the Arabs he did not admit it; he gave them instead a lively tale of dupe and bribery and casually excused his shocking physical condition upon his return to Azrak after a night away by ascribing it to some unlikely accident. But later, in his history of the Arab Revolt which was also the history of himself in that Revolt, he devoted a chapter to it which makes uncomfortable reading even today.

With meticulous detail, saved from morbidity only by its cool and almost sad objectivity, he described his ordeal: his reconnoitering from Azrak around Hauran and the Der'a junction in the garments of one of his Haurani boys; his capture as a deserter near the airfield; the incredible masquerade as a Circassian in which his true identity was concealed; the insistence of his captors that as a deserter he should go and satisfy the frantic lust of the Der'a military governor; and his disgust and revolt against even the preliminary indecencies of sexual perversion. In the end the Anatolian soldiery, who were not fundamentally vicious but only brutalized by their conditions of service, took him outside to the head of the stairs to "soften him up" by processes which are now all too familiar. After a preliminary pummeling, they flung him face down on the guard bench, held him fast, and with a whip began to lash his proud and resilient body into subjection and the betrayal of the mind which it had been schooled so admirably to serve.

He bore it for what seemed an interminable time while the soldiers took turns to punish him, quarreling among themselves who should be next, playing unspeakably with him, he said, between each series of lashings. While he possessed the will to order them, the cries which they forced out of him were in Arabic, and afterwards, when will could no longer fight against the agony, sickness mercifully choked him.

There followed an incoherent and yet oddly tranquil interval when his body, broken at last, rested on the dirty floor; and then a kick of revival and more punishment until every nerve screamed out for mercy. Yet he did not by any sign divulge the secret of his identity, though there was a moment earlier when he thought the governor knew it; and when later he escaped, he left behind no clue but the remembrance of his white skin and his seeming inexhaustible appetite for punishment.

At Der'a Lawrence ate of a fruit of knowledge so shameful that ever after he shrank from the memory and yet could never forget it. It was not alone the discovery that physical punishment could arouse in him that ecstasy of nerve and blood which his mind so violently rejected. If that had been all, as indeed from his description of the episode it would, superficially, seem to have been all, the morbid horror might not have lasted. But his body betrayed him into even graver dishonor. In his war history he was to say that mishandling made him too frightful an object even for the Bey's depraved senses, but years later, in a private letter to the wife of George Bernard Shaw, he was to admit bitterly how on that night in Der'a he had given away the only thing we may validly call our own, which we come into life possessing: bodily integrity, and this in order that he might gain a few moments respite from pain.

This is a solemn admission, but not a surprising one; it is implicit in the Der'a chapter as he eventually wrote it. For that reason alone the interpretation which has been put on it—that he yielded to the Bey's pederasty—is a false one. He yielded certainly, or felt he had yielded, to the assault of one or more of his punishers,[11] but the ac-

[11] The clue is surely to be found in that horribly evocative scene: ". . . but I next knew that I was being dragged about by two men, each disputing over a leg as though to split me apart: while a third man rode me astride. It was momentarily better than more flogging." (*The Seven Pillars of Wisdom.*)

count he gave of the Bey's refusal of him after the flogging is undoubtedly an accurate one. From so ghastly a denouement the mind recoils, and the wonder is not that he was unable to bring himself to relate the story honestly in his war history, but that he was able to tell even a part of it. And the wonder too is that after so violent a physical and psychological shock he could continue to play his part in the military campaign.

In harsher days when soldiers of the British Army were flogged on parade for their defaults, there are incredible records of men receiving a thousand or more lashes and surviving. Lawrence lost count of his after twenty, and though he has been accused, often with justice, of embroidering the account of his Arabian exploits, there is every reason to believe that his description of the flogging at Der'a was understated. There are some of course who will be grossly offended by the revelation of this expurgated incident from the Der'a episode; they should not be. Life being cheaply held in the East, in his pose as a Circassian deserter, there was no reason why the Anatolian soldiers should not have flogged him to death if he had not at some point yielded; and if death had been all there was to it, he could doubtless have borne it. Pain of the slightest, he said, had been his obsession and secret terror since boyhood; and he recorded how he took a vial of corrosive sublimate from the Der'a barrack dispensary to serve against recapture. Had he possessed the means to take his life earlier, during his torture, it seems likely he would have done so. But the way to death and release then was more of the intolerable agony that lapped his body in a livid flame and from which his mind would not save him by mercifully imposing unconsciousness between him and the flame. His will broke and he was despoiled, but the surrender was dearly given. The toll of his great powers of endurance was at Der'a paid in full.

He left Der'a broken, bloody, led by weakness of the flesh into unspeakable defilement, and at the moment of escaping he discovered, belatedly, the hidden roadway into Der'a which he had sought. Short of death no higher price has ever been paid for a piece of military intelligence. At the end of the short and repellent chapter he appended his judgment of the event: how in Der'a that night the citadel of his integrity had been irrevocably lost, and no one who saw him immediately afterward and knew the truth could ever have doubted it. Together with his growing conviction that the Arab cause—now so nearly won on the field—was already lost in the council chambers, this rape at Der'a was the corrosive that bit ever deeper into his serenity and destroyed his inner balance. Even after he had freed himself from the Middle East in 1922, its nightmare episode remained to harrow him sleeping and waking. "There was," said Sir Ronald Storrs in his Memoirs, "the element of dismay at the standard expected of him by the public; and I doubted how far even his nerves could ever be the same after his hideous manhandling in Der'a."

Since that November night in Der'a, so many men have been beaten and put to torture with a colder, more calculated malice than the Anatolian peasant soldiery was capable of that our minds have become dulled to the shock of compulsive terror. And Lawrence's ordeal, measured by the fearful annals of Büchenwald, the unspeakable brutalities of the Nazi SS and the Russian MVD, may not seem very great; indeed, his sensitivity to it as he struggled to free himself of it may to some seem unnecessarily tender. Yet there was something apocryphal in his scourging; it was a deeply traumatic experience patterned inexplicably in sacrificial myth: a ritual mortification of the flesh and spirit, and at the same time a solemn exaction of retribution for his imposture. It was as though he had to bear on his body forever after those awful lesions of pain: the image of his still more terrible scarring of mind and spirit. That it was for him also a sexual defilement cannot be doubted.

Lawrence was now twenty-nine, and Azrak found him on the verge of fulfillment of all he had ever hoped for. The years still sat upon him lightly. Privation, wounds, and tropical sicknesses brought on by drinking foul water, were, by 1918, to cut down his weight to less than a hundred pounds, and hollow out his facial contours. Yet he still looked a boy, the more so in Arab clothes perhaps by reason of his clean-shaven, sunburned face—a freak among the hirsute manhood of the Arab world. Only when he drew up the corners of his headcloth through the royal gold and scarlet agal, swathing his face in its folds, did the severity of his features become immediately apparent. Then surprisingly, the "street-arab" could become regal; the youth with the shy Irish grin could yield to the forceful man whose quiet authority was not to be overruled. "He could be severe," wrote his friend Vyvyan Richards; "there was a mastery in his voice and eye when he was roused that few could withstand; but it was not by fear that he swayed others." [12]

The scourging and exposure afterward enforced a brief period of recovery in which he lay face down in his tower and listened to the skirling of the wind and the percussion of the rain; the murmur of voices continued about and below him: the pounding of the coffee mortar, the clatter of coffee cups, and the slap of sandals on the bare ground. For it was taken for granted that if a man slept in the daytime he did so under compulsion and needed no quiet to lull him into sleep. Nor was he left quiet for long, for the bad weather did nothing to halt the perpetual stream of visitors to the fort. Undaunted by it they came endlessly across the mud flats: Bedouin cameleers, distraught or curious peasants; Druzes on rearing, whinnying horses; suffering Armenians; Arab deserters from the Turkish levies; glib Syrian townsmen from Damascus—all to be sorted out by the guest masters and presented to one or other of the two chiefs of the fort: Lawrence and his companion, the dashing young warrior-prince, Ali ibn Hussein, who between them bore the weight of authority.

"I had never been a lofty person; on the contrary I had tried to be accessible to everyone, even if it continually felt as though most of them came and saw me every day," he wrote of this time. Like the Hebrew psalmist, he complained he had ever kept himself lowly, with no tents, no cooks, no body servants, and yet there came these daily delegations of Syrian townsmen—far differently nurtured and conditioned than the rough, often chivalrous Bedouin—with their saccharine hailing of him as Prince and Lord and Saviour, spreading

---

[12] *Portrait of T. E. Lawrence.*

corruption, he felt, with every word, and exacerbating the incongruity of his role as alien *agent provocateur* in a national uprising. The road to Damascus seemed paved with gold and frankincense and myrrh. He was overharsh perhaps in his censure of Levantines, but for their like it seemed an imposition for him to have to sit upright on the coffee hearth, his head swimming with giddyness, and buckle on the heavy gold ceremonial dagger, symbol of his authority and prestige among the sherifs of Mecca. Angrily he thrust them aside. On November 23rd, three days after his manhandling, he exchanged half of his Arab wardrobe and the kiss of peace with the Sherif Ali and took his departure southward across the brown and barren hills of Moab toward the Dead Sea.

Earlier, in June, 1917, Lawrence had ridden secretly and dangerously in the company of an old sheik of his prewar Syrian days, northward from Wadi Sirhan in a rough triangle which encompassed Ain el Barida near to Palmyra, ruined *entrepôt* of the ancient East, whose empty towers, like eyeless skulls, kept watch still upon their promontories against the drifting waves of sand; Homs, Ras Baalbek—the more glorious ruin—and up to the outskirts of Damascus; thence to Salkhad in Jebel Druz, Azrak, and down to Nebk, his starting point. Though for his own reasons he never divulged more than a fragment of its adventures, this ride was in itself a full-scale odyssey in which he made clandestine descents upon leaders who were sympathetically disposed toward the Emir Feisal but had not yet shown their hand, and reconnoitered key positions for future operations. Once he was nearly captured, and not incognito, when an ill-wisher, the sheik of the Beni Sakhr, sent to the Turks to disclose his presence. The difference between that northward journey and the one he now undertook to the south was the difference between a heart and will intact, despite lost illusions, and a will almost broken. In June he had vowed to lead the Arab Revolt "so madly in the final victory that expediency should counsel to the Powers a fair settlement of the Arabs' moral claims." [13] In November the vow still held, but his heart had

---

[13] *The Seven Pillars of Wisdom.*

gone out of the enterprise. Still wracked with fever, his punished and lacerated flesh revolting against long, hard hours in the saddle, he reduced to tears of self-pity his young companion-guard, Rahail, a rider of some prowess who had made himself unpopular on previous marches by deriding everyone else's fatigue.

The real victim of this harshness was himself; and he was now reaching the end of his strength. As they rode from ridge to ridge, descending into the valley only to rise again over jagged limestone and basalt slabs and cross the glittering gravel wastes, the black gulf opened before him—yet not black this time, gray rather, with that falsely soothing monotony of numbed senses when pain and weariness have become too great to bear. On the other side of the gulf lay delirium, and into that he now slipped. Time past and time present piled up like a massive causeway which he must somehow scale before he could find himself back in that ineffable kingdom of light from which he had come. About him, released from the limits of time and space, his many selves now were grouped: grinning, frowning, and posturing before him—all he had been, all that he would ever be, in a ghastly nightmare multiplicity.

A sharp blow on the face by Rahail, who by now had become stoic, recalled him to life and saved him from toppling out of the saddle. They were lost in the desert with darkness cloaking them, their camels floundering, and stumbling recklessly near to the Turkish lines at Abu el Lissan. After this incident there was peace between himself and Rahail, and having by this straying from their intended path lost all chance of achieving Aqaba, their goal, in the three days planned, they made a detour in order to ride up the incredible Valley of Rumm, planted in a gardenlike grace and artfulness with mature tamarisks rooted in pink sand, and flanked by its guardian cliffs of serrated rose sandstone. Aqaba was reached on the fourth night out from Azrak, at midnight, just in time to contact the British patrol camped there.

On October 31 Beersheba had been captured by the British forces and Jaffa was occupied on November 16. On December 9 Jerusalem fell, nearly completing the Palestine Campaign, and General (later

Field Marshal Viscount) Allenby, for Lawrence the one great and rugged god in the British military pantheon whose feet (to say nothing of his head) were not of clay, entered by the Jaffa Gate two days later, accomplishing after a lapse of more than seven hundred years what Richard Coeur-de-Lion had failed to do. But he came not in the manner of a conquerer, but humbly on foot as he felt was befitting a Christian soldier, and in his entourage, by his own invitation, walked Edward Lawrence decked out with the aid of friends in the uniform of a British Army major, which rank he now held, even to the scarlet band and tabs of a staff officer. It was perhaps the first and only time he was properly and completely accoutered as an army officer, but on his own admission the occasion was worthy of the effort.

> I never saw him at his heights of action nor in his depths of disillusion [wrote Field Marshal Lord Wavell later]. I met him first when he came to Allenby's headquarters in December 1917, just as Jerusalem fell. At the official entry into that city I walked beside him: he was gay that day, with jests at his borrowed uniform and the official appointment that had been loaned him for the ceremony—staff officer to Bertie Clayton.[14]

Behind the gaiety however was bitter disillusionment indeed, could his companions have known it.

The interlude in Jerusalem was significant for more than Allenby's triumph. It saw the beginnings of the Lawrence Legend which after the Armistice was to burgeon and blossom into a fantasy as preposterously gilded as any in history. Lowell Thomas, the American journalist who launched the legend, encountered Lawrence in Jerusalem in December, 1917, and, seeing a young man in Arab dress who was obviously not an Arab, walking through the Damascus Gate, he let his curiosity and journalistic enterprise lead him on to exploit Lawrence as a romantic figure. In 1917 Major Lawrence was unknown beyond the geographical limits of the Egyptian Expeditionary Force; by 1920, he had become the "uncrowned King of Arabia" whose word was law in the desert; a brilliant adept at fanci-

---

[14] *T. E. Lawrence by His Friends.*

ful disguises and unmatched for guile and cajolerie with any tribe among whom he was let loose. The legend was full of half-truths and distortions; it gave rise to a host of lesser popular myths like the Ahmed of Mrs. Hull's *The Sheik* and Sigmund Romberg's Pierre in *The Desert Song*, and worse, the whole resultant and ridiculous ostentation of well-bred young men dashing off in native dress to succor oppressed peoples and redress imperial outrages.

Between them, Lowell Thomas with H. A. Chase, his photographer, and Raymond Goslett, the British supply officer at Aqaba, produced an incredible picture gallery displaying Lawrence in Arab dress and out of it; mounted on a racing camel and standing barefooted in the Arabian sand. Apart from being numerically remarkable, the collection contains some extraordinary theatrical poses [15] which have often puzzled sincere admirers of Lawrence, and which raise the suspicion that he was indulging, with the photographers, in a little sly leg-pulling. While it seems clear that he acquiesced to being photographed out of bemused irony, it seems equally clear that he wanted to satisfy his curiosity, to see what he might look like if he actually *were* Mr. Thomas's "mystery man of Arabia." And here is exposed that odd form of self-consciousness that was his particular affliction, causing him as an introvert to shrink from notoriety and yet perversely to seek it; to deprecate self and yet always be willing to have that same self revealed in photograph or painting, out of an insatiable longing to see it as others saw it, outwardly at least. This sort of behavior made some otherwise tolerant people impatient with him, feeling that a truly great man would not be trapped into all these subterfuges. Greatness, however, is as difficult to define as genius, and both expose their bearers to strains and provocations beyond the understanding of normal men.

In Jerusalem then and whenever he returned, Lawrence basked briefly in the luxury of Sir Ronald Storrs' bachelor quarters, sleeping in a bed, looking to the paraffin lamps which refused to burn properly, listening to his friend, a fair pianist, play the piano, but melting away

[15] But consider General Sam Houston's portrait posturing as Marius, barefooted and in a toga with a backdrop of ruined Carthage.

at the mere threat of other guests. "He had Shelley's trick of noiselessly vanishing and reappearing," said Storrs. "We would be sitting reading on my only sofa; I would look up and Lawrence was not only not in the room, he was not in the house, he was not in Jerusalem. He was in the train on his way to Egypt." [16] The analogy of the Cheshire Cat comes readily to mind, and with those instincts inherent, it is not surprising that he should afterward liken Eric Kennington's black and white drawing of him—a face without neck or shoulders but with an enigmatic smile—to that fabulous Carrollian creature.

The Campaign continued after the fall of Jerusalem with raid and counterraid and increasing demolitions on the Hejaz railway which as late as 1954 was still not entirely restored to order, and with inevitable conflicts of temperament among its protagonists. Indeed, the characters who move in and out of the story of the Arab Revolt are as rich an assembly as any to be found outside Scriptural legend. The doughty old warrior-chief, Auda abu Tayi, who died in 1927, has been described by many, and by none so well as Lawrence himself. His loyalty was steadfast and enduring, as was his irascibility. Not long after the Emir Abdulla became ruler of Transjordan, he found it necessary to shut up the old desert chief in the Amman prison for intransigence in the matter of taxes.

And there was the Sherif Ali ibn el Hussein, the Harith prince and Lawrence's companion at Azrak, who would have none in his company save they could do as he did: mount a racing camel in a single leap with one hand on the saddle, the other grasping a rifle, and who "dressed spotlessly, all in black or in white, and studied gesture." [17] No touch in Lawrence's history of the Revolt is more exquisite than his description of Sherif Ali running on bare feet through the unfamiliar grass at Azrak. There was, too, Sharraf with the drooping eye which made him fearful of countenance even after a British naval surgeon had attempted to make straight the crooked; Sherif Nasir, the delicately nurtured man of gardens and gentle living, who

[16] *T. E. Lawrence by His Friends.*

[17] *The Seven Pillars of Wisdom.*

bore the discomfort and hardship of their campaign together stoically and with little complaining; and Sherif Shakir, who put off his dark cloak and, dressed dazzlingly in white, stepped within the campfire ring to perform in ritual gesture the action of a tribal song to the accompaniment of drumbeats, handclaps, and a rousing male chorus. And there were, aloof in their princely eminence yet always accessible, the four emirs: Feisal, tall, frail, charming, looking like the statue of Richard I at Fontevraud; prone to quick anger and mercurial thinking, but full of constancy; Abdulla, urbane and shrewd, who played a skillful game of chess and teased his court jester by shooting a coffee pot off his head every now and then; Ali, the eldest, pious and book-learned in law and religion, viewing with obvious distaste all this traffic with infidels; Zeid, who had a Turkish mother, an unformed, shy, and pleasant youth who languished not a little in this protracted war of his elders, but played a man's part nonetheless. Above all, there were the Ageyl, those elegant Nejd townsmen from whose ranks Lawrence's bodyguard was recruited. Handsome, keen, they "talked a delicate and elastic Arabic, and were mannered, often foppish." [18] But they were constitutionally tough and able to endure calmly the harshness of their existence and the physical punishment which in the East, he said, were the outward proofs of discipline.

The pages of his history swarm with bearded prophets, long-haired, cross-eyed bandits and barefooted, bandoliered youths flaunting their lovelocks, whose prowess and wild beauty evokes ancient pictures of the youth of Israel, the pride of Judah arraigned before the Philistines. In his preface to the catalogue of drawings and paintings by Eric Kennington exhibited at the Leicester Galleries in 1927, Lawrence was to write:

> He has drawn camel-men and princes of the desert, donkey-boys, officers, descendants of the Prophet, a vice-president of the Turkish Chamber, slaves, sheikhs and swordsmen. They represent a fair choice of the real Arab, not the Algerian or Egyptian or Syrian so commonly palmed off on us, not the noisy, luxury-loving, sensual, passionate greedy person,

[18] *Ibid.*

> but a man whose ruling characteristic is hardness of body, mind, heart and head.

It was a rich world but, significantly, it was a man's world. Except for the occasional amorphous women of the tribes who receive scant mention, no women are found woven into the tapestry's fabric, and female gender is limited to the camels, noble or intransigent, who bore the full ardors of the desert march. Above all, it was Arabia, as Charles Doughty had known it, as Edward Lawrence had dreamed of it.

In the measured biblical cadences which open Doughty's classic and set its mood are the words:

> Tell me . . . since thou art here again in the peace and assurance of Allah, and whilst we walk, as in the former years, towards the new blossoming orchards . . . how couldst thou take such journeys into the fanatic Arabia?[19]

The aspect has changed since Doughty's time and since the days when Edward Lawrence raced his thoroughbred camels across deserts of flint and volcanic detritus. Her fastness broken at last by American oil drillers trailing their lavish caravans behind them like Himyarite kings of old and altering radically the face of the landscape, Arabia is no longer quite fanatic. One day she will be open and accessible to all and her mystery will be no more inscrutable; the Campaign of 1916–18 was only the entering wedge. No one will or should regret the resulting amelioration of the desert Arab, so often in the past ravished in middle life by sicknesses brought on by malnutrition and exposure. Yet with the passing of hardship and the softening of life by contact with the West, something noble in a way of life is passing too. As Cadillacs replace camels and radios supplant *ghrazzus*, it is inevitable that they will sweep away the rich sanguinity of the true Bedouin, in which guileless innocence, patriarchal wisdom, Labanian wile, fierce loyalty, and weak vacillation are conjoined in a most extravagant archetype of human strength and frailty. For this, most in the Arab world will be glad, for the Bedouin is the symbol now of backwardness

[19] *Travels in Arabia Deserta* (New York, Random House, 1937), Vol. I.

and inferiority to the West which all Eastern peoples are resolved to slough off at whatever cost.

By January, 1918, there was a stiff price on Lawrence's head, making imperative as he approached more populous regions and the greater risk of betrayal, the complete mustering of his Ageyl bodyguard. Disciplined, daring, colorful—"like a bed of tulips"—for the rest of the war they served him with enthusiasm, with faith and honor, and when necessary, died for him. Cutthroats the British called them, but, he said, "they cut throats only to my order."

The year 1918 was a year of decision, both on the Eastern and Western fronts. The Arab forces, so long dismissed by some at General Headquarters as a tatterdemalion army, scarcely worth the gold expended on it, became one of the hinges in the gate which Allenby was inexorably closing on the Turkish Army. Early in the year, at Tafila, Edward Lawrence fought his first and only pitched battle, a miniature classic, for which he was gazetted with the Distinguished Service Order. In February they were forced to shore up again in the face of bad weather, and during this second period of idleness, tension gathered like an electric charge on a sultry day and burst in sharp flashes of primitive lust and wild dissension among the members of the bodyguard champing restlessly at the bit. Then the Zaagli, one of their two disciplinarians, set about restoring order with the whip.

It was too much for Lawrence's still-raw memory; he stopped it and then broke away from Tafila, descended into the Wilderness of Zin once more, and rode to Guweira to wait there for the gold being sent up from Aqaba in readiness for the spring offensive. Here is Captain Samuel Brodie's description of his arrival at Guweira:

> It was a dark, wet and very stormy night and, for the Guweira plain, exceptionally cold. The tent was rocking and flapping with the storm and we were huddled in our greatcoats, doing our best to keep the candle lighted, when someone said, "Is that somebody calling?" We held our breath and listened and we heard a quiet voice asking if Captain Gilman was there. Being nearest to the door I pulled open the flaps and stepped

out into the inky night only to bump into the shoulder of a camel. A small figure was seated on its back. This was Lawrence. His camel barracked down and he came into the tent. We asked him if he would take some food but he said, "No." However, we pressed him to have a cup of tea which he accepted.[20]

On the return journey, after he had shed his two reluctant guides whose blood was chilled by the bleak cold of the northern heights, he came back alone along the stony paths of the Edom escarpment on the eastern flank of Sinai. Here the snowdrifts had banked up, deep and impassable, so that he was forced to scoop out a path for Wodheiha, his pedigreed, cream-pelted camel to save her from perishing in the cold, and himself from frostbite and death. The pains of Arabia were numberless; scraping wrists, knuckles, and ankles against the hard crust of snow, he left behind a delicate pink trail—"like water-melon flesh."

There was an interval at Shobek, halfway between Petra and Tafila, where he rested on the coffee hearth of his warrior-host, Abd el Muyein, who was just newly married, and taunted him with the futility of cohabitation whose purpose is procreation—the old crying out against birth and being—and quoted the example of Dionysius of Tarsus: "Here lie I of Tarsus never having married; would that my father had not." The epitaph might well have been his own.

Days later, after a reconnaissance as far north as the Jordan Valley, he returned to Tafila and discovered to his horror that the young Emir Zeid had already spent his portion of the gold, so arduously transported, on a tissue of foolish causes. It was more than the frayed edges of Lawrence's nerves could bear, for it meant at worst the ruin of his spring plans and failure to fulfill his pledge to Allenby. His friends Colonel Joyce and Dr. Marshall had ridden up from Guweira to surprise him, but he would not stay. Irritated beyond endurance by Zeid's improvidence and prevarication, despairing of the falseness of his own position and still mourning his defilement, he rode off eighty miles to Beersheba to surrender his command and ask for reassignment. It was Hogarth, his old patron, who received him at Allenby's

[20] *T. E. Lawrence by His Friends.*

late headquarters, the man who more than any, perhaps, understood him. Zeid, who after all was young and inexperienced, a likable youth who was later to row creditably for Oxford and in maturity become the Iraqi Ambassador in London, was entirely exonerated from blame by Lawrence. The fault lay in himself, he said—a knave whose tricks were exhausted. His will moreover was gone; he confessed he feared to be alone, lest the wind of circumstance, or power, or lust, blow his empty soul away. It was a real *cri de coeur*. Hogarth however received it noncommittally and told him of Jericho's fall on February 21, wooing his mind away from his own dilemma to the larger issues of the Arab war. Slowly, painfully, the pivot of his will, damaged but not destroyed, was brought back to the Arab enterprise, but not his enthusiasm. He resigned himself stoically to see it through, come what may. Damascus was ripe for the taking, and after it Aleppo—and who knew? The victorious allies, British and Arab, might yet storm the gates of Constantinople. Only the first two of these objectives were to be achieved, for the war did not last long enough to make the other necessary. The bitter winter surrendered to spring which in turn gave way to summer, the torrid, flaming, merciless summer of Arabia, the Dead Sea Valley, and the Wilderness of Zin.

On July 15 the guerrilla leader sat down to write a strange, disquieting letter to his friend Vyvyan Richards in which he compressed his agonies, foreshortened and rationalized, and revealed the aching futility that had him in thrall. He had carried Richards' letter which he was answering, from Aba el Lissan to Aqaba then to Jidda and beyond. For himself, he said, he had been so violently uprooted and plunged into a job too big for him that everything felt unreal. He lived only as a thief of opportunity, snatching the chances of the moment when and where he found them; and he lived night and day in fancy dress, in a strange language, with the price of failure on his head if the part was not well played.

It was a long road far removed from the quest of the Well at the World's End; and, he said, "these years of detachment have cured me of any desire ever to do anything for myself. When they untie my bonds I will not find in me any spur to action." [*Letters*, No. 103.] It was, he said, like one of those dreams which seem to go on for infinity and yet which leave nothing but a blank on the screen of the waking mind. He longed always for change, and yet that was idiocy, "for I change my abode every day, and my job every two days, and my language every three days, and still remain always unsatisfied. I hate being in front, and I hate being back and I don't like responsibility, and I don't obey orders." This was in every sense a new note, a foreshadowing of the man to come: the postwar Lawrence who was a fugitive from happiness and only intermittently acquainted with contentment.

His thirtieth birthday in August, 1918, found Edward Lawrence at Bair, between Wadi Sirhan and Wadi Anab, by a pool, musing over the rare comfort and the novelty, after so many months in alien company, of being surrounded by his own kind. And as the unbelievable multitude of the British Camel Corps watered their animals, he brooded over his changed ambitions, his regrettable shortcomings, developing in retrospect out of this reverie the most provocative, misleading, and yet paradoxically revealing confession that ever a man made. In it he set himself to sound out his being, letting down the line little by little until he touched bedrock: until he knew who and what he was; and he did it in a species of code. Like all codes it is easily broken, once you have the key, but that key is not homosexuality, as so many have fancied it to be.

He begins by revealing his ambition in its crudest form—the truth was far too tender to expose to light—how he had determined to be a general and knighted by the time he was thirty: General Sir Edward Lawrence, odd-sounding and incongruous; and how, now that these honors were within his grasp he no longer desired them. Sufficient that they were within grasp; he could let them go. This disregard, this easy relinquishment of the honors his war role had brought him was not new. In the previous September he had written home: "Tell Mother they asked for that twopenny thing she likes [the Victoria Cross] but fortunately didn't get it. All these letters and things are so many nuisances afterwards, and I'll never wear or use any of them. Please don't either. My address is simply T. E. L., no titles please." [21] And the dream? That too was dust and ashes. The vision which at Oxford and later at Carchemish had bloomed in a mind most favorable to its fruition, was withered. And here a mystery rises up veiled and nameless. Who was "S. A." who received the long but cryptic dedication of his war history, and how far were S. A. and the dream synonymous?

Robert Graves believed that S. A. was a woman, and produced a letter which seems almost to prove his claim, if the conversation which preceded it was remembered accurately.[22] (And there is a story at once romantic and mysterious of a Palestinian Jewess named Sara—the same name as his mother—whom Lawrence is supposed to have known and loved ideally before the war, but it is a fanciful enough story to be dismissed.) Vyvyan Richards on the other hand saw in S. A. a lay figure introduced by Lawrence to salvage his freedom—having revealed so much of himself—by interposing an insoluble riddle between himself and the reader. To some, of course, S. A. will always be Sheik Ahmed, the boy Dahoum, companion of his early manhood who loved him well and shared his halcyon days in Syria; but there is too the literary allusion of Shakespearean sympathy, and this should not be entirely discounted.

"S. A. was a person, now dead, regard for whom lay beneath my labor for the Arabic peoples," he told Colonel R. V. Buxton in 1923. [*Letters*, No. 219.] There the matter rests. If, as he later said, "S" was a place in Syria and "A" a person, this should not be taken too literally. Lawrence's mental processes, hence his motives, can never be reduced to a simple formula, and the truth is likely to be more complex rather than less. The strongest motive throughout had been a personal one, ever-present until near the end, he confessed in the epilogue to his history. The dream evaporated in the heat and the cold, the thousand deaths of the Arabian desert. "S. A. 'croaked' in 1918," Lawrence told Captain Liddell Hart, but the dissolution may have been gradual

[21] *The Home Letters*, p. 340.
[22] *T. E. Lawrence to His Biographers.*

and prolonged, beginning in 1917, and one of the death blows may well have been delivered at Der'a that night in November.

After ambition, he sets up for contemplation the absolutes of women and animals, and confesses that he has never been capable of achieving them. A soldier with a girl, a man with a dog, were what made him most despair of himself, for they showed him the gulf between what he was and what subjectively he desired to be. The subject of women has already been broached and must inevitably return. By some Lawrence has been described as frigid, but this is really a clinical term and requires a trained faculty if it is to be properly understood. In any consideration of Lawrence's attitude toward women certain quite obvious facts must be taken into account. The first has already been mentioned—that he grew up in a singularly masculine household. The second and equally obvious fact is that his choice of existence from 1911 to 1914 gave him little opportunity to meet any women but the wives of consular officials and missionaries. In his leisure hours Lawrence was not the sort of young man who craved the distractions of society; his pleasures were otherwise. The only possibility then would have been a chance encounter with a woman as unique as himself who might early have broken through the screen of his prejudice. After the war it was already too late; his extravagant romantic reputation, the gulf which he felt separated him from the conditions of ordinary men—even ordinary gifted men; the disharmony of mind and body which was the wages of his war effort, were insurmountable barriers. And in any case, after the war, he was to retrench himself solidly in a society as uncompromisingly masculine as any in his previous existence.

As for animals, he feared "animal spirits" more than anything else, he said, and he resented deeply the animal nature imposed upon man. During one of his absences in Syria before the war, when a handsome blue Persian cat had attached itself to the family in Polstead Road, they wondered, said his eldest brother, Bob, how Ned would take to it. They found him after his return with the cat on his knees, stroking it gently and saying: "I think this is the most beautiful animal I have ever seen." [23] It was not that he disliked animals; one has only to

[23] *T. E. Lawrence by His Friends.*

read his almost tender accounts of the hardships endured by Wodheiha and Ghazala, two of the pedigreed camels which served him so well in Arabia, to know this is not so. But he was simply not a man given to enthusiasm over dogs, or horses, or even birds as Hudson was, though birds probably made a stronger appeal than any creature by reason of their shyness and aerial elusiveness.

But there is another absolute, and from this too he shied away. At Rumm, that rose-red valley of enchantment, when in September of the previous year he had stripped off his soiled, verminous clothes to bathe in a fresh-water pool, he found a hermit sitting on his discarded garments pronouncing what, for Islam, was a heretical creed: "The love is from God; and of God; and towards God." The holy man vanished soon after, leaving room for speculation that he might well have been an extension of Lawrence's own metaphysical reflections.

As for religion, there was Christianity in which he had been nurtured; there was Islam, the third great revelation of the Semitic East, constraining its followers to surrender utterly to the will of God, a faith peculiarly suited to the desert which gave it birth. He wore the Arabs' clothes, he lived their life as arduously and as naturally, seemingly, as they themselves. Why then, demanded Auda abu Tayi on more than one occasion, did he not give in wholly and embrace their faith? It was only stubbornness, the old chief felt, that kept him from doing so. But in the summer of 1917, after a sultry afternoon and evening spent on a hillside with some tribesmen of the Juheina, being shot at and trumpeted at by the Turkish garrison, he and his companions came out of their ambush and solemnly leading their camels along the railway line, within sight of the enemy, knelt down and performed the sunset prayer. "This was the first and last time I ever prayed in Arabia as a Moslem," he remarked in his history. Indeed, he never at any time posed as a Moslem, never made any elaborate pretense, fiddling with prayer beads in the company of the faithful. He was as uncompromisingly himself among the tribesmen as Doughty before him had been. He was in any case too much of a Hellenist in sympathy and education ever to be able to give himself up to the stark, monolithic creed of Islam, however much it might have appealed to him in the same way that the bareness of Bedouin life appealed to him, a complex Englishman. Yet, reading this chapter of his history, there seems no doubt that his longing to surrender himself to an absolute was very great. For men of Lawrence's temperament there is an almost irresistible desire for submission. In part it is the dark and obscure urge in strong wills for domination, in part the unassuagable longing in men of religious impulse to find their desires gathered together in a sudden illuminating focus: the longing for love, not earthly, carnal love, but the devastating love of the spirit experienced by saints and mystics. Lawrence knew that he possessed a will to suffer, and he realized that it lacked a proper motivation. There was a burden of glory laid on him, a burden which he repudiated with all the strength of his intellect, shrinking back from it, not out of fear but out of repugnance, for that particular path to the ultimate of all desires, the Beatific Vision, is marked by blood and flame.

Meanwhile, there was the problem of sex which he found so shameful by reason of its equation of man with animal. "Sex is an integer in us all," he wrote Lionel Curtis from Bovington in 1923, but he would not recognize sex as a basic human fact, a clue to the meaning of life and a symbol of human redemption: fulfillment by surrender, completion by sacrifice, the losing of self in order to find self. In defense of his attitude he says: "I liked the things underneath me and took my pleasures and adventures downward." [24] This is interpreted generally as a taste for low life, and so it was, but not in the superficial sense that so often is read into it. His vagabond wanderings in Syria and Mesopotamia, his harvesting in the fields and coaling in Port Said, "curling up by night to sleep on the breakwater by De Lesseps, where the sea surged past," [25] were routes in a search for that final level beyond which he could not sink, and yet at which he could retain, still intact, his own secret identity. The particular pleasure of these downward adventures came from achieving a perfect equilibrium in a hostile element with no dependence on artificial aids: like a man walking on the floor of the ocean without the benefit of oxygen. And the piquant humor always inherent in such situations was for

[24] *The Seven Pillars of Wisdom.*
[25] *Ibid.*

him an added titillation. Yet negatively, it was an acknowledged impulse toward debasement always latent in him even before Der'a transformed it into a virulent and masterful impulse. And the key there is masochism, with all it entailed in self-disparagement and self-abuse.

Always, he complains, there was his will waiting like a beast of prey to break out of the cage, to seize and destroy; and there were his sluggish senses. This lack of sensibility which he deplores constantly should not and will not be confused by discerning readers of his history with a lack of sensitivity. Time and again he displayed perceptions so refined, so sharpened, that the impact of them was nearly painful. The truth is that his standard of sensibility began where most men's leave off. What he complained of, what he lamented the lack of so in himself and desired so ardently was a suprasensitiveness transcending the ability of physical senses and passing over into the inexpressible realm of the spirit.

How bitter it was to confess to a longing for admiration, and yet it was there undeniably. He wanted to be liked, to be admired, and yet when admiration was proffered him, he shied away. Not only did he distrust its foundation but he feared its encroachment—if it went too far—upon his freedom. Better loneliness than an assault upon independence which he would have to fight. Possessiveness was one of the aspects of Woman that repelled him. And he desired peace, the contentment of a man at ease with his own spirit, but there stood between him and the content he craved the sham circus piece which was his effort in Arabia as a man of action: the shame of all the deceptions he had practiced on those who trusted and followed him. And all that shame was compressed allegorically into the memory of a reeking, narrow room made nauseous by the fetid crowding of hostile bodies around him; made ghastly by the suffering and the hideous agony of his own body which his strong will could do nothing to curb, as one by one his scourgers bent over him wielding the thin and terrible lash. He saw himself with loathing and yet with morbid satisfaction, stripped of all intellectual refinement, all civilized aberrations—a writhing mass of pain, debased and longing for the ultimate debasement of oblivion; a return to the nothingness out of which he had come.

Eric Kennington who met Lawrence after the war and was to contribute so many fine portraits of him, thought he detected a deeper and more transcendental cause for Lawrence's anguish in Arabia and afterward. For him, this rent in the inner fabric came not so much from exhaustion or disillusionment or even defilement as from an experience tantamount to a vivid experiencing of the Third Temptation of the Wilderness to which Lawrence, in part, succumbed at the cost of that exquisite balance of mind and body that had been his. "*Noli me tangere*" is what in essence he says in this personal chapter: "I am all thorns and briars and you will only injure yourself if you touch me." What is more nearly certain is that in Bair that August, Edward Lawrence had already decided upon his future course: degradation, the dark expedient he had accepted once before in the face of a recondite and painful predicament.

The solitariness of his part in the campaign which had haunted him for a year was now over. Henceforth, he was never far removed from his own countrymen as regulars and irregulars joined forces for the final assault on Syria; and seldom lacking a kindred mind with which to exchange opinions—a relief after the vagaries of Oriental minds. S. C. Rolls of Rolls-Royce car fame, Major (later Colonel) R. V. Buxton with his three hundred strong Camel Corps precariously mounted on their Manchester-made wooden saddles, Colonel W. F. Stirling, and Peake Pasha, were his associates now. It was a curiously mixed army broadcast over the way from Aqaba and the flood bed of Wadi Ithm along the red, undulating land that led to the Maan Plateau and Abu el Lissan: a strange melee of camels, horses, armored cars, and airplanes amid which Lawrence moved back and forth—now riding with the British, now with the Arabs—always accessible yet ever elusive, melting away and then as suddenly returning. Yet to be among his countrymen was a pleasure not unmixed with discomfort. In the nearly two years he had spent among the

Arabs he had become detached, ill-at-ease almost, in the presence of Englishmen. To ease his disquiet and anesthetize his mind, he now zigzagged over the flint deserts and the mud flats between Azrak and Aqaba in an armored Rolls, the "Blue Mist," careening along in the loose sand between tamarisks that fringed the edge of Wadi Sirhan, and being shot at occasionally by Turkish snipers. And there were wild airplane rides, making mock of the long marches by camel he had undertaken over the same ground. For the moment, at least, life assumed a shadow of its old zest. To those who accompanied him on these jaunts, he was an easy, acceptable companion whose needs were few and whose departure each time left a sense of vacancy. The men who found themselves serving under him discovered him to be a most unconventional military commander, with no parade of rank (he was now a lieutenant colonel), no condescension: a slight figure in white and gold which occasionally, and with startling effects, became a still slighter figure in khaki drill shorts and tunic, distinguished by a soft, low voice that wooed rather than ordered their compliance with his wishes. "Here was a power who seemed to command one's very soul, of charming persuasive manner, to reduce one's rebellion and counteract all obstinate ideas," wrote S. C. Rolls of him afterward.[26] And in the glow of the campfire he appeared one night, in immaculate white, to brief the British troops in a rousing talk on their role and their conduct, now that they were in "fanatic Arabia."

The conquest of Palestine was complete. In September, 1918, there began the last great march northward for which thousands of troops waited in their tents dressed along the Plain of Sharon. Then Damascus, pearl of the Arab East, tempted, set in its verdant gardens up to which the desert sweeps but cannot encompass; whose cream domes and gold-tipped minarets within sight of Mount Hermon palpitate upon the dry and burning air with all the insubstance of a mirage. "Damascus had not seemed a sheathe for my sword," he wrote in his history, but Damascus was, he saw, the fitting crown of triumph for the Arab Revolt, and he bent all his flagging efforts, which were still dynamic by ordinary standards, toward its attainment. Will and

[26] *T. E. Lawrence by His Friends.*

heart were set on it. At Azrak where he rested again, this time with twelve of his countrymen and the gentle Sherif Nasir, his mood altered and his nerve springs uncoiled. It was a precious interval.

> The preciousness would seem to have been partly in myself, for on this march to Damascus (and such it was already in our imagination) my normal balance had changed. I could feel the taut power of Arab excitement behind me. The climax of the preaching of years had come, and a united country was straining towards its historic capital.[27]

But the flaw was already implicit:

> In confidence that this weapon, tempered by myself, was enough for the utmost of my purpose, I seemed to forget the English companions who stood outside my idea in the shadow of ordinary war. I failed to make them partners of my certainty.[28]

While the British 4th Cavalry Division slowly and with painful precaution wound itself up the Pilgrims' Way, the Arabs, more mobile, raced ahead and engaged some of the remnants of the Turkish Fourth Army. Der'a, scene of his agony, fell on September 27 after the demolition—his seventy-ninth so far—of the bridge at Tell el Shehab above it. The path of retreat by which columns of the enemy now moved out was laid waste with hideous massacre and pillage: the savage brutality of war stripped of chivalry and glamor and all its imposed ethics. The rape of the Arab village of Tafas was almost the final agony. On the last day of September the crimson silk standard of the Emir Feisal was raised in Damascus, and in his name Edward Lawrence governed for three days and nights. This was the city he had known in his youth, with its crowded *suk* where he had shopped for carpets and Hittite seals, and searched out armorers still taught in the craft of chain-mail-making. There stood the great mosque of the Ummayads with praying space for twenty thousand, built on the hallowed ground of the Christian church of St. John the Baptist; one of whose minarets was named in honor of the prophet Issa, and where above a disused and sealed gate was still visible the Greek inscription: "Thy Kingdom, O Christ, is an Everlasting Kingdom and Thy Dominion Endureth throughout all generations."

---

[27] *The Seven Pillars of Wisdom.*

[28] *Ibid.*

From the grilled windows of the harems as they rode up the street in the "Blue Mist," flowers and attar of roses showered down on himself and Shukri el Ayubi, a Syrian patriot who had suffered greatly in the cause of Arab freedom. Years later Lawrence wrote to Mrs. Hardy, the wife of the poet: "That day we reached Damascus, I cried, against all my control, for the triumphant thing achieved at last, fitly." [*Letters*, No. 333.] The crowded hours of drama, tragi-comedy, and nightmare horror that followed were on epic scale, and it required all his great strength of mind and will and hand to bring some order out of chaos. Moments of quiet were rare, and when they came he recoiled from them as from an opulence too great for comfort. "I felt restless as the dusty sunlight which splashed a diaper over the paths through chinks in the leaves because, after a long spell of the restrained desert, flowers and grass seemed to fidget, and the everywhere-burgeoning green of tilth became vulgar in its fecundity." [29] So he had written of his experience at Allenby's headquarters in Palestine earlier in the month.

During the eventful tumult of the three days, the will to power raised its head again, and he feared. "More than three arbitrary days would have quickened in me a root of authority," [30] he wrote, and so he made his plans to leave, his task completed, believing one should never outstay a climax. And the worth of the Arab Campaign? "Its value to the British commander was great," wrote Field Marshal Lord Wavell in 1928, "since it diverted considerable Turkish reinforcements and supplies to the Hejaz and protected the right flank of the British armies in their advance through Palestine. Further . . . it removed any danger of the establishment of a German submarine base on the Red Sea. These were important services and worth the subsidies in gold [31] and munitions expended on the Arab force." [32] And Lord Allenby himself was in agreement.

> Lawrence was under my command [he wrote], but after acquainting him with my strategic plan, I gave him a free hand. His co-operation was

[29] *Ibid.*

[30] *Ibid.*

[31] In all about eleven million of which Lawrence expended four hundred and ninety thousand pounds.

[32] *The Palestine Campaigns* (London, Constable, 1928).

> marked by the utmost loyalty, and I never had anything but praise for his work, which, indeed, was invaluable throughout the campaign.[33]

So much for military opinion which ought to be able to judge its exponents on their own ground. Strangely, in spite of military opinion, Lawrence's qualities as a leader as well as his achievements, have been acrimoniously challenged. The fault rose with the exaggerated claims made for him, and it may be well to emphasize again that though the field of his action encompassed a thousand miles or more of territory —a formidable battleground—its scope was limited by the purpose it was made to serve and the strategy conceived by him to achieve his purpose; and it was as a strategist rather than as a leader in the popular sense that Lawrence showed that rare brilliance which commanded the respect of regular soldiers. In 1933 Liddell Hart who in spite of his great admiration held to this soberer view of Lawrence's capabilities was to write:

> By general recognition the supreme art of the strategist is to convert his opponent's advantages to their disadvantage, while minimizing his own disadvantages. By this test Lawrence has no peer. For the dominant idea in his strategy was to turn the weakness of the Arabs into an asset, and the strength of the Turks into a debit.[34]

It was as simple as that, but like most simple truths, behind it stood an intricate body of thought and a dynamic energy without which execution would have been impossible.

As a leader he was afterward to be compared to Gordon, but Gordon, that "strange compound of pugnacity, religious fanaticism, contempt of fame and riches, and vast ambition of power," [35] was less subtle, less devious, for all his blend of ill-assorted paradoxes, and less tender toward those weaker than himself. "Why Gordon?" Lawrence asked George Bernard Shaw who made the analogy in 1922. "There is only a superficial likeness I think: though my mother was a Gordon." [*Letters*, No. 184.] In truth, so soft-spoken, ardent yet boyish, a leader must appeal on other grounds than authority, and in

[33] *T. E. Lawrence by His Friends.*
[34] *Colonel Lawrence, the Man Behind the Legend* (New York, Dodd Mead, 1934).
[35] *History of the British Army.* Fortescue.

doing so he pressed his demands no less successfully than the fanatic or the martinet. "His example made it impossible for any of his force to let him down," said W. H. Brook—the gunner "Stokes" who was to figure prominently in Lawrence's war history. "To do well in his eyes was the ambition of every single one of us. He typified all that was best in man." [36] This is high praise indeed.

The Syrian autumn was golden, Lawrence's mood black, and the taste of triumph was wormwood on his lips, doubly so, for when his release was reluctantly granted him, he beheld the beauty of Damascus and saw how hard it would be to leave. Like a lover he took leave of it, fondly, seeing it soft and lucent in the evening light; and ever after he was to remember how its white dust gently lapped over his bare, sandaled feet as he walked along the quiet paths by shaded walls.

"As we hoped, we got to Damascus and there I had to leave the Arabs—it is a pity to go and it would have been unwise to stay. I feel like a man who has suddenly dropped a heavy load—one's back hurts when one tries to walk straight." [*Letters*, No. 106.] So he wrote from Cairo when his Arabian travail had ended.

[36] *T. E. Lawrence by His Friends.*

❊

5

THE HOUSE OF WISDOM

The war was over; with it had vanished, blasted in the holocaust, all those bright promises which the twentieth century had seemed to hold. Peace had come suddenly when acceptance of war as the normal state had become ingrained habit, reinforced by the grim tally of the fallen which day after day appeared in the columns of *The Times*. No one was really prepared for peace; yet at five minutes to ten on the morning of November 11, 1918, Lloyd George in jubilant mood, his white hair waving like a plume in the damp November air, proclaimed from the steps of No. 10, Downing Street, the magical, unbelievable words: "At eleven o'clock this morning the war will be over."

Between November 11 and January 18, 1919, when the Paris Conference finally opened, there was to occur an anxious jockeying for position and power by the greater and lesser statesmen of Europe, while over their heads loomed, like a crusading banner, the Fourteen Points of Woodrow Wilson. And while the great statesmen of Europe and their supernumeraries were attempting to grasp the significance of the peace, the stage was being set in Paris for the greatest international gathering since the Congress of Vienna.

In his war diary which was later published as *The War Office at War*, Sir Sam Fay made a significant entry under the date October 30, 1918: "Colonel Lawrence of Arabia called at the War Office." The second phase in the life of Edward Lawrence, that of guerrilla leader, was ended and the third about to begin. He was now to attempt to vindicate his hot resolve to fight for the Arab cause in the Council Chamber with the same verve and energy that he had fought for it in the field, and he lost no time in beginning. In November he wrote a secret report for the British Cabinet in which he pointedly stated that the Hejaz Campaign had ended in August, 1917, with the capture of Aqaba, and that thereafter, the Emir Feisal, as a sealed member of the Syrian Revolutionary Committee, had undertaken the liberation of Syria with a regular army of Syrians and Mesopotamians, returning to the Hejaz all his Arabians. Feisal, he wrote, could not be militarily independent, however, and had made himself "the handmaid of General Allenby." In so doing, he had enabled the British commander-in-chief to throw in his cavalry from Jaffa to Aleppo in pursuit of the routed Turks, without the necessity of maintaining long and costly lines of communication. This report was Lawrence's first real assault upon the lines which were forming and hardening against the Arab claims, more damaging by implication than the secret Sykes-Picot Agreement drawn up in May 1916 by Russia, France, and Britain, and exposed by the Bolsheviks after the Russian Revolution of 1917. Knowledge of the Sykes-Picot Agreement had come to Lawrence early in the summer of 1917 and contributed to the dark and bitter mood of his subsequent campaigns. In partitioning the Arab portions of the Ottoman Empire—Syria to France, Mesopotamia to Britain, the rest to be divided into British and French spheres of influence—it went contrary to the British undertaking to the Arabs during the negotiations which led up to the Arab Revolt. The Cairo promise of 1915 had been: the Arabs shall keep what they take. The Emir Feisal had entered Damascus as a liberator, enthusiastically and joyously received by the Syrian population, and it was in Syria, said Lawrence, that the Arab Movement became relevant, its purpose being to prevent the manpower and strategic advantage of that country from falling into the hands of any continental power. ("The French insist upon Syria—which we are conceding to them," he had written Hogarth in March, 1915; "there remains Alexandretta, which is the key of the whole place as you know. It's going to be the head of the Baghdad line, and —— the natural outlet for N. Syria and N. Mesopotamia . . . In the hands of France it will provide a sure base for naval attacks on Egypt." [*Letters*, No. 81.])

Syria in the hands of Syrians was preferable to Syria in the hands of France was the subtle intimation of his report to the Cabinet, and Feisal, he urged, being well educated and clear-sighted, was capable of fulfilling all the needs of Syria, so far as self-government was concerned.

This, then, was the underlying motive of Lawrence's intervention in politics in 1919. He had raised his wave in the great sea of history, and he had now to insure that its subsidence would not find the current flowing contrary to his desire. He was not concerned with Arabia proper, for which however, his report offered a number of sane and practical specifics; and certainly not with Arab unity which he called "a madman's notion for this century or the next probably," but he was concerned with Syria, joyous land of his youthful adventuring. And by Syria he meant the whole of the coastal line from Alexandretta to Tripoli in a southward sweep that embraced Damascus and then turned eastward across the steppe to the Euphrates boundary, leaving the predominantly Christian Lebanon to the French. (Monsieur F. Georges Picot had already gone to Beirut as French High Commissioner in Syria and Armenia.) All of this area, including the Lebanon, was claimed by France under moral and historic rights reverting back to the Latin Kingdoms of the pre-Crusader period, and the Sykes-Picot Agreement had to some extent acknowledged and reinforced that claim, though it reserved the interior portions of the old Turkish vilayets for Arab independence with the benefit of French and British advisers. In support of their new position, the French refused to recognize the Emir Feisal as ruler of Damascus and the other Syrian cities over which he claimed kingship, and had shown by their cool disposition toward Colonel Lawrence their annoyance at his presuming to interfere in the political sphere. So it was that the elements of a first-class international wrangle were already present by the time the plenipotentiaries took their seats in Paris.

In Paris itself, in the strange glitter of rekindled lights, the fragility of peace seemed almost threatened by the exultant fervor of victory which stimulated emotions and sometimes stifled reason, but even the fervor of victory was tempered somewhat with discontent and misgiving, exacerbated by the unwelcome presence of large numbers of Allied troops waiting in France to be demobilized. Yet peace it undoubtedly was. The Conference opened in the New Year at the Quai D'Orsay with such fanfare, prodigious organization, and impressive paper work as had never before been known. It was as though the war, which had begun with horse-drawn artillery and cavalry, and ended with tanks and armored cars, marked the beginning of the modern world as it is now known, and the Paris Peace Conference with its imposing galaxies of experts, its intricate telegraph systems, motorcycle messengers and shuttle of fast airplanes plying between Paris and London, emphasized the break with the past which had occurred since 1914. The plain man, who was becoming known as "the man in the street," showing how utterly the Victorian ideal of hearth and home had been destroyed, knew little of what went on in Paris in 1919. He recognized the central point at issue: the Treaty of Peace with Germany, and he wanted it to be a hard one; he knew that the British Delegation and its unwieldy entourage had established itself in the Hotel Majestic which, with an extraordinary gesture to national prejudice, had been provided with a British catering and domestic staff imported from provincial hotels in Britain, and that Lloyd George and Clemenceau—the Welsh Lion and the Tiger of France—were the twin pivots on which the delicate issues of peace revolved. Of the Syrian question and of Colonel T. E. Lawrence of Arabia, his hopes and his fears, the plain man knew nothing.

Lawrence came to Paris in January as a member of a delegation from the Foreign Office under Louis Malet whose business it was to handle Eastern affairs. It was the only position in which he was *persona grata* to the French government, which had vigorously denounced his meeting with the Emir Feisal when he arrived at Marseilles in November, 1918, on a British cruiser. Only in the uniform of a British colonel would Lawrence be welcome in France, said a French Foreign Office directive in November, but in this matter of dress at the Peace Conference, there seems to be some confusion of memory, deliberate or not, on Lawrence's part. "In Paris," wrote Liddell Hart in *Colonel Lawrence, the Man Behind the Legend*, "he did not don Arab dress but wore an Arab headcloth with khaki uniform and British badges on a few occasions—to the Council of Ten when interpreting for Feisal, to be photographed with Feisal." But in 1933, Lawrence himself told Liddell Hart he wore Arab dress in Paris when with Feisal and British uniform when he was functioning as a member of the British delegation, and a photograph reproduced in Robert Graves' book, *Lawrence and the Arabian Adventure*, shows him at Versailles in silk skirts, camelhair cloak, the Arab *kuffiya* half veiling his face. One convenience of this guise was that it enabled him to slip in and out of Feisal's headquarters at the Hotel Metropole without question, past the Nubian guards with their drawn swords, and there seems no reason to doubt that he did wear Arab dress in Paris whenever it pleased him to do so.

The Syrian contretemps was to continue throughout January and February, plaguing French, British, and American statesmen alike, and Edward Lawrence, "the undergraduate with a chin" as (Sir) Harold Nicolson later described him, would stride along the decorous halls of the Hotel Majestic, his displeasure reflected ever more formidably in the hard glitter of his pale blue eyes. Yet no doors were barred to him; he had the sympathetic ear of Lloyd George of whom he said afterward that he towered above everyone else at the Peace Conference. Sir Henry McMahon who as High Commissioner of Egypt had engaged in the celebrated McMahon Correspondence with Sherif Hussein of the Hejaz, told Robert Graves later how, when he arrived in Paris, no one seemed to know anything about what was actually happening, and that he could not even discover who were his rightful colleagues. The only person who appeared to know everyone and everything and who had access to the "Big Three"—Clemenceau, Lloyd George, and Woodrow Wilson—was Edward Lawrence. How he achieved it was a mystery to Sir Henry McMahon, but it was simply his old trick learned at Carchemish and perfected in Arabia of managing men without their knowledge. He approached Lloyd George as a minor British delegate, exceptionally well versed in Arab affairs and possessing a useful store of knowledge on other subjects. But when he spoke for Feisal at the meetings of the Council of Ten, he was Feisal's mouthpiece and, not being a notable linguist, his feat there of speaking alternatively in English, French, and Arabic may be regarded as something of a linguistic *tour de force.* It did not unfortunately forward the Arab case, though Feisal's charm and his zeal and eloquence, his clearheaded grasp of detail, made a lasting impression on many people, including Colonel House, the leading American plenipotentiary.

As for Lawrence, he made new friends in Paris, but he also made enemies among French statesmen and army officers, for in his zeal he went beyond reason, and though his political knowledge and acumen were essentially sound, his ardor led him into a sort of political blindness that could not and would not see the Syrian problem from the French point of view.

Spring found the Syrian question still deadlocked. On the one hand there were Britain's ambiguous promises to the Arabs; on the other, the most unambiguous contracts with the French. By then, however, French aspirations in Syria and British aspirations in Mesopotamia had rendered the Sykes-Picot Agreement unworkable and unacceptable. The Anglo-French Declaration of November 9, 1918, had put forward the rather more benign intent of encouraging native governments in Syria and Mesopotamia, out of which, like a jinni from a bottle, the mandates system was to issue. But mandatory government is not independence, and the Arabs were not satisfied.

To France, who had lost over a million of her sons in the war just ended, Britain's wartime pledges to the Arabs did not seem relevant at all in the light of later thought and political expediency; nor did it seem unreasonable to the French that their colonial aspirations be fulfilled. Under the 1916 Agreement, France would have retained under her control the coasts of Syria and Lebanon while the interior of Syria would have remained in Arab hands. Now, under the proposed mandates system, they were demanding the whole of Syria as well as of Lebanon; and as a riposte to any show of reluctance, the question was inevitably asked by Frenchmen: Would Britain be willing to surrender her claim to Mesopotamia with its potential oil riches for the sake of those same promises to the Arabs? The answer of course was that Britain would not, and that Mesopotamia did not in any case figure in the Arab Revolt. But the stirring slogan "*partant pour la Syrie*" was already popularly impressed on the mind of the French public; it was a relief from the mud and blood of the trenches. France was not greedy, she was not being petulant. Frenchmen were simply caught up and borne away by the glittering vision of Saint Louis in crusading armor, and British objections, in view of their own crudely materialist determination to participate in the spoils of the disintegrated Ottoman Empire, seemed almost sordid by comparison.

To counter Feisal's declaration that the Syrians wanted nothing but their independence and this most emphatically, M. Pichon, the French plenipotentiary, produced a Syrian poet who had lived in Paris for the past twenty years and who affirmed with equal passion that the Syrians would welcome nothing less than a French mandate. A proposal for an international commission to investigate the validity of both these claims became lost in the vagaries of the antechambers; the French refused to appoint their delegate and only the two American representatives, Dr. H. C. King and Mr. C. H. Crane, left for the Levant and ultimately made their report which was quickly shelved and forgotten. These do not appear realistic attitudes today; they may, in the welter of contemporary problems, even seem irrelevant, but the mandates question was to shape and bedevil Middle East politics for years to come, vexing future statesmen with an unhappy legacy of bad feeling which required years to expiate.[1]

[1] It is still not expiated.

To all these aspects of French opinion Lawrence remained quite cold and most bitterly censorious. He was later to write in his history:

> Even in situations of poetry the French remained incorrigible prose-writers, seeing by the directly-thrown light of reason and understanding, not through the half-closed eye, mistily, by things' essential radiance, in the manner of the imaginative British: so the two races worked ill together on a great undertaking.[2]

In Arabia he had sought to foil the French at every turn; in Paris he fought them relentlessly, and even Britain's deflections in the Arab affair seem to have been regarded by him as the result of French pressure rather than culpable ambition. By 1921 his attitude to the French was permanently soured. From Amman in that year he was to write to Colonel Newcombe:

> There's only one thing to tell the French: that the catching of assassins is no doubt desirable, and one of the functions of government: but that we in Transjordan have first to make the government, and then to make public opinion disapprove of political assassination. After this the capture of assassins becomes timely. Meanwhile it would be silly, and I'll have no part in it. We cannot afford to chuck away our hopes of building something to soothe our neighbour's feelings: and the French have made our job here as difficult as possible—if it is possible at all—by their wanton disregard of the common decencies observed between nations. [*Letters*, No. 148.]

The "dirty-dog" business had been equally shared, he thought, by Arabs and French, and he thanked what gods he had that he was neither—but only the poor brute who had to clean up after them. "Drop over here friendly-fashion sometime," he said, "and I'll show you the French picture from underneath. Not lovely."

The recrimination was mutual. The French were as bitterly critical of this sanguinary and infuriating Englishman who at every opportunity and without waiting for his government's sanction interfered in matters which were of their, but none of his, concern. They awarded him the Croix de Guerre (which he returned when he surrendered his British decorations), but it was a gesture to his military reputation, not approval of his political activities. There is a tale of

---

[2] *The Seven Pillars of Wisdom.*

his tying the ribbon of his Croix de Guerre on Hogarth's dog one day at Oxford which if true is sad, for it is a caustic marrying of his cold displeasure with his love of whimsical tomfoolery and spoils the whimsy utterly.

Early in May, the Emir Feisal, delicate, regal, seeming, said Mr. Lansing, the American Secretary of State, "to breathe the perfume of frankincense," feared for his desert kingdom and returned to Damascus. On April 7, Edward Lawrence had received word from his youngest brother, Arnold, that their father, the impeccable Anglo-Irish aristocrat, had died of pneumonia following upon an attack of Spanish influenza, the scourge that was beginning to ravish all of postwar Europe. He returned briefly to England to attend the funeral, and later that month took off for Cairo from Carnin near Lille in a Handley-Page 0/400, one of fifty-one "trail-blazers" bound for Egypt by way of Italy and Greece on a route that was soon to be flown by commercial aircraft. This adventure by air was to cost him dearly; it had a strong motive besides its appeal to his imagination and his enthusiasm for air transport, for it was undertaken to collect his diaries and all his papers relating to the Arab Campaign which he had left behind in the Arab Bureau at Cairo in 1918. The twin-engined plane carrying Colonel Lawrence, two pilots, and two airmen was in the first flight. Apart from a near ground loop in the long grass at Pisa, the flight was uneventful until they reached Rome and tried to land at Centocelle in semidarkness. The pilots, peering ahead, made a fatal error of judgment in estimating the length of the field, and the Handley-Page capsized. The first pilot was killed instantly, and the second was so badly injured that he died on the following day. Lawrence, who had sat in the rear with the two airmen, escaped with a broken collarbone, some bad rib fractures, and a mild concussion. But it was a close call, for he had been pressed by the pilot-lieutenants to sit to the fore of the machine with them rather than aft with the airmen.

He came out of hospital in time to continue his journey in one of the 0/400's of the second flight which reached Rome in May after being delayed by bad weather. And it is a measure of his cool and steady nerve that he took his seat calmly in the second Handley-Page, still encased in plaster, and continued his writing as unperturbed as though he had boarded the Orient Express. In all, with delays for bad weather and repairs, and stop-overs in Albania, Greece, and Crete, it took nearly three months for the "trail-blazers" to reach Cairo.

It was during this flight to Egypt that Lord Allenby, by then High Commissioner in Egypt, received a confidential Foreign Office telegram which he showed to Lord Wavell, informing him that Lawrence had been "lost" after leaving the Peace Conference, and that the French were persuaded he was on his way to Damascus to aid Feisal in a revolt against them. Allenby was enjoined that if Lawrence did arrive in Egypt he was on no account to permit him to proceed to Syria, and Allenby in turn made Wavell responsible for the supposed renegade. Once Lawrence had arrived at Shepheard's Hotel, Wavell immediately sent a staff officer to collect him, and he appeared before his superiors "dressed in uniform but without belt or cap—as a subaltern in something," [3] very indignant until the situation was explained to him. Within forty-eight hours he had collected his papers from the Arab Bureau and was on his way back to Paris, where he moved himself over completely into the Arab Delegation headquarters near the Bois de Boulogne and continued working on his history of the Arab Revolt.

On Christmas Day of the previous year he had written Charles Doughty from the Carlton Hotel, London, to let him know that he had been over much of the same country as his distinguished predecessor, though more securely and comfortably—which was hardly the case—meeting the men and the sons of the men whom Doughty himself had encountered years before. "It has been a wonderful experience," he wrote, "and I've quite a lot to tell. I'm afraid it is not likely to be written for publication, since some of it would give offence to people alive (including myself!) but I hope to get it put

[3] *T. E. Lawrence by His Friends.*

on paper soon." [*Letters*, No. 108.] This is the first intimation of a book to come. He had drawn up the outline before leaving Paris in April, 1919, and in Paris once again, where the spring turned slowly to summer and the crowds, many of the men still in uniform, strolled along the Champs Élysées enjoying the novelty of peace, the first draft of his war history took form. It was written in marathon sittings of twenty-two, sometimes twenty-four hours each, during which his mind gulped hungrily at the words and set them down on paper at an average of one thousand to fifteen hundred an hour. Generally, he worked for twelve hours at a stretch without food and then rested a little like a runner before going on to the next heat. And as he had measured his stride while walking in Mesopotamia in 1911, so now he took measure of his literary stride with the same curious interest. The first draft of his book was completed before he left Paris. It was a herculean task and he might well have been gratified by its accomplishment; but the awful, the agonizing, truth was that his labor had only just begun.

In July Lieutenant Colonel T. E. Lawrence, D.S.O., was demobilized, and at the end of August he returned to Oxford, his hopes in President Wilson's power to obtain self-determination for the Arabs shattered. But his efforts in the Arabs' behalf did not slacken. Early in September he was writing to *The Times* and enumerating the British promises to the Arabs and to the French as embodied in four controversial documents: the McMahon Correspondence, the Sykes-Picot Agreement, the British assurances to the seven Syrian citizens in Cairo in June, 1917, and the Anglo-French Declaration of November, 1918. It was for England and France to consult the Arabs, as the third party concerned, in any proposed revisions; for the Sykes-Picot Agreement was, he said, in a sense the Arab "charter," providing as it did for independence in Damascus, Homs, Hama, Aleppo, and Mosul. But the truth was, the Sykes-Picot Agreement—concluded without the Arabs' and until 1917 without Lawrence's knowledge—was rather less satisfying to Arab aspirations than he implied.

"The Sykes-Picot Agreement is a shocking document. It is not only the product of greed at its worst, that is to say, of greed allied to suspicion and so leading to stupidity; it also stands out as a startling piece of double-dealing." So wrote George Antonius in *The Arab Awakening.* In 1919, however, it was still worth more to the Arabs than the depredations they then felt themselves threatened with. Meanwhile, a member of the American Commission to Negotiate Peace, Professor William Yale, had been making an independent study of the Syrian situation, and now came up with what was subsequently known as the Yale Plan, which made a neater disposal of the former Turkish possessions than did the Sykes-Picot Agreement. Palestine was to come under British mandate with provisions for Zionist immigration; Mount Lebanon was to be a French mandate; Syria, from Maan and Aqaba to Aleppo, together with portions of Tripoli and Latakia, was to be constituted into what was ambiguously called a "provisionally" independent state with a representative Arab government. This too was to be under French mandate, while Mesopotamia (Iraq) was to be divided into two areas: the north, including the former vilayets of Mosul and Baghdad, the south including Basra and the emirate of Mohammerah. The northern state would be "provisionally" independent while the southern state would be granted a measure of local self-government under British mandate.

Lawrence, in a meeting with Professor Yale in October, expressed a qualified approval of the plan, and there was good reason to believe that, *imposed* by the United States, the plan would be acceptable to all the parties concerned. The British Cabinet accepted it without any formal imposition, but when Professor Yale returned to Paris to present his plan to the French, he was told by his own commission that he could not be permitted to do so since the President, who by then had returned to Washington, had left the American Commission without authority to make decisions or to take any action. It was a fantastic situation and quite inconceivable by contemporary practice in American diplomacy.

In a last effort Edward Lawrence wrote a memorandum to the Foreign Office and a private note to Lord Curzon, the Foreign Secretary, embodying his views, but in the absence of American decisiveness, adherence shifted back to the Clemenceau–Lloyd George Agreement of September 13, 1919, which would establish French military administrative hegemony throughout most of Syria, and British control in all of Mesopotamia, leaving the Arabs with that debatable "provisional" recognition of their control in Damascus, Homs, Hama, and Aleppo—as long as they could keep it.

"I am afraid my entanglements are going to keep me in the Near East a certain part of each year," Lawrence had written Vyvyan Richards in 1916; [*Letters*, No. 89.] but by the end of 1919 his Near East entanglements seemed to have been loosened. He intended now to let himself become caught up with his friend in that other dream of youth: the Morrisonian hall and the printing press, and to this end he obtained title to a field at Pole Hill, Chingford, as a possible building site. The hall would grow, starting with a printing shed, around the teakwood doors he had brought from Jidda: simple yet boasting a fine sophistication in its heated floors and its provision for hot baths. "You know Coleridge's description of the heavenly bodies in the 'Mariner,'" he had written in that same letter of 1916—"'Lords that are certainly expected' etc——I don't want to be a lord or a heavenly body, but I think one end of the orbit should be in a printing shed."

He had now been elected a fellow of All Souls and his future seemed assured—a logical development of his past: he would complete his history and live in academic tranquility for the rest of his life, pursuing in a quasi-professional fashion his hobby of book-printing, and beginning possibly with his own book: after the storm a safe harbor and peace. It was a dream, and the realization that it was an unattainable dream came to him slowly and painfully at home in Polstead Road as he sat quietly and without urgent distractions for the first time in nearly five years. At that house in Polstead Road, scene of his childhood, familiar as of old and for that reason stranger and lonelier now than any place on earth, he would remain silent and quite still for hours at a time, gazing off into what unknown horizons, what hidden vistas, his mother could only guess. And who could have lived through the tumult of the Arabian adventure, the physical and mental anguish of those two eventful years, and be set down again in the place from which it had all started years ago without feeling lost and bereft? The rudder was gone, and at times during the next few years, his ship was to yaw dangerously.

And there were saddening alterations at home. Will and Frank Lawrence were both gone, the one shot down over France, the other killed in action at Richebourg l'Avoué; Thomas Robert Lawrence was gone, and the four members of the family who remained trying to close ranks could but feel the agonizing gaps in their fellowship which the permanent loss of the others had created. There is an apparent coolness in Lawrence's acceptance of his father's and his brothers' deaths, but this coolness is only superficial.

"Frank's death was as you say a shock, because it was so unexpected," he had written Will Lawrence in July, 1915, adding: "I don't think one can regret it overmuch, because it is a very good way to take after all. The hugeness of the war has made one change one's perspective, I think, and I for one can hardly see details at all." [*Letters*, No. 87.]

Will's death only five months later was an even greater shock, jarring him the more because of his own security in Cairo, and imposing a dread of returning to Oxford to find him gone. By 1919 when he did return, the details were very clear indeed, and together with the sense of his defeat in the Council Chambers of Paris, their bleak finality conspired to depress his spirits. Because there is no published record of his reaction to these losses, it should not be taken for indifference. That letter to his mother written after Frank's death contained the words: "If you only knew that if one thinks deeply about anything one would rather die than say anything about it." [4] It may be argued that he belied this by saying much about things on which he felt deeply, but Englishmen are notably reticent about their families even when most expansive on other topics. While his letters to his parents from Cairo and later from Arabia seem inconsequential minutes about maps, stamps, and the Cairo weather; requests for

[4] *The Home Letters*, p. 304.

shoes, books, and odd Arab garments left over from his Carchemish venture, they are precisely the sort of letters a young man would write home if he were drawing a veil over his inner thoughts and emotions. From Cairo on December 14, 1917, he had written: "I wrote you last from Azrak, about the time we blew up Jemal Pasha, and let him slip away from us. After that I stayed for ten days or so there, and then rode down to Akaba in 3 days: good going, tell Arnie: none of his old horses would do so much as my old camel." [5] Within that casual "ten days or so" was concealed the wrack and sorrow, the pain and defilement of his Der'a capture.

But it was upon Sarah Lawrence that the weight of grief fell heaviest. With husband and two of her sons dead, she turned instinctively to the two elder sons who remained and, perhaps, because he was above all strong and resourceful, to Ned, the deep, the obscure one. It was for both a tragic appeal; it laid open a temporary field of dissent and fretted in Lawrence the wounded core that could find no rest or sanctuary. Home had become a prison, but too tender and memorable a prison for his present state; and from home he escaped into All Souls.

At All Souls where he went into residence he indulged in outbursts of wild, almost undergraduate exuberance, as when he leaned out of the window one tranquil afternoon and loudly clanged the iron bell taken as booty in his raid on the Tell Shahm station. And for a season he lightened the sobriety of his oak-paneled sitting room with five or six colored balloons floating free against the ceiling. The prayer rugs on the walls, Augustus John's portrait of the Emir Feisal, and a statuette of horse and rider taken from a child's grave at Carchemish, showed only his past interests. The future was dark, but intuitively he knew what it would be and waited only for the propitious moment.

Meanwhile, he had acquired many new friends: statesmen, poets, painters, writers. Among them was Robert Graves, huge and slightly stooped in the manner of the scholarly tall, with tousled hair, burning eyes, and an eccentric viewpoint, suffering keenly from the eco-

[5] *Ibid.*, p. 343.

RIGHT: Lawrence in the white silk robes of the Sherifs of Mecca. (*Courtesy of the Imperial War Museum.*)

BELOW: Aircraftman Ross on one of the family of "Boanerges." (*Combine Photos.*)

LEFT: Captain Lawrence at Aqaba.

RIGHT: The guerrilla leader barefooted in the sands of Aqaba.

BELOW: The ruined fort at Azrak. (*Photos courtesy of the Imperial War Museum.*)

LEFT: Colonel T. E. Lawrence and the Emir Feisal at the Paris Peace Conference, 1919.

RIGHT: Lawrence with a Bedouin chief and his young son. (*Photos courtesy of the Imperial War Museum.*)

nomic strictures of the postwar world; and there was the scholarly Lionel Curtis, editor of *The Round Table,* who encountered him after the Armistice and at the Peace Conference, and who was to buy his gold Hejazi dagger for All Souls. Later there was Eric Kennington who with John and Rothenstein was to paint him, to contribute much to his war history, and, perhaps, to catch his spirit in paint, crayon, and stone more perfectly than any artist who tried. When in 1922 Lawrence wrote Charles Doughty: "Of the present ministry, three or four are Fellows of All Souls, and most of the others friends of mine," he did not exaggerate, for by that time he was a private citizen no longer, but a public figure.

That autumn, in a Wildean variation of the famous catastrophe of Carlyle's *History of the French Revolution,* his own history was nearly lost to posterity. On a train journey between Oxford and London he left the manuscript in its black bank messenger's bag under a table in the refreshment room at Reading. It is open to speculation whether he lost it purposely, either because he was dissatisfied with the draft as it stood, or because he wanted an excuse for abandoning the project.[6] At any rate it had vanished entirely never to be heard of again by the time he reached Oxford and acknowledged the loss, and in high glee he reported to Hogarth: "I've lost the damned thing." But Hogarth, annoyed at his apparent negligence, only told him firmly he must write it again. It was a crushing order, but he obeyed. All but a few chapters were gone and he had to set about recreating the rest from memory, using his diaries as signposts, little realizing as he worked that this book was destined to hang about his neck like the Albatross around the neck of the Ancient Mariner, with whom he felt a secret identification, at once his curse and his means of redemption.

In August of 1919 an event had occurred that was to change his whole life: Lowell Thomas' illustrated war lecture opened at Covent Garden and marked the public launching of the Lawrence Legend.

[6] See Robert Graves in *The News Chronicle,* January 31, 1955.

It continued throughout January, moving into the Royal Albert Hall to accommodate an overflowing audience. All of his indiscrete poses in Arab dress at Jerusalem and Aqaba were now flaunted before a delighted public, and his Arabian exploits, which had been incredible enough without any gilding of fact, were given a distorted and often inaccurate airing. With the help of a clever presentation and title—"With Allenby in Palestine and with Lawrence in Arabia"—the lecturer succeeded in blowing up the obscure Colonel Lawrence into an oversized national celebrity, a figure so romantic—in the wrong sense—that the war-weary, hero-hungry British public gasped in its admiration. Who was this exciting young army officer who had spent the war in fabled Arabia leading an Arab revolt that few people had ever heard of? Why had not the public been told of his existence before now; why was it left to an American to unveil the most provocative, sensational figure turned up by the war? The distortion and the fanfare were a pity, for in a very real sense, in his attitudes toward history and toward himself, Edward Lawrence *was* romantic to a degree beyond the most extravagant conception of popular fancy.

The implications of the Lowell Thomas legend were enormous. Lawrence was the man who, singlehanded—a boast which exercised him more than any other for its slight of all those who had shared the Arab Campaign with him—had led the Arabs in their revolt against the Turks; who had harassed the enemy in the desert, aided by a band of cutthroats who could be controlled only by himself; who was so adept at disguise that it was impossible to tell who and where he was at a given moment: he might be the dervish who demanded baksheesh in the market, or the dancing girl who hid seductively behind a yashmak and slipped in and out of secret councils through the doors of the harem. He went himself to the Albert Hall to see and was made hot and embarrassed by the spectacle. And yet he returned time and again, secretly fascinated by his own romantic capering. Hearing this journalistic nonsense about himself—which in a sense he had helped to propagate—he was even more ashamed of the part he had played, since it could lend itself so readily to fraudulent exhibition and travesty, and make of himself a jackanapes figure whose practiced deceptions were even more gaudy than he had thought.

"I'm a sublimated Aladdin, the thousand and second Knight, a Strand-Magazine strummer" [*Letters*, No. 120.], he wrote Colonel Newcombe in February, 1920, half humorously, half despairingly, regretting both the unwanted notoriety and his own failure to do better in the effort that had precipitated it. But "Lawrence of Arabia" was now his identity, fixed and permanent; he could not lose it no matter how he turned and twisted. By 1920 he was distinguished by an entry in the *Who's Who:* Thomas Edward Lawrence, Archaeologist, Arabic Scholar; C.B. 1917; D.S.O. 1918; 2nd Lieutenant 1914; Lieutenant Colonel 1917. In 1921 the "Colonel" was followed by the lofty title, "Prince of Mecca" which has been the source of much acerbent comment. A Prince of Mecca, strictly speaking, is an emir, of the Family of the Prophet and of the House of Bani Hashem. This, Edward Lawrence could never be, though he wore the clothes of an emir and was invested with an emir's honor. No doubt it was vanity which dictated its inclusion with his honors in 1921—vanity and the irresistible impulse to pull the legs of solemn readers and romantic enthusiasts alike. In the entry for 1922 the Archaeologist and Arabic Scholar has become Adviser on Arab affairs, Middle East Division Colonial Office; the "Colonel" is dropped in favor of the 2nd Lieutenant, and the "Prince of Mecca" has vanished! Because of criticism—or because he had tired of the joke? Probably both. (Correspondence in 1951 and 1953 with the publishers of *Who's Who*, however, suggests that the entries with the list of honors may have been prepared by the editors, and that Lawrence petitioned for their removal.)

Meanwhile, the "Prince of Mecca," the "Uncrowned King of Arabia" continued to work quietly at Oxford on a shortened version of his history which he jokingly referred to as "my Boy Scout Book," to be published in America where, he said, it would undoubtedly have great appeal for Boy Scouts. To the astonishment of those who now met him for the first time, fed on his legend, he was not at all cast in heroic mold. Eric Kennington who first saw his future subject at Lowell Thomas' exhibition—"all glorious photography, glamour and oratory," and came out drunk from it all—discovered the fabulous Colonel Lawrence of Arabia to be a "small grinning, hatless kid, bothered by a lot of untidy hair falling over his eyes," [7] with a habit of teasing and chuckling over his victims' discomfort like a delighted schoolboy. But he quickly discovered too that his subject could and did on occasion unsheathe a power of mind and will which were not easy to oppose. As for the propensity for youthful mischief, it seemed as strong as ever. At Fullers' Restaurant for tea with Robert Graves, he caused a momentary flurry amid the teacups by clapping his hands, Eastern fashion, to summon the waitress; and once he indulged again in his old sport of roof-climbing in order to hang a crimson Hejazi flag from the pinnacle of All Souls. He had one scheme to rob Magdalen of its herd of deer; another to present a peacock to All Souls bearing the name of Nathaniel, after Lord Curzon who was then the Chancellor. He was visited in his rooms at All Souls by *avant-garde* poets and American oil men, and it was clear that his presence bestowed a luster on the college beyond that of mere talent or achievement, and a piquancy not normally associated with serious men of letters. These were pleasant or frivolous pastimes which anesthetized his mind; they did not bring peace of soul, but even so they might have led him into the way of that peace, given time. Had he not set out with all his energy to recapture the events of the past two years, those events might in time have faded naturally into a perspective whole, monotone instead of all hectic scarlet and purple. It is a law of life that highly concentrated and eventful living shall not, granted sufficient time to follow, seem greater in the balance than what has gone before or what comes after. For Lawrence, however, this leveling off was not to be; Hogarth who had once before moved fatefully in his destiny, urged upon him unceasingly the duty of writing the history of the Arab Revolt as he had seen it from his unique position. But even if Hogarth had not pressed him, he might

---

[7] *T. E. Lawrence by His Friends.*

still have been impelled to do so by his own strong historical consciousness and his desire to write a "great" book.

In May, 1921, Lawrence wrote to his new friend, Robert Graves: "Our schemes for the Middle East are doing nicely thanks. I wish I hadn't gone out there: the Arabs are like a page I have turned over: and sequels are rotten things: do you want to make a happy ending to a tragedy? On paper it isn't virtuous, but in flesh and blood? I wish I knew." [8]

He was reluctant indeed to become entangled in Eastern affairs again, but when Sir Winston Churchill took over the Colonial Office in 1921 and invited him to join a panel of experts, Lawrence's conscience would not let him refuse, though he had to be persuaded. The last doubting question in his remarks to Graves is the key not only to his hesitation but to his author's sense and judgment of what was fitting. His book was designed originally as a personal tragedy on an epic scale; instead it was now to bear the superscription, "A Triumph," and he was uncertain how far this would mar its poetic wholeness. Syria it was true was lost, but there was still a chance of redeeming honor in Iraq and the marginal states. Should it be redeemed? He could not forebear to try.

In March, therefore, he was in Cairo, one of a distinguished fellowship of conferees which included Sir Herbert (later Viscount) Samuel, the first High Commissioner of Palestine; Sir Percy Cox; Gertrude Bell; Jaafar Pasha, an Iraqi and an officer in the Turkish Army who had volunteered for the Arab Revolt; Sir Hugh (later Viscount) Trenchard and General Sir Geoffrey Salmond. The question of Iraq had already been discussed and disposed of before the Conference assembled in the Semiramis Hotel. It was agreed that the Emir Feisal should be invited to take the throne in lieu of the one he had forfeited in Syria, and that thereafter the keeping of order in the country should be entrusted to the Royal Air Force. But another

---

[8] *T. E. Lawrence to His Biographers.*

thornier question developed even as the Conference took its seat. Transjordan, originally part of the Palestine Mandate but later excluded from the undertaking of the Balfour Declaration, had become the rallying point of disaffected Syrian nationalists driven from their government posts by the French. Unexpectedly and without warning, in March, the Emir Abdulla arrived in Maan traveling up by uncertain stages from Mecca on the maimed Hejaz railway, burning up telegraph poles for fuel as he came—there to be welcomed by the Syrian nationalists who needed very little urging to seek redress. Abdulla, accompanied by Lawrence's old comrade-in-arms, the Harith prince Ali ibn Hussein, was there, so ran the rumors in the bazaars, with one avowed purpose: to raise volunteers in Transjordan to fight against the French in Syria and regain for his brother the lost throne and prestige of Damascus. True or not, it was an embarrassing and altogether insupportable position for the British with Transjordan under mandate, since the French in Syria took the threat seriously and protested vigorously from Damascus to the Conference sitting in Cairo. Lawrence listened to the reports, asked questions, and as usual absorbed the situation rapidly, seeing it not as a calamity but as an unforeseen event which could be turned to advantage. First, he urged a meeting in Jerusalem between his chief and the Emir Abdulla who, across the gap of alien environment, culture, and language were not wholly dissimilar in temperament. The meeting was the success he expected it to be. Out of it after half an hour's talk on the Mount of Olives came a provisional agreement to recognize Abdulla as the ruler of Transjordan and the beginning of a new state in the Middle East. The effort "to make straight the tangle" was progressing. Of his meeting with the "Jonathan" of his Azrak days there is unfortunately no record. Perhaps it was unrewarding and strained, as such meetings are apt to be. It was not so much the gulf of time—which was not great—which separated them, but the difference now in the conditions under which they confronted each other: "Lurens Bey" stripped of all his power, his incredible prowess, and Ali ibn Hussein the warrior whose pace, swift though it was, had never outrun him.

To Charles Doughty to whom Lawrence never revealed any of his doubts or his private agonies, but always adopted the air of a happy schoolboy reporting his adventures respectfully to an admired elder, he wrote after the Cairo Conference: "I'm back in England for a little bit (next move probably Jidda) after spending six weeks across the Jordan, most of it in Amman where conditions are strange and rather exciting." [*Letters*, No. 142.] He was in Arabia again by July, in Jidda at the height of the sweltering Red Sea summer, to treat with King Hussein who in his old age was becoming more fractious than ever and was demanding unreasonable concessions with a petulant, childish obstinacy. It was during these futile and exasperating negotiations that the famous cable exchange between Lawrence and Lord Curzon occurred which is supposed to have resulted in the word "wangle" being added to the Foreign Office cipher book.[9]

From Jidda he sailed south to Aden and then in October, "Lurens Bey," in a dark blue lounge suit and gray Trilby hat, was back in Transjordan, traveling over much of his old ground in a model-T Ford. It was a strange and unsettling experience; this was the desert where he had striven mightily, endured stoically for the sake of an ideal. Here was the mute evidence of carnage: the twisted rails of the wrecked Hejaz railway, ghostly now without its trains, haunted by the complaining shades of all the Turks he had killed. To return to it now was to find it a shadow-box, as unreal as a pasteboard scene when the curtain is rung down. His deeds in retrospect seemed not epic at all but sham, and the house he had hoped to erect as a tribute to Wisdom was a tawdry violence built on shifting sands.

Peake, then still unmarried, was immured in a stone house in Amman, on the site of a Byzantine church whose shattered nave pillars stood in the garden amid quinces and flowering japonicas. Into this demesne of ruined Byzantium and English fireplaces built to order by Arab laborers for English tastes, but with a scornful disregard of the laws of flues and up-drafts, Lawrence came, another bachelor, and the two of them lived with a semiwild Egyptian cat for

[9] See Robert Graves, *Lawrence and the Arabian Adventure* (New York, Doubleday, Doran, 1928).

company. The office of the British Political Resident put at his disposal he scorned, packing up the official typewriter and throwing away the files which, as it happened, contained a number of passports waiting to be endorsed, whose owners, not unnaturally, were somewhat chagrined at his unorthodox handling. With Peake in the model-T (which once, in a fuel crisis, ran for miles on sunflower-seed oil) he toured the new desert kingdom, unsteady as yet on its foundations and plagued with poverty and banditry.

"Lawrence was an amusing guest to entertain, but he was a man of moods," wrote Major C. S. Jarvis in his biography of Peake Pasha. On some occasions he was the most ingratiating of companions, ready with humorous anecdotes about the Peace Conference—the Foreign Office official who went off to Paris with seventy lady typists and a Harley Street obstetrician as Medical Officer. At other times he was uncommunicative, burdened under the weight of his contemplation and visibly depressed. He would disappear then for several days and return eventually with a lively cohort of Bedouin friends. On those occasions there were huge feasts of saffron rice spiced with pistachio nuts and raisins all heaped over a baked sheep which, Peake's house being too small to accommodate, were served in a large goat's hair tent set up in the garden.

Why did Lawrence not remain in Transjordan or in some other Arab country as Peake had done, as St. John Philby was to do? The answer in part is that it was psychologically impossible. He had done with the Arab adventure and he could no more retrace his steps than he could rekindle the mood which begat it. Other British officers concerned with the Arab war, some of them regular soldiers, could return to the Middle East and help to shape its future policies. They had not been in the Arab Revolt from beginning to end, caught up in it heart and soul in a special and intimate fashion. To them it was simply a military adventure; to Lawrence it was the summation of all he was, and all that he had become.

> What more? Nothing [he had written to Eric Kennington from Cairo, before going on to Transjordan]. I'm bored stiff: and very tired, and a little ill, and sorry to see how mean some people I wanted to respect have

> grown. The war was good by drawing over our depths that hot surface wish to do or win something. So the cargo of the ship was unseen, and not thought of. [*Letters*, No. 146.]

And too, the role of government official came awkward to him. Not only were his actions closely watched by Whitehall, but his thoughts were also bound, and to be really effective in all his power, Edward Lawrence required to be untrammeled and free from all official restraints. How unfitted he was for the role of Political Resident may be seen from Philby's account of the transfer of office and authority when, in 1921 he went to Transjordan at Lawrence's request to relieve him: no records, no memoranda except an initialed copy of the secret McMahon Correspondence and a sheet disbursing £100,000 in gold which he had used up during his short term of office. And on this, £10,000 was listed unaccounted for—"lost, I forget how or where." It was later found in a safe buried for security in the sands of Aqaba. But, said Philby, a month spent in his company was an exhilarating experience. He was strong as steel, incredibly enduring, incredibly ascetic, with all his belongings fitted into a little suitcase. It was cold during that winter month across the Jordan, yet he possessed no overcoat, though he appeared correct and clean always in a stiff collar—made of celluloid, with a dicky: the cheap gentility of clerks and commercial travelers in the Brave New World.

Major Jarvis has suggested that Lawrence saw in Transjordan in 1921 the problem in microcosm of all the Arab states, and realized that those who had now come forward to assume control were not the men he had fought with—the inevitable development in nationalist movements once the days of blood and strife are over. Perhaps; the dream in any case had died long ago and what he did now he did to quiet his conscience. His return to the scenes of his wartime triumphs and defeats was a painful and exasperating anticlimax, though not without its own achievement, which was why he alternatively regretted and approved it. Feisal was firmly established as King of a partially pacified Iraq; Abdulla was installed as Emir of Transjordan; he felt that due honor had been paid to the sherifs and that Britain was out of her wartime adventure with clean hands, though "three years too late to earn the gratitude of the Eastern peoples."

Was he really satisfied with the 1921–22 settlements? In 1929 he was to write to Professor Yale:

> The Sykes-Picot Treaty was the Arab sheet-anchor. The French saw that, and worked frantically for the alternative of the mandate. By a disgraceful bargain the British supported them, to gain Mesopotamia . . . By the mandate swindle England and France got the lot. The Sykes-Picot Treaty was absurd, in its boundaries, but it did recognize the claims of Syrians to self-government, and it was ten thousand times better than the eventual settlement. [*Letters*, No. 397.]

But rebellion, financial pressure, and perhaps, he said, conscience aroused by his own agitation, did persuade Britain to abrogate *de facto* the mandates of Iraq and Transjordan, though she still was *de jure* the mandatory power. "It is my deliberate opinion that the Winston Churchill settlement of 1921–22 (in which I shared) honourably fulfils the whole of the promise we made to the Arabs, in so far as the so-called British spheres are concerned," he concluded. Not all Middle East students, and certainly few Arabs would agree. They did not then agree. In the draft preface to the revised Oxford text of his history he wrote:

> Some Arab advocates (the most vociferous joined our ranks after the Armistice) have rejected my judgment on this point. Like a tedious Pensioner I showed them my wounds (over sixty I have, each scar evidence of a pain incurred in Arab service) as proof that I had worked sincerely on their side. They found me out-of-date: and I was happy to withdraw from a political milieu which had never been congenial.[10]

As for those who expected great things of Islam:

> I don't believe in any form of religious revival in the Western Islamic countries [he wrote in 1923]. Their present passion for nationality has driven out their former fanatical interest in creeds—and I do not believe that anything will make political a faith which has become, like our Christianity, a purely ethical concern. Ireland and Poland are the two Christian parallels to India, where Islam is still a power at the polls. In

[10] See *Letters*, p. 346.

> Turkey, Egypt, Persia and the Arab countries, orthodox Islam is no longer a fighting creed. [*Letters*, No. 194.]

His later views were often illuminating:

> Our aim was to free from Turkey and make self-governing, not the Bedouin, who have a secure, unenvied freedom: but the settled peoples of Syria and Irak [he wrote to a former officer of the Camel Corps in 1928]. To avoid upsetting places like Egypt and Algiers, the Arab Movement had to be kept within these dykes. In the Middle East religion has completely yielded to nationalism as the motive in politics. So our job was relatively easy. [*Letters*, No. 342.]

But Arab federation was a fantastic hope for generations to come—unless the tempo of the East was quickened. "I agree their only future is that they should join but it must be a natural growing-together. Forced unions are pernicious: and politics, in such things, should come after geography and economics." The nearest approach to an Arab Empire was Ibn Saud's, but, he said, "It is a figment built on sand. Nothing static will rise in the desert, which has seen hundreds of such tyrannies as his, all cemented (less liberally, perhaps) with blood. It will pass." Ibn Saud's empire, thanks to war and oil, held, however, and this was a long and inaccurate shot. But the awakening of Asia which he did foresee is still in progress.

On the subject of Palestine he had no strong views except to welcome the Zionist experiment whose protagonist, Dr. Weizmann, he had met and much admired, and to look upon it as the irritant which would spur the Arabs on to greater effort in their own behalf. History has not proved him wholly right in this, but history in the Middle East is still being made, and in any case, he could not be expected to anticipate the Palestine debacle of 1948.

When at Der'a, to which he returned in October, 1918, on his way out of Syria to make his farewells to Peake, he rose up to take his leave, a strong earth tremor shook the house and left them both awed.[11] Was it an omen? There is no record that any similar phenomenon marked his ultimate leave-taking of the Middle East, but

[11] Major C. S. Jarvis, *Arab Command.*

he was quit of it utterly and forever after 1921, except in the haunting vistas of his book and the still darker regions of his dreams.

Lawrence had crowded much into the past three years: the Peace Conference, the flight to Cairo, the writing of the first and second drafts of his history, and all the arduous work he gave to the Colonial Office, and it had taken its toll of his health. Lord Keynes who saw Edward Lawrence at the Peace Conference wrote David Garnett: "When I knew him in the spring of 1919, I should have said that he was a man fully in control of his nerves and quite as normal as most of us in his reactions." By 1921 it was clear he was not normal in his reactions. For David Garnett, the airplane crash and the subsequent disillusionment of the Peace Conference were the chief contributing causes of Lawrence's deterioration, but it has been shown how steady his nerve was still when he started his flight from Rome in the second Handley-Page bomber after the crash of the first, and indeed, there was another, more relentless ravisher of nerves. In 1921, while still at the Colonial Office, he worked by night on the third draft of his history, often far into the early morning hours without regard either for food or sleep; and it was this reckless pouring out of himself on a task which by alternatively raising him to a fever pitch of excitement and casting him into abysms of despair, sapped away his vitality. George Orwell has said that writing a book is "a horrible, exhausting struggle like a long bout of some painful illness." For Lawrence to relive his Arabian adventures meant reliving their emotional impact upon his spirit, and it was an excruciating and under the circumstances psychologically dangerous experience which left him spent and empty. Night after night he sat in his attic in Barton Street, Westminster, over the offices of his friend Sir Herbert Baker, the architect, retching out his soul and then goading himself on to even more prodigious efforts of soul-draining. It was not sufficient merely to recreate the atmosphere and the *mis-en-scène* of the Arabian Campaign; he must dragoon the words into a perfect fulfillment of his creative will and, employing all the splendor of his wide and rich vocabulary, evolve a poetic synthesis which should catch up himself and his moods, the awe and grandeur of the Arabian landscape, and the unpredictable, blood-stirring hazards of irregular warfare. The result was to be an unforgettable cyclorama in which he himself was both protagonist and spectator, victim and judge, which carried the reader across the deserts of flint and sand through stark physical privation into the more bitter agonies of his soul.

> No man ever yet tried to write down the entire truth of any action in which he has been engaged [he was to write to Lionel Curtis in 1927]. All narrative is parti pris. And to prefer an ancient written statement to the guiding of your instinct through the maze of related facts, is to encounter either banality or unreadableness. We know too much, and use too little knowledge. [*Letters*, No. 331.]

He did not write the whole truth in his history; he did not write of the hidden dream which had quickened his action, nor of its dissolution—that would have been too painful. And there were adventures in Arabia too wild, too ghastly even for him to record; all the more surprising then that he should have chosen to record in part his defilement at Der'a. Ever after he was sorry and ashamed.

> If that Der'a incident whose treatment you call severe and serene (the second sounds like a quaint failure to get my impressions across, but I know what you feel) had happened to yourself you would not have recorded it [he wrote Edward Garnett in August]. I have a face of brass perhaps, but I put it into print very reluctantly, last of all the pages I sent to the press. For weeks I wanted to burn it in the manuscript: because I could not tell the story face to face with anyone, and I think I'll feel sorry, when I next meet you, that you know it. The sort of man I have always mixed with doesn't so give himself away. [*Letters*, No. 162.]

While London dined, danced, flocked to the theater to see *The Lady of the Rose*, *The Dover Road*, and *The Beggar's Opera*, and then slept, he sat at his table and filled foolscap sheets with his vigorous, legible handwriting, using a large black fountain pen and India ink. To keep warm in his eyrie, he wore a fleece-lined flying suit and sometimes gloves. Direct vision is often blinding, and the reflection in the glass, offering a subrogate image is less shocking, to the viewer. So

Perseus looked into his shield to slay the Gorgan; and Edward Lawrence, unable to bear the image of himself as he was, held up the polished mirror of High English prose in which to view himself and his actions. Robert Graves felt afterward that he had unconsciously emulated Doughty and strived for some ultimate consummation in prose-writing, poetry being beyond his reach. He was striving for perfection certainly, and after the experience of most writers, the conception he succeeded in committing to paper did not reach high enough quite to encompass the inner vision that had fired him. The fault, he felt, was innate in the book's structure. "All the revision in the world will not save a bad first-draft: for the architecture of the thing comes, or fails to come, in the conception, and revision only affects the detail and ornament, alas!" he told Bruce Rogers in 1931. [*Letters*, No. 451.]

"I nearly went off my head in London this spring heaving at that beastly book of mine," he was to write Robert Graves from Farnborough late in 1922. How near to complete collapse he was during those last few months of his freedom he did not himself fully realize until they were over. He was haggard, strained, dangerously withdrawn, with a fever raging in his brain beyond the cure of any but a most drastic antipyretic. When he was not writing at night he roamed the London streets with steady-pacing policemen and prowling cats. Graves who saw him in those critical months was alarmed at his appearance and urged him to take himself in hand, to end his experiment with solitariness "and to find some appropriate woman who would help him to a settled life." It was no use; Lowell Thomas' spectacle at the Albert Hall had made him the romantic object of irrational pursuit by foolish and fashionable women alike, and left him shying off feminine society to an even greater extent than before.

Was his history worth the effort? Is any work of art—and within its limitations this was a work of art—worth the pain and ardor lavished on it by its creator? It is a question the creator cannot stop to ask if he is impelled by an irresistible creative urge. Writing was the means of sublimation and self-justification which he craved, as once he had wanted to sculpt; and he craved it so avidly that he could not bear the thought of failure and yet could not believe he was able to attain to the high level of achievement which as a purist he set as his ultimate goal. As his war history took form, he developed toward it an ambivalence more violent than that normally felt by an author toward his work.

> Do you remember my telling you once that I collected a shelf of "Titanic" books (those distinguished by greatness of spirit, "sublimity" as Longinus would call it): and that they were *The Karamazovs*, *Zarathustra* and *Moby Dick*. Well, my ambition was to make an English fourth. You will observe that modesty comes out more in the performance than in the aim! [*Letters*, No. 164.]

So he wrote Edward Garnett that August. His ambivalence drove him from pole to pole, alternatively defending and then rejecting his work with an exasperating variability.

> I should have warned you before I sent it (only it seemed so remote a contingency) that if your opinion was favourable it would be wasted on me [he wrote Edward Garnett in another August letter]. The thing is spotted in nearly every line with blemishes of style, and while my critical sense doesn't reach as far as subject matter and construction, I judge them equally bad, by analogy. [*Letters*, No. 162.]

And again a day later:

> Don't call me an artist. I said I'd like to be, and that book is my essay in the manner of an artist: as my war was a decent imitation of soldiering, and my politics chimed well with the notes of politicians. These are all good frauds, and I don't want you to decorate me for art, over the book in which I explode my legend as man-of-war and statesman! [*Letters*, No. 163.]
>
> It reads to me inferior to nearly every book which I have found patience to read —— and that is many [he was to tell E. M. Forster in 1924]. If it is the best I can do with a pen, then it's better for me to hump a rifle or spade about: and I fear it's the best I can write. It went through four versions in the four years I struggled with it, and I gave it all my nights and days till I was nearly blind and mad. The failure of it was mainly what broke my nerve and sent me into the R.A.F. . . . [*Letters*, No. 243.]

Yet if friends to whom he submitted his history criticized it, he was quick to suggest that it was better composed than most books written by retired soldiers—though he was scarcely a typical soldier —and that there might be some obscure merit in it after all. All this made it difficult for those of his friends who genuinely admired his history and wished it to be read by a wider audience to help him to see it in a more balanced light. It had its faults of course; it was overwritten in places, fastidiously delineated, almost precious in style, with every word fitted into place like pieces of a mosaic work, and never a careless phrase or a crooked clause. But it remains, as Sir Winston Churchill has said, an English classic, and through its closely meshed and jeweled pages, the person of the author—the incredible "I"—veiled as he intended himself to be—shows forth; tantalizing, seductive, and ever evasive.

Early in 1922 the third draft of his manuscript was set up in type at the Oxford Times Press, and eight copies were run off, printed two columns to a page, at a cost of about eighty pounds. This is the so-called Oxford text. By then the history had acquired a title: *The Seven Pillars of Wisdom*, after an earlier "youthful indiscretion book" written before the war and destroyed, he said, when he joined up. The earlier book had recounted his adventures in seven Eastern cities: Cairo, Smyrna, Constantinople, Beirut, Aleppo, Damascus, and Medina—which he apparently intended visiting but war intervened. Afterward he said that it "arranged their characters into a descending cadence: a moral symphony" and was a queer book. The borrowed title was a memorial to his lost youth, actual and metaphysical, as well as the record of his triumphs and his failures. Within the suggestive frame of this cryptic allegory, "Wisdom hath builded her house, she hath hewn out her seven pillars," the reader could impose what symbolism he would; just as he could read what he would into the allegorical poem which was its dedication.

His work with the Middle East settlements was finished; his war history was finished—at least he had achieved a perfect but rough cast which he could refine and burnish at leisure—and already it was illustrated by a lavish collection of portraits of those who had participated prominently in the Arab Campaign, drawn by Eric Kennington, Augustus John, and other artists whom he commissioned when he first considered printing. He asked now for his release from the Colonial Office, and when Churchill, reluctant to lose his Eastern expert, refused, Lawrence resigned but continued to go into the Colonial Office until his chief should find it convenient to give him a formal release.

The home in Polstead Road, Oxford, was sold in 1921, and with it the little garden house where he had dreamed his dangerous daylight dreams before the war. In that same year his eldest brother, Dr. M. Robert Lawrence, went out to China as a missionary doctor. His mother, who with Bob and Arnold had met Ned in Jerusalem in the early autumn of 1921 and driven with him to Es Salt, was to join the eldest son in China a year later. Thus there were no loose ends left to be gathered up; the way was clear at last for the downward experiment he intended to make.

When in 1933 Liddell Hart asked him what he did immediately after leaving the Colonial Office, Lawrence's answer was: "Nothing at all, except tramp London." Poverty, self-chosen, now pressed hard upon him. He was a national celebrity, but so far as material gain was concerned, his position had netted him nothing at all. During the war his army pay, when he had claimed it, had been sent home to his parents or thrown back into the Arab cause, and after 1917, his wages were so tainted by the dishonor of his cause that they were barred to his own use. As for his Colonial Office emoluments, he felt he could not use them to his profit, and they too were put to official use, while the fund from his All Souls fellowship was devoted almost entirely to financing the illustrations for his book. In 1922, therefore, he was very nearly penniless, though Colonel Newcombe has described this complaint of penury as a mental aberration, since he could, had he wished, have drawn on family funds. In fairness to Lawrence it should be said that the penury was of his own choosing, and he never claimed it was otherwise. In his hands was the key to a fortune; his book when finally it was published in abridgment netted a clear £14,000 for the trustees after the payment of income tax and his overdraft of £7000 incurred in the publication of the subscribers' edition of *The Seven Pillars of Wisdom;* and it would have earned much more had he not withdrawn it soon after. The book, however, was in the same category as his wages, tainted and dishonored by his part in it.

He had come out of the war and the peace as Colonel T. E. Lawrence, C.B., D.S.O., and when it was proposed to add a "K" to the C.B. fulfilling exactly his old craving for the distinction of knighthood, he refused while surrendering his previous honors in a private letter to the King—not at a formal investiture as has so often been claimed. At the same time the High Commissionership of Egypt was also being considered for him as successor to Lord Allenby, but this too, like all other political offices, was unacceptable. It may appear like wilfull intransigence on his part that while His Majesty's Government were busy trying to find a position for him that was acceptable, he was scheming determinedly to discover a way of making himself professionally unemployable. Archaeology was out; he would, he said, be suspect in every country he might wish to dig in, except in Central America where he did not apparently wish to dig; and the truth was that archaeology could not serve him in his present state of mind. Friends stood ready to help him in any way they could; Colonel Newcombe offered him the peace and refuge of his home in Devonport, or the solitude of bachelor's quarters on Drake's Island, if solitude was what he wanted; but it was no use. He had been drawn into a shadowed continent, and it was by no means certain that he could return. If he did, it would be by a route undreamed of by his friends. And so he tramped the London streets, a slight, hatless, nondescript-looking young man in an old army raincoat, his mind convulsed with anxiety: the terror of walking into the unknown—yet not quite unknown; of taking the most solemn decision of his life.

"Seriously," he had written in that letter to Colonel Newcombe deploring his inflated reputation, "I am changing my own name, to be more quiet, and I wish I could change my face, to be more lovely, and beloved." [*Letters*, No. 120.] On the night preceding his enlistment he kept a vigil of the hours like a condemned criminal waiting for dawn, and wrote out all his reasons for taking the step he planned. It was a calm night of late summer with a waxing moon which earlier sailed over Westminster through a wrack of cloud in omniscient brilliance, detached, remote, oblivious of human uncertainty, bringing again to his mind his favorite side note from "The Ancient Mariner." Like the Mariner, he yearned in his loneliness and fixedness toward the journeying moon, and the stars upon their everlasting courses, with the heavens their appointed home, their native land which they entered as lords expected. More than anything now, he longed for a refuge, for annihilation, the negation of all that he was; and he desired peace, a peace so deep that it would be like drowning. And he desired, if possible, the usefulness of plain work. In the whole of the boisterous and jangling era upon which the world was launched, only one challenge had any real value: conquest of space above the earth. In that conquest he was moved to play a part, however small, and the gods and demigods, the giants and pygmies, the braggarts and dissemblers, could have the stage to themselves; he, Thomas Edward Lawrence, the archdissembler, was finished.

The next morning he went down to the Royal Air Force recruiting station in Henrietta Street and presented himself as an airman recruit under the name of John Hume Ross. According to W. E. Johns, who, in 1922, was chief interviewing officer of the London Recruiting Depot, the air force did not receive him with enthusiasm. To the interviewing officer he seemed suspiciously bogus, and he was sent away for written references which, when produced, proved to be genuinely bogus, for he had written them himself.

After this failure to achieve his ends privately and by his own efforts, Lawrence had no recourse but to secure the powerful support of the Air Ministry through friends, and to present the chief interviewing officer with a genuine "reference" from an authority who could not be overruled. But he had still to pass the medical officer and undergo the shameful exposure of his Der'a scars. Explaining away the lesions of his other wounds was difficult enough in the circumstances of his incognito—no war service; internment as an "enemy alien" in Turkey; for the flogging which had furrowed his back with broad, deep welts, he could neither tell the truth nor invent a plausible fiction.

There is a popular legend that Lawrence was weak and ailing all through his youth and had to overcome these constitutional deficiencies in order to perform his incredible feats of endurance during the war. Nothing could be farther from the truth. In 1927 he was to write:

> In 1914 I was a pocket Hercules, as muscularly strong as people twice my size and more enduring than most. I saw all the other British officers' boots off in Arabia: they went to base, or to hospital, while I did two years in the fighting areas, and was nine times wounded and five times crashed from the air, and had two goes of dysentery and suffered enough hunger and thirst and heat and cold and exposure, not to mention mistreatment, to wreck the average constitution. [*Letters*, No. 311.]

Whether, as W. E. Johns relates,[12] it was necessary to call in an outside physician to pass him, since the R.A.F. Medical Officer refused, is immaterial. In 1922 it was the ruin of strength which presented itself to the examining doctors; even so, the ruin was firm enough to hold up under the rigors of Uxbridge and not to break—and there were some there who did break. There is in any case more than one standard of physical fitness by which the Royal Air Force deems recruits suitable for service, and he was able to pass the standard for an ordinary aircraft hand which was all he desired.

He was formally enlisted on August 30. In a subsequent letter to Air Vice-Marshal Sir Oliver Swann—the "power" which had steered him between the Scylla of medical fitness and the Charybdis of square roots—he apologized for the mess he made at Henrietta Street. "If I'd known I was such a wreck I'd have gone off and recovered before joining up: now the cure and the experiment must proceed together." [*Letters*, No. 166.] Sir Oliver Swann who was ordered unequivocably to get "John Hume Ross" into the Royal Air Force and disliked the whole business, seems not to have recipro-

---

[12] In *The Sunday Times*, April 18, 1951.

cated Lawrence's attempted friendliness, but his position, like that of the chief interviewing officer, was a difficult one.

It was done. He felt a sudden and exhilarating sense of relief. The uncertainty was ended; his future was assured. Colonel Lawrence of Arabia, that monstrous creation, was erased, and in his place stood Aircraftman John Hume Ross, a new name, a new identity, a new adventure. In a mood of unsteady jubilation he went into the nearest Fullers' and ordered a cup of coffee as a libation to the life about to begin.

6

DESCENT TO THE PIT

Over the portal of hell is inscribed the legend:

> Through me is the way into the doleful city
> Through me is the way into eternal pain
> Through me is the way among people lost.

It was incredible that hell could be entered in broad daylight, upon a limpid afternoon in late summer, when dust and dried leaves lay underfoot; when sea and mountain waited serenely under the blue eggshell sky for the first breath of autumn; when children, hopping in and out of chalk-drawn squares moved aside to stare curiously at the little band of recruits shuffling with embarrassed steps down the road to the R.A.F. Depot under the casual shepherding of a trim air force sergeant. Nevertheless hell was entered, though the inscription above the gate at Uxbridge was less poetic, more stark, and noncommittal. It did not promise that hope should cease upon entry, or that pain there should be unremitting, but if a man entered already without hope, there was little solace it could offer him; and its deliberately inflicted pains were sharp or dull according to his capacity to bear them.

What seems most precious to the man who surrenders freedom at the instant of its surrender? Not the beauty of earth, for that remains, however restricted his opportunity for its enjoyment. Not possessions when he has jettisoned what little of the world's goods he ever possessed. But the treasured privilege, until then little considered, of being able to move at will: the luxurious choice of stirring or not stirring as mood dictates. The five who went through the gate at Uxbridge were as lost to freedom, to volition, for the next weeks as any but virtual prisoners. They were really lost to the world for the duration of their active service, long or short, for the life which they had chosen would gradually impose its own barrier between them and the outer world of civilians, with its own opposing standard of values. Henceforth, they belonged to the machine to which they had voluntarily surrendered themselves, and which alone had legal warrant to order their actions. For John Hume Ross it was a novel prospect not to be able to order his actions or engage his will in voluntary decision.

As inconspicuously as the other five recruits he skirted the high, bomb-encrusted walls and entered the gate with its sentry stiffly poised and alacritous, with mingled feelings: relief that the uncertainty of his postwar career had ended, and apprehension over what he had done, what he had now taken upon himself. Yet behind the apprehension was the calm surety that accompanies a twice-lived experience. He had done it all before; it was not a new adventure; it was not even a strange one except insofar as its details differed from the other. The essentials were the same. Had it not been so, it may be doubted whether even his resilient and adaptable spirit could have withstood, at thirty-four, the severe shock of Uxbridge. There at last he was to touch that bedrock existence he had half earnestly, half romantically craved. Arabia had been an epic of pain, of sweat and blood lavished without stint on a great enterprise. Uxbridge was a martyrdom of petty causes, a heroism called forth at the whim of sergeant and corporal instructors by whose unrelenting efforts the recruits were pressed into the required shape, like *bois-durci*—with their own life's blood.

The camp, which had come into being as a mustering center during the 1914–18 war, was set in the wide and beautiful park surrounding Hillingdon House. Broad-leafed elms leaned over the walls in summer and dappled the pavement with vibrating webs of light and shadow; trams darted past it, clanking down the main road of what was then still a country town on the outskirts of London with country lanes and a distinctly rural atmosphere. Everywhere on the periphery of the camp, away from the huts and the tarmac of the square, were trees, grass, and open sky. The park itself sloped down in green swathes to a tinkling stream—the River Pinn—and there tumbled headlong into a tangled undergrowth of fern, dock, and foxglove. Thus, in spite of its foreboding aspect, it was not hell but a place of purgation. The trees encouraged the birds: thrushes sang their fanfarons in the high elms; communities of rooks quarreled noisily over the heads of marching airmen; and in the last opaque light before nightfall the swifts wheeled in twittering aerobatics over the corrugated iron hutments, teaching the embryo airmen by sublimation the art which they were being nurtured, harshly, to serve. The air was still; over the park seemed to brood a divine serenity, a hint of the gold and purple glory of September, a promise of heaven to come. But to the raw recruits, raw in nerve and experience, being drawn ever deeper into the Uxbridge maw, the calmness was sham. It taunted and eluded across a barrier as irrefragible as that which cleaved Dives in torment from the peace of Lazarus. For they belonged to the air force body and soul—since the soul was compelled to bear some of the brunt of the body's discipline—and were its creatures to do with as it saw fit. John Hume Ross was to write a poignant little description of his first impression of Hut 2 when he saw it, remarking on its surprisingly delicate coloring—whitewashed walls, red brick, and light green pillars, brown blankets over hard beds, a strip of black linoleum running down the center of the gray cement floor. It seemed faintly hostile at first as well as strange, though the day was to come when he would return to it, after defeat, as to a home, feeling nothing but its warmth and friendliness. But these were the outer lineaments of Uxbridge; beneath them ran a deep sea of pain.

In that same letter of September 1 addressed to Air Vice-Marshal Sir Oliver Swann which commenced: "I can't ask the corporal how an aircraft hand addresses an air vice-marshal," Lawrence, assuming his old identity to overcome the difficulty, commented humorously, "Would you tell the C.A.S. that he's given me the completest change any mortal has had since Nebuchadnezzar."

It was assuredly a change from the solitary vigil of Barton Street, from the milieu and attitudes of the introverted protagonist of *The Seven Pillars of Wisdom*—this living in a hut with fifty men, sleeping, eating, washing, exercising, burning, suffering in inescapable intimacy: a tumbled, dirty existence in which no provision was made for privacy even in the most personal functions.[1] In the desert at least escape into solitude had been possible; at Uxbridge escape into solitude was almost unattainable. It was a motley crew which gathered in Hut 2 that first day: out-of-work laborers, ex-officers down on their luck, ex-lorry drivers from Wolverhampton, ex-sailors from Tyneside, and here and there a bewildered farmer's son. They were broken men, he said, but capable; unemployed but not unemployable. They boasted of their past jobs and backgrounds in defense of their present helplessness: ex-lorry drivers became chauffeurs and laborers not wishing to own up to meniality passed as unskilled mechanics. Among them, with a sincere not an assumed humility, Lawrence classed himself—a failure in the game of life. Thrown together in Hut 2 they evoked a pathos in spite of their crudities.

Those crudities which Lawrence told Sir Oliver Swann were far less than he expected, worried him far more than he had anticipated. But food, sleep, and the anathema of physical training were the paramount difficulties he had to contend with. For a man to whom

[1] Latrine cubicles had no doors.

food had never been important and who ate a bare minimum, preferring al fresco meals to any formal spread, the set meals of the Depot were too hefty both in quality and content. As for sleep, a lifetime of abstention and the practiced alertness of desert nights had turned him into a chronic light sleeper, so that not only was he prone to wake at the least augmentation of sound in the vibrant, restless, dreaming hut, but he lay awake half the night as a matter of course in those slow, fearful hours of the predawn when agonies are long-drawn and fears lope like predatory beasts over the defenseless mind. Whenever he could, with impunity, he rose, dressed in trousers, shirt, and gym shoes, and crept outside to wander about the camp, startling guards and sentries with his soft, incredible prowlings. This was eccentric, puzzling behavior in a recruit for which he was teased and scolded by the guards and ordered back to bed "like a good lad."

Eventually he learned to stomach the food, though never to wolf it down with the relish of his fellow recruits, and to sleep for somewhat longer intervals without waking. But P.T., this ordering of his stubborn body into prescribed movements—he who had hated regulated games and sports at school and at Oxford had refused to take part in them—remained an excruciating ordeal. "I had taught myself," he wrote, "that display of the body was a prostitution, our credited shapes being only accidents until by taking pleasure or pain in them we make them our fault." [2] Reluctance and fear paralyzed him and made him clumsy, but the source of his dread was not merely mental revulsion. It was to him a severe physical hardship ending nearly always in pain and nausea, thanks to the air crash of 1919 which left the end of one rib jagged and sharp against the wall of his chest. The terrible sickness that caught him up after P.T. made him miss breakfast on most mornings. He would go to the hut instead of the mess deck and, lying face down on his bed, endeavor to pull himself together for the remaining stress of the day. Drill on the square when it came punished him averagely with less severity; cer-

---

[2] *The Mint* (New York, Doubleday, 1955).

tainly he suffered less from it than the other recruits who were flayed by it.

The new recruits were processed, kitted, shorn to the scalp, and their training begun under the large, dour, watchful but roughly kind Corporal Abner. The first lesson was a hard forcing of the bit, the inculcation of humility and obedience through the discipline of drudgery. "What of it," says Ishmael, "if some old hunks of a sea-captain orders me to get a broom and sweep down the decks? What does that indignity amount to, weighed, I mean, in the scales of the New Testament?" But the recruits at Uxbridge, driven through a course of senseless fatigues for five weeks of their training, would hardly have concurred. The truth was they did all the heavy and dirty work of the camp, one raw contingent after another taking over as its predecessors moved up and on to the drill square. There were no distinctions made, as indeed in this place of purgation distinctions could not and should not be made. Laborers and public-school men were driven equally hard and humiliated with the same monotonous frequency.

The days commenced early with reveille at six-thirty, and physical training at six-forty-five followed by breakfast one hour later. Then came the ceaseless round of humping and carrying, sweeping and scrubbing, of literally wallowing in filth and refuse, and a running to and fro at the call of bugles sounding the charge imperatively across the expanse of park and hutments. Their time was not their own until after five, and not even then if they had been unfortunate enough to draw extra fatigues or pickets as a penalty for misdemeanors. Lights out at ten found most of them ready to sink into welcome oblivion. Even John Hume Ross could sleep away the first half of the night, though he might lie awake during the second and listen to the sighs and dream-talk of the supine men around him; for hard beds made them sleep uneasily, turning many times and always with great effort as though, he reflected, the body was active by day only through some wholly unnatural compulsion which, once released in sleep, let it betray its inherent reluctance to make any movement without complaining always. Sometimes the moon showed herself through the hut windows and bestowed her favors in a light caress of his pillow; or the autumnal rains drummed against the glass and drowned out the restless stirrings of the hut.

At the end of a month of back-breaking labor, scrubbing floors, cleaning out pig sties, and emptying dustbins, it is possible that even his best friends would scarcely have recognized Edward Lawrence in his prison garb: a pair of soiled overalls from which rose an effluvium suggestive of his prison tasks; his prison manner of shrinking from bullies and "leaping into the air" whenever accosted sharply by authority. Even he looked like a convict with his fair hair cropped close to the skull. It was a far cry from the long hair and youthful aestheticism of Oxford and Carchemish, and from the romantic figure in Arabia preaching and fighting in white silk. Yet there was a startling propinquity between Lawrence at Uxbridge and the hurt boy of seventeen doing his few weeks' stint in the Royal Artillery. The hurt even was in a sense a magnification of the earlier one, but there was no one now to buy him out. Meanwhile he had begun the notes for the book he was to call *The Mint* and which in his hope was to redeem him from the failure of *The Seven Pillars*, and thereby he counted off his Uxbridge days on its rosary of pain.

"Don't be shocked by the accidence of this letter," he wrote Edward Garnett in September. "It's being written in the barrack room, and there are 27 lusty people doing jobs about me and muddling me up." [*Letters*, No. 167.] Twenty-seven men cleaning boots, polishing buttons, blancoing webbing, arguing, singing, erupting into wild, unrestrained horseplay that respected no one and recognized no sensitivities. And in the morning at reveille, fifty men to dress in sleepy haste, scramble for the latrines and wash basins, and present themselves with gym shoes and sluggish minds and bodies to be thoroughly awakened by the physical-training instructor. There was squalor, there was obscenity, but there was also fellowship, and slowly he began to be aware of that fellowship and to experience its efficacy even while he complained of the penalties it imposed.

A letter from Edward Garnett forwarded to him at Uxbridge and received by him on a day of dismal laboring which forms one of the most pungent chapters of *The Mint*, called bluntly and evocatively

"Shit-Cart," invited him to become the editor of a new literary magazine to be titled *Belles-Lettres.* With three other luckless slaves he had finished emptying Saturday's refuse bins, forty in all, from the cook house, the officers' mess, M-Section, and the hospital, a disgusting conglomerate of coke, ashes, bones and paper, rotting food, tin cans, and broken pots congealed in a thick black syrup poured over the mass; and they were next detailed off to collect swill for the pigs. In the pig sty where he read it, Garnett's invitation seemed more than inappropriate; it was a rich joke and he enjoyed it hugely as he always enjoyed the inept union of incongruities. He would not, of course, accept the invitation, pleasant relief from the pigs though it was to contemplate. T Squadron possessed him, and though he might sometimes protest that possession, he was willing for the present to accept it. This deliberate quest for degradation need not shock; it was in complete accord with his self-confessed habit of seeking his pleasures downward. In *The Seven Pillars* he had written of his fighting, daring, and suffering bodyguard: "The lads took pleasure in subordination; in degrading the body: so as to throw into greater relief their freedom in equality of mind; almost they preferred servitude as richer in experience than authority, and less binding in daily care." Care was removed from him by his act of enlisting, all, that is, except care lest his body crack under the strain he now imposed on it. As for literature, it could and would survive without him.

The prescribed course of drudgery at Uxbridge wore on interminably throughout September, and there seemed no hope of ever escaping it, for until the recruits were squadded and sent to the square—a fearfully anticipated but necessary ordeal—the Depot could never be conquered and left behind. It was a day they labored and sweated for, as they labored and sweated toward their ultimate destiny, though the only sign of that destiny was one Bristol fighter with faded roundels, standing inaccessible and neglected behind iron bars. Melancholy and discouraged he wrote:

> A month, two months of these senseless fatigues and we will accept the R.A.F.'s dictum that our time weighs the same whether spent in work or wasted. Then we will present to our instructors a blank grey sheet on

> which to draw up, by drill and instant obedience, an airman. Let us see if the Air Force can build as well as it has destroyed.[3]

Eventually the day of the last fatigues came. With his squad mates he went off in a lorry to collect supplies from an abandoned airfield, racing down the road with joy at the conclusion of this first trial of servitude. The younger men, merry and in the mood for a lark, leaned out of the lorry shouting "Beaver!" at elderly men—the inane craze of the twenties, and heckled airmen, women, and policemen along the road. And John Hume Ross? Crouched down in the lorry, hands over face, he cried silently for the first time in years at the thought of this new beginning. After a delay, what in his R.A.F. notes he called a perverse "humbugging about," their separateness began to cohere, their awkwardness was shed, and they began to feel like a real squad.

The regime was still a harsh one. (The badge of Uxbridge is the bugle and the pace stick, its motto: "*Juventutem Foramus.*") Because it was so harsh it requires some explanation.

The Royal Air Force in 1922 was a very junior service, its age, four years. In the period immediately succeeding the war, it was regarded by the more senior services as an anomaly, albeit an anomaly which had fulfilled a useful role during the war. In the fever of disarmament after the war, it was encouraged to quietly run itself down, though not before Marshal Sir Hugh (later Lord) Trenchard had managed to submit a memorandum to the government laying down the minimum requirements for an effective air arm, and to get his minimum accepted. Ultimately this running down was all to the good, but in 1922, when the Royal Air Force was faced with the task of meeting its new commitments—Lawrence himself had been instrumental in persuading the government to give the control of Iraq into the keeping of the air force—the pressure of building up and of training airmen to man the outposts of Empire in the new air age was great indeed. In its urgent groping to find a discipline suited to the training of technicians and mechanics, the Royal Air Force, itself

[3] *Ibid.*

an elite corps, took the one nearest to hand: the old tried and proved Guards' discipline, one which was however clearly not suited to an air force.

The admitted aim of the Guards' discipline is to take away a man's self-will, his pride in himself, and to replace it with a collective will, a pride of unit, what is popularly called *esprit de corps*. To accomplish this, a man's self-will and individual pride must first be broken; only then can the end be achieved of molding him into a disciplined soldier whose instant obedience and trained reactions can be relied on. The men who ran the Depot at Uxbridge were thoroughly cognizant of these principles; many of them were themselves ex-Guards' officers and within the scope of their vision they were quite correct, but not objectively so. With the help of a hundred-odd N.C.O.'s, some good, some bad, and some the harassed victims of the system themselves, determined that their charges should not have an easier time than they had had, they managed to impose upon the Uxbridge R.A.F. Depot a near-penal system which cannot have been equaled even at Caterham in that period. The watchwords were haste and dispersal, with everything done at the double and no margin allowed for error. ("Here we tame lions," the instructors boasted to them, but, Lawrence remarked, they were indeed lambs, and the regimen of lions struck hard on lambs.) [4] The decent instructors who, if given a free hand, might have efficiently brought the recruits up to squadron standard were thwarted by a higher mandate which ordered their charges off on irrelevant and degrading labors at all hours when they might profitably have been schooled in the niceties of military behavior and practice. Frequent charges and stiff punishments were a part of the system—the short cut to acquired discipline which was economical of words and repeated explanations. The effect on the recruits was to inspire in them confusion, bewilderment, and despair in a descending cadence; the more so as after squadding, they were sent to school literally, to a civilian schoolmaster who urged on them the virtues of independence and initiative,

[4] *Ibid.*

as though to subvert them from their true course of dependence, surrender, and subjection of will. So to the physical hardship was added a conflict of duty: Did the air force really intend to make automatons of them, and if so, why had it misrepresented to them their role as technicians; and why did it now permit this revolutionary doctrine of the schoolmasters to undermine their earlier training which had taught them not only their utter worthlessness as individuals but their crying need for a strong hand to rule them at all times?

That commissioned officers at Uxbridge were totally ineffectual was due, Lawrence thought, to their elusiveness; for they were rarely seen except on parade, or when the hapless recruits were hauled up before senior officers on a charge. In default of their presence, the noncommissioned ranks maintained a deathgrip on the rank and file for which, he felt, the Uxbridge system of training officers by keeping them apart from the men they would ultimately have to lead, was wholly to blame. Fortunately, even in the hours of their worst discouragement, the recruits were buoyed up by the conviction that once the Depot was left behind, the R.A.F. would be different in form and intent, and, happily, they were right in their conviction.

The recruits' course was hard on all, but doubly hard on a man of thirty-four who had endured the privations of Arabia, undergone torture, suffered scores of bullet wounds and lacerations, had been subjected to four or five minor and one major air crashes in the capricious aircraft of the day, and whose nerves were stretched taut to the breaking point. *The Mint* should be read always with these facts in mind. But *The Mint* is an unforgettable and disturbing portrait of the Uxbridge R.A.F. Depot in 1922 and of Lawrence under authority. The mood is dismal in spite of ephemeral gleams of humor which are thrown in to lighten its somber chiaroscuro. The sights and sounds and smells of the Depot are so sharply portrayed that the reader is transported into its innermost recesses to experience vicariously its terrible sensations. The sweat, the straining, the physical anguish of the recruits, are there made articulate for them all by one who endured it all with them and was able to dissect his sensations which were partly those of the mass, and partly and more acutely the result of his own dilemma. He was their spokesman and defender, but with them he was also a victim and suffered proportionately. "I want to cry out," he wrote, "that this our long-drawn punishment can subserve neither beauty nor use." [5] The inmates of Hut 2 would not have been quite as fastidious of phrase, but they would have agreed.

His R.A.F. notes were written at night in the hut, in the half-hour of freedom before "lights out," slowly and painfully at first; later, with more facility as his impressions accumulated. But they were written always in a condition of weariness and exhaustion, and there is a brevity and circumscription about them despite later polishing. He repeats barrack-room conversations with no sparing of their obscenities. This gave rise to the claim that *The Mint* out-Joyces James Joyce, but the difference between Lawrence and the Dublin rebel is very marked. Lawrence uses these raw scenes and lewd dialogues, the elemental dregs of human thought and impulse struggling for articulation, as foils for his own introspective and ornate style, and the result is a breath-taking olio of crudity and polish, at once dramatic and incongruous. But whether in a pithy, fastidious comment ("Do you in reading my complete works notice that tendency to do up small packets of words foppishly?" he asked Lionel Curtis in the following year) he sums up some fearful aspect of the Depot or, with a skillful economy of line, sketches its inmates in a striking gallery of miniatures which range from the controversial commanding officer, "under whose stark skull and crossbones the Depot sailed," to the ubiquitous sergeants and corporals who had charge of them, and the driven, harassed recruits of T Squadron, the central figure of the drama is always himself. This was not intentional when the notes were written, for they were simply to depict the life at the Depot as it was, but it was the inevitable result, being what he was and unavoidable, as in *The Seven Pillars* it had been unavoidable.

An intense emptiness, a loud and clattering loneliness bore down

---

[5] *Ibid.*

upon Lawrence at Uxbridge day and night, in the midst of all its milling throng of men, caught up as he was by the harsh system and by his own strange predicament which had brought him there. There is a Kafka-like aura of nightmare frustration in *The Mint's* description of the ardors of Uxbridge, its pains and penalties, neurotic, yet without the dream neurosis of Kafka's fantasies. For comic relief there is a scene in the canteen where the patriotic photographs adorning the walls—King George, Admiral Lord Beatty, Earl Haig, Trenchard—included one small picture of himself. He describes pleasurably how he moved aside the dirty crockery on a nearby table, sat down with his cup of "cha," and when no one was looking, quietly took the offending photograph off the wall and tossed it in the incinerator.

As Ross, Lawrence shared fully in the harassment, the humiliation, the chastening, that was meted out to all, and if he seemed to suffer more, it was only because of the dual dimension of body and spirit in which he endured it, as it was also in his sufferings in Arabia. He cut and blistered his hands on galvanized iron bins; sprained a foot, split a thumb and fractured a little finger carrying heavy sacks of flour. Boots were heavy—they weighed five pounds a pair, said Lawrence; the rough wool of the tight R.A.F. uniform fretted his skin; the webbing harness weighted down in punishment drill with full pack chafed his much-broken collarbone intolerably; and there was the constant attrition of rifle drill at which he acknowledged his clumsiness. These may seem trivialities, the penalty of an overfastidious nature, and Lawrence is the master cataloguer of pains when he sets himself to it. But hardship and discomfort were not new to him. He had spent a lifetime toughening his body and denying to it even the occasional softness of living most men crave, and the fact remains, his sufferings at Uxbridge were very real.

David Garnett has said there is nothing in *The Mint* to shock anyone but a fool except this revelation of Lawrence's readiness and desire to suffer. The veil is there withdrawn completely and his masochism lies revealed. He was not balanced; his preoccupation with and appetite for pain and punishment are proof of it. At Cranwell in 1926 he was to break his wrist on the kickback of a crank handle on the car he was obligingly trying to start for an old man, and to return to camp without divulging the accident until hours later. Garnett perceived and condemned the pointlessness, the abnormality of an educated man behaving like a boy too proud to make a fuss. And the truth is no one makes so much of punishment or the effects of punishment unless they have come to assume an obsessive importance in the mind, either as pain desired and willingly endured, or as pain illicitly enjoyed. It seems certain that both aspects were present in Lawrence's attitude, though the second was subdued to the first, which was paramount. He knew both aspects, however, and the third which completes the triad: the perverted pleasure of the punisher, but this he knew only as a victim. The bitter knowledge which had taught him that severe maltreatment could unleash in himself impulses which normally were repressed had taught him also the full horror of sadism, that most degenerate form of man's inhumanity to man.

But here too the lines are closely drawn; the masochist may enjoy vicariously the spectacle of pain and punishment inflicted on others while still recoiling from it in guilty horror. Enjoyment of cruelty—to others, not himself—is a sin which some have laid to Lawrence's discredit. It is not evident in *The Mint's* frank dissection of his raw feelings; there he records bitterly that some of those who day by day exercised their authority over the recruits did so out of lust of cruelty. There was a glitter in their eyes and a tautening of muscles which betrayed the satisfaction of their passion. He did not know if the others saw it; the hut, he said, was full of innocents who had not eaten of his fruit of knowledge: had not "laid their wreath of agony to induce—the orgasm of man's vice." [6]

Eric Kennington has related how his old metaphysics teacher Bowhay described Lawrence as a man who had found a false "I" and of being merely a pipe through which life flowed but did not quicken or regenerate. Certainly, in *The Mint* he did not show forth the whole,

---

[6] *Ibid.*

in the sense of being healthy, cogent life he was capable of showing. But amid his melancholy self-searching-and-never-finding are constant evidences of the humor which was his saving grace, even as his compassion, his kindness to others weaker and less able than himself, were the crowning garland of his strength and his unnatural powers of endurance. Average opinion, of course, will protest as terrible waste all this suffering without cause, which seems almost suffering for the sake of suffering, but in the inscrutable calculations of the eternal, it may not be accounted valueless.

Of all the letters written throughout the straining days of his Uxbridge ordeal, none seem more piquant than those he addressed to Charles Doughty which hinted at his changed state—"I leaped off on a new line, which makes itself master of my time and movements"—but never troubled him with any of the details. David Garnett has mentioned how E. M. Forster drew his attention to Lawrence's attitude toward Doughty which was ever one of kindness and consideration. In 1921 he had written an introduction for a new edition of the *Travels in Arabia Deserta* which he was largely responsible for getting into print again, and in 1922 he was instrumental in obtaining a Civil List Pension for Doughty. His own Arabian book he withheld until 1924 when the old man had already petitioned him twice for it. Even then it was offered with great reluctance, only because the alternative was to offend him by a third refusal.

When Lawrence enlisted in August, 1922, only a handful of his wide circle of friends and acquaintances knew of his action and Doughty was not one of them. Most people believed, plausibly enough, that he had gone abroad on business relating to either archaeology or politics. "The World doesn't know of me now: and God forbid that the Press should. Only three people have both my old and my new name, and I don't propose to enlarge that circle," he wrote Colonel Newcombe on October 15, breaking the news of his enlistment. [*Letters*, No. 170.] Edward Garnett was one of the three.

He had undertaken to assist in making an abridgment of *The Seven Pillars* for publication, and Lawrence's letters to him during these Uxbridge weeks reveal completely his dilemma: whether to go through with publication or not. They reveal too his heavy judgment on it and on himself, and above all, they reveal his loneliness at Uxbridge.

> What you say about the oddity of my brain doesn't surprise me—but it helps to explain the apartness of myself here in this noisy barrack room. I might be one dragon-fly in a world of wasps—or one wasp among the dragon-flies: it's not a comfortable place: but if the oddity of my standing produces a fresh-feeling book, I suppose I shouldn't grouse about my luck. [*Letters*, No. 169.]

One of his objects in joining the air force had been to break down that dragonfly apartness. Shy, mannered, and nurturing his oddity up to the age of twenty-five, he had scrupulously avoided the society of his fellows unless they happened to share his hobbies and interests, or contribute to them. At thirty-four he was in the midst of the third and greatest adventure of his life, plunging headlong into a sea of humanity in the hope that he would rub off by contact with ordinary men who were neither scholars nor intellectuals, all his inbred and nurtured oddity and so acquire the common touch. Yet he wrote: "I'm odder, here, than when by myself in Barton Street: the oddness must be bone deep." [7]

But squad mates took his digestibility for granted: he could be as odd as he pleased, he was still acceptable; that was the difference. He had privileges; he was deferred to—but he was quick to add, deferred to not because of his "pound note accent," but because he possessed the only watch in the hut that went regularly and kept time. The tolerance and kindness of squad mates astonished him; they also on occasion embarrassed him and made him recoil, as he always recoiled from too close a human contact. Yet they were a challenge as great as any he had met.

The worst aspect of Uxbridge was its animalism. It was this order-

---

[7] *Ibid.*

ing of bodies, this straining and suffering of bodies in communion, this rank bodily intimacy imposed by authority, and the carnality of mind which it evoked that most disturbed Lawrence. To some extent this is the execration of all military life, yet at Uxbridge, it was something perverse and wanton implicit in the system.

> I hate this dirty living: and yet by the decency of the other fellows, the full dirtiness of it has not met me fairly. Isn't it a sign of feebleness in me, to cry out so against barrack-life? It means I'm afraid (physically afraid) of other men: their animal spirits seem to me the most terrible companions to haunt a man: and I hate their noise. And yet I'm a man, not different from them, certainly not better. What is it that makes me so damnably sensitive and so ready to cry out, and yet so ready to incur more pain. [*Letters*, No. 178.]

So he wrote Edward Garnett from Farnborough later in the year. In pitting his overeducated brain against the bedrock of reality at Uxbridge, it seemed to him that this carnality must be real and that the fastidious, sensitive scholarly attitudes fostered in him and his peers by birth and upbringing were sham. This was the ultimate reality from which there was no escape. And yet by the inevitable paradox of human sympathy, he found loyalty and devotion and comradeship even among the dregs. As John Hume Ross he was, like all the recruits, singled out for special abuse and often bullied outrageously, but in justice to those who abused him, it should be said that with the possible exception of the Depot's commanding officer, it does not seem likely that they knew his real identity. During these hecklings squadmates who recognized and admired his superior mind and tongue would urge him to defend himself, but his sense of duty came ever blankly between him and any possible defense of himself. He could not even look his persecutors in the eye,[8] and it was not cowardice but a fearful recoiling because he had set himself to follow a given course and would not be deflected from it by rebellion or violence of feeling. Similarly, he would not complain about his physical disabilities lest the already-reluctant authorities should

---

[8] But see *Letters*, No. 186.

think him unfitted for service. "Till this year my ungainly body has met life's demands; if it fails me now I shall break it," he wrote.[9] It was a tight and most vicious circle in which he had enclosed himself without allowing any avenue of escape.

Why did Lawrence subject himself to the hardships and discomforts of Uxbridge and later of Bovington Camp and to this life in the ranks which was so unsuited to a man of his background and temperament? The motives were curiously involved, and we are not provided with that useful tally of them as he wrote it out in Barton Street the night before his enlistment. Hogarth, his friend and patron who knew him better than most, wrote explaining his actions to George Bernard Shaw: "He will not work in any sort of harness unless this is padlocked on to him. He enlisted in order to have the padlocks rivetted on to him." That is one aspect, but only one.

To his old schoolfriend, E. F. Hall, he gave as his reason for enlisting his desire "to forget and to be forgotten"; to Colonel W. F. Stirling he once said that the Royal Tank Corps in which he was later to serve was "a hefty penance for too rich and full a youth"; while to Robert Graves, after summarizing his reasons—"an inclination towards ground level"—he concluded: "I wanted to join up, that's all: and I am still glad sometimes that I did. It's going to be a brain-sleep, and I'll come out of it less odd than when I went in: or at least less odd in other men's eyes." [*Letters*, No. 177.]

These are all valid reasons, but within them are shades and overtones of meaning. At the beginning of 1923 Lawrence told Robert Graves who had passed on to him an invitation to go and live in an Eastern ivory tower: "Partly I came here to eat dirt till its taste is normal to me, and partly to avoid the current of other men's thinking; and in your hill court there will be high thinking." [10] And in the same year he was to write Lionel Curtis from Bovington:

> Free-will I've tried, and rejected: authority I've rejected (not obedience, for that is my present effort, to find equality only in subordination. It is

---

[9] *The Mint.*

[10] *T. E. Lawrence to His Biographers.*

> dominion whose taste I have been cloyed with): action I've rejected: and the intellectual life: and the receptive senses: and the battle of wits . . .

He would, he said, have gone to prison literally if he could have got there without committing a crime, since prison was the ultimate of degradation.

The real motive by his own admission lies hidden in his war history, and this has led many people to make the fundamental error of supposing that Lawrence enlisted because of his disappointment over the Arab affair. This is far short of the truth. Men do not enter the strict Cistercian and Carthusian orders because of failure in some enterprise of life. Nor was it out of a sense of pique that Edward Lawrence, a lay monk of singularly severe persuasion, put himself under authority to learn obedience and root out of himself every vestige of free will and pride. There are two keys to his action: first his enlistment as a boy which showed his strong moral compulsion and his acute sensitivity to any suggestion of unworthiness or defilement; and second the actual sexual defilement he suffered on the night of his capture at Der'a. It was an impulse deeper than conscience, a masterful, penitential instinct which drove him to seek, in the abysms of squalid and dirty living in the ranks, atonement for the misuse of power and a corresponding purification of body and spirit.

At Uxbridge he wondered half fearfully what years of this life of subjection would make of him and his habitual willfullness. "I haven't the impulse and the conviction to fit what I know to be my power of moulding men and things: and so I always regret what I've created, when the leisure after creation lets me look back and see that the idea was second-hand," he confided to his friend Lionel Curtis. [*Letters*, No. 205.] But no one reading *The Mint* or the letters written later from Farnborough and Bovington can fail to realize that submission did not come easy to him. Whether he liked it or not, he was better suited to command than to submit, though to command in his own fashion; and it is difficult for the unique, self-disciplined leader to transform himself into an ordinary well-disciplined and obedient soldier. This was his handicap throughout his penance. Of the monk's triple vow of poverty, chastity, and obedience, the first two were his natural habit, but the last was a mortification of will hard to brook, and the sergeant and corporal instructors at Uxbridge were not the best of novice masters.

The late summer moved invisibly into autumn, but except for occasional and sudden tempests of equinoctial rain, it was sunny and warm—warm enough to lay out of a Sunday afternoon after the hated church parade on the grass behind the huts, smelling the hay scent that mingled with the acrid smells of warm iron and fresh paint. "The feel of sun-warmed iron and the scent of deep brown grass are not the least of my Uxbridge memories," he wrote in his R.A.F. notes.[11] The coalition government of Lloyd George fell, but for all its effect on the recruits training at Uxbridge, they might have been encamped by the Dudh Kosi in the Himalayas instead of by the Pinn in Surrey. Talk in Hut 4 into which they had now moved up, when it was not a putrescent jargon of midden words which shamed and mocked and yet made absolute the alimentary and sexual functions of man, was all of cup finals, the newest films, free passes, and the bloody-mindedness of certain N.C.O.'s; and always there was music—a banjo, a mouth organ, paper-covered combs, and a beaten stove lid for tympani. Their music, like their conversation, was pathetically simple; a clumsily articulate expression of yearning, of ill-defined longing, of girls left behind, of happiness for two, love for two inanely compared with the love of honey bees.

They were being drilled a grueling five hours a day now in preparation for the ceremonies of the fourth anniversary of the Armistice, drill being, in the words of the manual, an exercise whose triple goal is muscular control, alert mental responsiveness, and spiritual cohesion; but passes to leave the Depot were issued, and it was possible to find some relief from the grimness of Uxbridge outside its walls. London was out of bounds for recruits, but Lawrence as Aircraftman Ross went up to London on the Metropolitan Railway with the aid of a little trickery and the connivance of the local railway employees, themselves ex-servicemen. To escape the Depot even for a few hours,

[11] *The Mint.*

to feel the familiar pavements under his unfamiliar hobnailed boots, was an exquisite interval of peace between torments. His fine scholar's hands were reddened and roughened with his weeks of hard labor, his body cried out for rest, but for all the physical hardship, his weight had increased, and to his surprise and amused disapproval, the constant exercising had developed muscles and sinews unexpectedly.

The blue wool uniform and the peaked cap were as effective a disguise as any he could have contrived; it precluded recognition by any but his most intimate friends. And he was a very trim airman in those early days of hooked collared tunics, pantaloons, and rolled puttees. "Every line always perfect, from set of hat to spacing of the puttees, never a dull button, or a speck on the boot, and how the well-cut uniform showed the strength of his neck and drive of his jaw," wrote Eric Kennington.[12] It was a contrast indeed to the young officer in Cairo dressed anyhow to suit himself with a gay abandon, in a uniform without badges, without Sam Browne belt, and as likely as not, with an unmilitary red tie and unpolished shoes. There were severe penalties at Uxbridge for any deflection from the normal in dress, but he was scrupulous always in the R.A.F. to conform to regulations, though later photographs of him abroad in "scruff order" show a return to something of the old abandon. In 1922, however, he was immaculate, but still a little shy of showing himself to his friends in his new livery which so clearly set the stamp of ownership upon him who had been owned by no man. Edward Garnett saw him, and Eric Kennington, but both of them were concerned with the preparation of his war history for publication.

The London he had left in August was little changed, though he felt keenly his own mutations. It lay before him—a devoted lover of its infinite moods—like a mellow fruit, all golden with bloom: the river tinted a delicate pearl gray with tongues of bronze lapping at its eddies wherever the sun struck; the strings of barques from the Medway cleaving the water in their soundless glide. The spires of the City stood poised in an instant of time between the holocaust

---

[12] *T. E. Lawrence by His Friends.*

past and the holocaust still to come, and not even Venice seemed more beguiling in the afternoon sun. Listening to the metallic rhythm of his iron-shod feet—for the British serviceman in the ranks, like a belled cat, must make audible his presence wherever he goes—Lawrence moved along the Embankment, one of his favorite London walks. There were more than a dozen-odd friends in London at that time, any one of whom would have been delighted to see him and meet him on his own ground in talk of books, painting, history. But Uxbridge to which he was bound to return was too raw a feeling, and he had not yet learned to live in two worlds as he was later to do. ("It was a hot day, my uniform felt as tight as an alderman's skin, my boots as heavy as lead, my legs like balusters. The embankment was really nicer than the tube to Golders Green," he was to write Ernest Thurtle in 1929, apologizing for not coming to see him. [*Letters*, No. 396.])

The walk around London which already was an improvement on his desperate tramping of the streets in August, a business call, a visit to his Barton Street attic to sort out the accumulation of papers, and he was gone again in a twinkling of blue—eyes and uniform. But if the exhilaration of momentary freedom was a short and rare bliss, the risk of encounter with the Air Service Police was well calculated. Uxbridge would make renewed demands soon enough.

The long, yet curiously abbreviated days of the recruits' course wore on. "Each day brings its breathless order and each night its breathless cancellation," he was to tell Robert Graves in November. He was writing then from the School of Photography, Farnborough, but how much more breathless the order and its nightly cancellation at Uxbridge where the discipline was tightly knit and a sense of violent urgency permeated all the hours. "*Per ardua ad astra*": The pace stick was the scourge which drove them and the bugle the clarion call which they followed, for life or death, in the frantic labor upward to the stars, though some of them were moved to wonder what they would be fit for by the time the stars were reached. On punishment drill which in one bleak penalty he drew for seven nights running, the less rugged bled at the nose or fainted and dropped out; for Lawrence there was no such relief for, he said, "I have searched myself exhaustively and know I can hardly faint." [13] Inwardly he was steadier, but his nerves were still raw. He was, he confessed to Robert Graves, easily made frantic. Uxbridge was an odd cure for bruised nerves, as he recognized, and there were times when he wondered if it was a certain one.

> I think that I may have to publish something after all [he wrote Edward Garnett in that letter already quoted], for I'm getting too old for this life of rough and tumble, and the crudeness of my company worries me a bit. I find myself longing for an empty room, or a solitary bed, or even a moment alone in the open air. [*Letters*, No. 167.]

The unbelievable tenderness of grass and sky at Uxbridge, the flight of birds, the tinkling water-sound of the River Pinn, after long and brutal hours on the drill square, were nearly shattering. It was necessary to be on guard always lest they betray heart and imagination into a vulnerable softness. Better the lusty songs and the not-too-tender horseplay of the hut where all were brothers in discomfort and Sons of Thunder. The question was: How long would he be able to stand it? It is an irresistible urge to wonder whether, if Uxbridge had been less of a martyrdom, Lawrence would have been able to disengage his obdurate will to suffer. As it was, the higher the flames licked, the more he settled back in his bonds to endure.

Submission to martyrdom is the chief theme of *The Mint*, but there are others. There is the ever-recurring debate on the conflict of flesh and spirit, the guiltlessness of ignorance and the concupiscence of knowledge, all built around his meditations at morning prayer in the Church of St. Margaret during the interminable levels of Trinity. He lets out like silken threads his telling little homilies which are at once revelations of his philosophy and a condemnation of the Pauline strictures. He remembers how, little by little, he has sloughed off all the declarations of faith in the Creed save the first four words: *Credo in unum Deum*, which, he says, he proclaims defiantly as if to evoke some last and permanent beneficence. And he is wrathful indeed

---

[13] *The Mint.*

with the ascetic-faced parson who Sunday after Sunday exhorts the ranks of shorn airmen helplessly arrayed before him like sacrificial victims to forsake their sinful ways. They were, he said, innocent and without sin, for all they did was done naturally and without reflection, untainted with guilt despite their animalism. As for the foulness of their language: "Words were like their boots, dirty on the fields, clean indoors: a daily convention and no index to the fellows' minds." [14] It is only when man begins to reflect that the concept of sin enters in his mind and pollutes his actions. Unthinking man is free and needs no absolution; it is thinking man who must bear the weight of guilt, for he has eaten of the fruit of knowledge and must henceforth accept responsibility for his deeds.

The Mint in its broader sense is his testament to the travail of man, to man's fumbling and agonized groping for truth, his confused reeling between faith and agnosticism, his bitter crying out to unseen angels. Yet Lawrence does not ask with Rilke: *Wer wenn ich schriee hörte mich denn aus der Engel Ordnung?* He does not expect to be heard. Instead, he says: man abundantly needs mercy and, in so saying, touches the very core of religious belief. To wish for mercy is to wish for God and to give worship, however involute. This is a long way, morally speaking, from the brash youth in Syria who shot his would-be assassin in the hand, rendered first aid, and then sent him off with a sound kick in the rear for the sake of prudence. Since then he had seen many men die, both at his own hand and as a result of his own actions. And he had not only been appreciably closer to death himself but had craved it—if not as the door that leads to light, then as the Sunday which should never end. This is a different thing to facing it with courage, bravery being so often a compound of recklessness and nerves excited into action by fear. He had seen his dearest dreams turn to ashes, and he had looked himself, his desires, his shortcomings, his sins, squarely in the face and seen how little there was to exult over, how far from the heroic and the exemplary his actions had been, how infinitely small he was after all. There had

---

[14] *Ibid.*

been times in the past when this overt self-depreciation acted as a spur to his vanity. At Uxbridge it was not so; there his humility was real and he drank of it deeply.

The R.A.F. notes had grown so in bulk by now that it was becoming difficult in the cramped quarters of the hut to keep them together. Remembering a blank loose-leaf notebook among his scattered effects, he sent off for it by post, and out of its pages, when he opened them in the hut, fell the august seal of 1921: "Our most trusty and well-beloved Thomas Edward Lawrence Esquire, Lieutenant-Colonel in our Army . . ." A chuckle, an improbable fiction—only a birth certificate—in reply to a prying question, and he whisked it up out of sight. How sharp were the prying eyes that saw it then is not known, but it seems an unfortunate oversight that David Garnett, his admirable and careful editor, should have attributed the presence of this document at Uxbridge to deliberate indiscretion rather than to accident. At Uxbridge his incognito was carefully preserved, and he did not himself do anything to divulge the secret. Later his behavior in the matter of his identity is open to question; but not at Uxbridge.

The pains and penalties of Uxbridge came to an abrupt end early in November when No. 352087 Aircraftman John Hume Ross was posted to the School of Photography at Farnborough. There is every reason to believe that he had written to the Air Ministry asking that his course at Uxbridge which had already run for ten weeks and was due to run another two, be expedited. Yet at once, when he was free of Uxbridge, he began to regret it for the sake of its fellowship and its poignancy in his mind as the scene of his hard forcing, his sufferings, and, through them, his growth. At Farnborough the discipline was less severe but still strict enough for him to find himself at odds with authority.

"I have laboured greatly, in a week which confined me to camp, fulfilling a fire-picket: for I am still an Ethiopian so far as my conduct-sheet goes," he wrote Edward Garnett on November 20. [*Letters*, No. 180.] To Sir Oliver Swann on the previous day he had written: "I'm reading German and Spanish to keep myself busy; for my nature doesn't second the demands of discipline very well, and unless I keep working at something I get Bolshie!" [*Letters*, No. 179.] The fact was that Farnborough was still a training center and not the real R.A.F.; he was still a recruit under training and made to wash dishes, scrub up kitchens, empty dust bins, and clean out pig sties.

Very little is known about Lawrence's sojourn at Farnborough, for he did not include it in his R.A.F. notes. It was too hard an experience for him to record—hard not in the sense of the physical hardness of Uxbridge but in the bleaker sense of deep frustration. For one thing, there was disappointment: he had arrived too late to enroll in the November class of photography and was told he must wait for the new class in the following January, adding two months to a nine months' course. With his usual aplomb, he assumed the old identity of Lawrence again in order to demur in a letter to Sir Oliver Swann and to set forth his qualifications as a photographer, which were considerable. Meanwhile, he had bought a motorcycle—"Boanerges" I—to give him that freedom of movement he delighted in and to enable him to escape his prison whenever confinement and discipline became intolerable.

Through the literary agency of Curtis Brown, he was, while at Farnborough, to sign a contract with Jonathan Cape covering the abridgment—Garnett's and his own—of his war history, and alternatively toyed with and rejected the idea of "buying" himself out of his servitude with the proceeds. For a few weeks at this time he was able to enjoy something of a domestic existence: his mother had returned briefly from China and was living with his younger brother in the borrowed London flat of his architect friend, Sir Herbert Baker, where he was able to run up two or three times a week to join them. It must have been an odd reunion, made all the more odd by Ned's reversion to his old schoolboy role of runaway.

Yet the hardness of his life now evoked in him a corresponding need for warmth and sympathy, and he began to look for that warmth and sympathy in his friendships to a greater extent than ever before. By now he was corresponding frequently with George Bernard Shaw whom he met before his enlistment, in March, when he went to Shaw's London house with Sir Sidney Cockrell to pick up an Augustus

John portrait which Shaw had agreed to exhibit. Of an impulse, in August, he submitted the manuscript of his war history to Shaw for criticism and thereafter the friendship of these two dissimilar beings, the one Irish by birth, the other Irish in spirit, was assured. By this time too, he had himself sat to a number of well-known artists: Augustus John through whom he met W. H. Hudson whose books he had long admired, and who had painted him in Arab dress to look heroic and falsely tall; Eric Kennington who drew and satirized him in paint and crayon with an uncanny insight; Sir William Rothenstein who revealed the gamin in him. Together with the photographs, war and postwar, these portraits and drawings form what is perhaps the most astonishing and diversified collection any public figure can boast of. They are his pictorial testament in which admirers and critics alike can search for clues to his personal complexities. One photograph, a motorcycling scene with George Brough, shows him astride "Boanerges" smiling broadly in a facial pose as strong, as ordinary, as vulgarly handsome as that of an Irish police constable. It is in startling conflict with Augustus John's ethereal drawing of him, and with the later powerful and sensitive Howard Coster photo-portraits.

Suddenly, in January, 1923, the prison gates opened wide of their own accord, and before he realized quite what had happened, he was on the other side of the high walls looking in, but with no right of entry. The news of his whereabouts leaked out, he said afterwards, through an officer at Farnborough who sold the information to the press; and the lurid headlines: "Uncrowned King as Private Soldier—Lawrence of Arabia Seeking Peace; Opportunity to Write a Book," put an end to his refuge. He has been accused, a little unfairly, of bringing this betrayal at Farnborough on himself, and a letter to George Bernard Shaw in December clearly indicates that he was known there. "They treat my past as a joke, and forgive it me lightly," he said. "The officers fight shy of me: but I behave demurely, and give no trouble." [*Letters*, No. 187.]

Sir Oliver Swann felt the exposure was due to Lawrence's love of drawing a veil of mystery over himself, as well as to carelessness on the part of the Colonial Office; and David Garnett, the editor of his letters, was inclined to agree. Perhaps he was culpable, but this does not alter the fact that he was recognized at Farnborough by someone who had known him in the East and who passed the word on to the press. For days the camp was seized with speculative gossip while photographers and newsmen, all trying to catch a glimpse of the fabulous Colonel Lawrence in R.A.F. overalls, milled around on the outside. The dust settled, but in its passing the upheaval left some bad blood and destroyed the surety of his refuge. His presence at Farnborough was felt to be an embarrassment to the officers under whom he would have to serve; his papers were forwarded back to Uxbridge, and his discharge was there effected in the teeth of his protests and his pleas to be posted to a remote station, like Leuchars in Fifeshire, where the sensation-hungry press could not find him, and where the commanding officer was "a solid and masterful person." At Uxbridge and at Farnborough, Lawrence's almost boyish ideal of service to the air flagged but did not wither. And after his dismissal from the air force he realized how devoted, in these few months, he had grown, and how much its challenge had got into his blood.

To B. E. Leeson who had been a member of the Royal Flying Corps in the days of the Arab Campaign, he wrote in February:

> When the Press let itself go in that hideous fashion the Air Ministry said, "Quite impossible to permit an A.C.2 to have such publicity." I was meek and said I didn't really want it: they might have it if they could get it. In reply they slung me out. Since then I've been in very low water (did you understand that I enlisted not to write books, but because I was broke?) and am not yet quite in the deep stuff, though three Government Departments exhaust themselves trying to find me a billet —— I turn down all their ideas, and ask for something poorer, and they think I mean richer. Soon they will burst themselves. You see, I'm fed up with being called Colonel in this ridiculous year 1923. [*Letters*, No. 192.]

This lighthearted, slangy exposition was a whistling in the dark: he was really quite desperate, and neither books nor the nerve-bracing thrill of riding over sixty miles an hour on a superb machine could serve him as an anodyne. In a moment of acute mental stress after the Farnborough incident, he abortively killed off the goose that would lay him golden eggs, if he gave it a chance, by canceling his contract with Jonathan Cape. There should be no book now even though financial embarrassment was added to his mental distress.

The Air Ministry was adamant. Reluctantly, after turning down an offer from the Irish Free State, he brought his considerable influence to bear on the War Office where he had many friends, among them Colonel Alan Dawnay and Sir Phillip Chetewode who had known him in Egypt and Arabia. In March he was enlisted as a private in the Royal Tank Corps and sent to Bovington Camp, Dorset, at which he was to labor, like Jacob for Rachael, waiting for his second chance in the air force. The process was much the same as before; the recruiting officers were simply ordered willy-nilly to enlist him, but once in, he conformed scrupulously to rule and order and asked no privilege for himself. John Hume Ross was gone into eclipse and his place was taken by T. E. Shaw, an identity he was later to legalize by deed poll, even as his father years before had legalized the name of Lawrence. All names are holy, says Greek theology, but "Lawrence" had lost for him whatever holiness it had ever possessed. As a public name it belonged more properly, he thought, to David Herbert Lawrence, his great contemporary to whom it brought luster and who was "an infinitely greater man than all of us rolled together."

He had entered still another circle in his long purgation, a dull and dispirited level where there were no contours, no color but gray, no feeling but hopelessness, no sense but that of despair. "One of my sorrows is the recruits' course," he wrote "Jock" Chambers [*Letters*, No. 197], a fellow airman at Farnborough who had helped to shield him against the importunate press photographers; "(a new name, naturally, new age, no previous service) and a consequent imprisonment in the camp for a month being damnably shouted at." The recruits' course ran eighteen weeks, a longer but less severe ordeal than Uxbridge; yet it was a worse one, for there was no promise at the end of it of that clean and splendid fellowship of technicians which he envisaged the air force to be. By comparison, life in the tank corps seemed drab and unrewarding, a depressing and lecherous dominion of ne'er-do-wells which he deplored. The R.A.F. had been crude, but it was a healthy crudeness. At Bovington he found that bedrock had sunk so deep he could hardly exist on its noxious substratum. It bred a feral, nauseous air where the phallus was no more a symbol but an openly cultivated fetish.

"We were really a decent crowd: and the present lot with me are the sort who'd always throw something at any cat they saw," he told "Jock" Chambers. It was a moral difference, he felt, and it threatened him with a return to the solitariness he dreaded. Yet the new prison on the Dorset Heath was more movingly beautiful than the old. It stood in the midst of "Egdon" Heath, in a wild and flinty landscape richly fledged with pine and oak and rhododendron—a brown, dank, undulating desert in winter, saturated with a brooding melancholy that only Hardy could adequately portray; but the summer transformed it into a flowering moorland of pink and purple in which only the heather clumps recalled its elemental sobriety. Yet, except in his leisure hours after the acquisition of his cottage, it did not gladden his heart.

> It's an odd penance to have set oneself, to live amongst animals for seven years [he told Edward Garnett in April]. Nebuchadnezzar did it, I suppose: the feel of tanks is so utterly unlike the R.A.F. and everything here disgusts me. My motor-bike is called into use when I find myself on parade facing an unconscious sergeant with my fists hard clenched. A hundred fast miles seem to make the camp feel less confined afterwards. Do you think Neb. made himself animal, like his companions? [*Letters*, No. 204.]

As at Uxbridge and at Farnborough, he was an odd, perplexing, and perhaps on occasion, exasperating recruit: a man of nearly thirty-five who often looked and in many ways behaved like an impulsive boy of twenty. Robert Graves, teasing him when he was still at Farnborough, had likened him to Coleridge serving in the ranks of the 15th Dragoons where he took the name of Silas Tomkyn

Comberbatch and wrote the other men's letters home in return for their services in grooming his horse and cleaning his equipment. Private Shaw did not so oblige, but he was markedly cut from a different cloth, and so betrayed his alien milieu by his manner of speech, his taste in books and gramophone records, that he could not but be conspicuous.

> From the day of his arrival he earned respect due principally to his quiet and reserved manner [wrote two of the men who had known him at Bovington]. It could be seen at a glance that he was older and far more experienced than the average recruit, yet he did not, at that time, speak to anyone of his former life. This silence in the recruit stage of service was so unusual as to arouse interest.[15]

But it was his interest in and knowledge of motorcycles which made him the object of instant regard by the other soldiers. Because of it, they were prepared to go to great lengths of tolerance of his aesthetic pursuits; also he did not by those pursuits set himself up as an exemplar. He was unassuming in spite of his legend, they felt, when they came to know him better—or perhaps because of it. And he was generous; always to be depended on in the soldier's chronic impecuniosity between pay parades. Moreover he was kind and thoughtful of those whose more urgent needs were beyond their means and their power to satisfy, opening doors which must have remained closed but for his intervention. And he indulged in schoolboy pranks: snow on the beds of grumbling sleepers; water sloshed by the bucketful over the hut floor to outrage a ridiculous orderly-sergeant who was forever sprinkling to lay the dust—the sort of jokes which soldiers, like schoolboys, highly relish. And though he did not set himself up as an exemplar, he was nonetheless an exemplar which soldiers, especially the more serious of them, could readily accept.

> Even his jollying in our company was a trial of strength, [wrote Regimental Sergeant Major H. H. Banbury]; for every energy went into these wrestles, and his spare frame took all our efforts to subdue; and

[15] Captain G. E. Kirby and Sergeant W. E. Jeffrey, in *T. E. Lawrence by His Friends.*

> competition with a pistol was severe, for he concentrated to overcome my highest standard: and succeeded everywhere.

(What is most interesting about this comment is the style and punctuation which are an attempted facsimile of Lawrence's own.)

Very soon he had assembled a little coterie of new soldier-friends in the ranks to add to the wide and exalted circle of statesmen, poets, painters, explorers, dramatists, and airmen who counted him as friend. There was Private Palmer, known by his nickname "Posh," who worked with Lawrence in the quartermaster's stores and with Sergeant Pugh contributed his impressions of his friend to Robert Graves' biography; there was Pioneer-Sergeant Knowles and his sons who were his near neighbors at Clouds Hill; there was Corporal Alec Dixon to whom he gave advice on writing ("Read plenty of Swift, and some Shakespeare every day—he's sheer music, you know!"). It was a life not without some fleeting pleasure, but it was not happiness nor even the shadow of contentment. And there were moments in it of bleak agony.

> He joked about his Tank Town troubles, so that I did not guess at his protracted torture there, but it was during his tank service that he paid us the most strange visit, as usual without warning, and with a soldier on pillion. This time—for the first time—he dropped all defences. There was a wall of pain between him and us. We both felt helpless, for he looked his disappointment at us. He almost might have come especially to quarrel. It was as if T. E. was giving an impersonation for two or three hours. Everything was attacked. Life itself. Marriage, parenthood, work, morality, and especially Hope . . . All we could do was to dodge and futilely make light of it. The young tank-man was more positive. He banged his fist on the tea table and threatened. "Now, none of that. How often have I told you? Look me straight in the face . . ." An animal tamer and T. E. a wild beast that partially obeyed him. . . . Aside, to my wife, the young man revealed his grief at T. E.'s suffering. I don't know who he was, but he had great courage and love for T. E."[16]

Bovington Camp was not included in *The Mint*, but it has left its own memorial in a series of letters to Lionel Curtis of All Souls written

---

[16] Eric Kennington in *T. E. Lawrence by His Friends.*

from March through June in 1923. In them Lawrence laid bare his soul, perhaps even more completely than in *The Mint*, but their confessions are transcendental rather than intimate, and their impact is correspondingly trascendent. "Lorde," he begins, "my mind moves me this morning to write you a whole series of letters, to be more splendid than the *Lettres de Mon Moulin*." Nothing would come of it, he prophesied, but he plunged then into the old argument of his enlistment, some of which has already been quoted and which, in turn, was to develop with gathering intensity like a swelling *passacaglia* into a relentless scrutiny of mind and attitudes.

There were his doubts: could he create well, or were all his creations marred?

> I'm not sure either that what I've said about my creations is quite true. I feel confident that Arabia and Transjordan and Mesopotamia, *with what they will breed*, are nearly monumental enough for seven years' labour of one head: because I knew what I was at, and the others only worked on instinct. [*Letters*, No. 205.]

And the book that was the real fruit of that labour? "Do you know I'm absolutely hungry to know what people think of it—not when they are telling me, but what they tell to one another. Should I be in this secret case if I really thought it pernicious?" Here was the tortured self-consciousness, the overscrupulousness, the curious desire to play spectator to himself and his works which so often betrayed his sounder judgment: how would he appear to others? How would his written words read? To some extent all authors share this natural concern for a work in progress or about to be printed, but most authors have lost the craving for opinion before the printer's ink is dry. Being prolonged, his was a morbid craving, and like all morbidities, it rode him hard and to his disadvantage in the eyes of others.

Eight days later he was holding up gross man and intellectual man and proving despairingly that the first was real and the second only the product of the mental accretions which had formed him, estimable in themselves perhaps, but not essential, and certainly not part of that bedrock of carnal existence on which he now lived; and carnality, he felt even as he shrank from it, was the supreme reality.

> You wouldn't exist, I wouldn't exist without this carnality. Everything with flesh in its mixture is the achievement of a moment when the lusty thought of Hut 12 has passed into action and conceived: and isn't it true that the fault of birth rests somewhat on the child? I believe it's we who led our parents on to bear us, and it's our unborn children who make our flesh itch. [*Letters*, No. 206.]

The old execration of creation and the means of creation—the shameful duality of man's nature: animal without the decent seasonal restraints of animals. And if he had willed himself into flesh, then the shame was all the greater. With Job he could say: Let the day perish wherein I was born, and the night in which it was said, There is a man-child conceived.

By May he was openly confessing to his masochism. The R.A.F. had been foul-mouthed but clean-minded; what he was up against at Bovington was stark bestiality which hurt and frightened him both.

> There is no criticism; indeed it's taken for granted as natural that you should job a woman's body, or hire out yourself, or abuse yourself in any way. I cried out against it, partly in self-pity, because I've condemned myself to grow like them, partly in premonition of failure, for my masochism remains and will remain, only moral. [*Letters*, No. 207.]

Denial, he said, gave him the gratification which others drew from indulgence, and everything physical was hateful to him and therefore impossible. But this does not negate the obvious: that he did in fact impose physical as well as moral suffering upon himself. His body was brought into subjection by the classic means, and though Lawrence may not have burned like St. Paul, nor was he made costive of spirit by his mortifications, there are aspects in both men which are near parallel.

Not only did he desire to suffer, but there was in him a desire to be mastered by other men, even if this meant voluntary submission to lesser men. It is one of the aspects of himself he makes quite clear in his ruthless analysis of himself:

> It was a part of my failure never to have found a chief to use me. All of them, through incapacity or timidity or liking, allowed me too free a hand; as if they could not see that voluntary slavery was the deep pride

> of a morbid spirit and vicarious pain its gladdest decoration . . . Allenby came nearest to my longings for a master, but I had to avoid him, not daring to bow down for fear lest he show feet of clay with that friendly word which must shatter my allegiance.[17]

The feminine desire for submission and the subjective longing for total annihilation of self are two interrelated modes, and the only satisfactory explanation of what seems a shockingly weak bias in so strong and willful a man, capable of exerting extraordinary influence over the minds and wills of other men, is that it was an inversion of his desire for an absolute: the ultimate submission of body and soul which leads at last to perfect freedom.

The travail wore on day by day.

> I consume the day (and myself) brooding, and making phrases and reading and thinking again, galloping mentally down twenty divergent roads at once, as apart and alone as in Barton Street in my attic [he wrote]. When my mood gets too hot and I find myself wandering beyond control I pull out my motor-bike and hurl it top-speed through these unfit roads for hour after hour. My nerves are jaded and gone near dead, so that nothing less than hours of voluntary danger will prick them into life: and the "life" they reach then is a melancholy joy at risking something worth exactly 2/9 a day. [*Letters*, No. 207.]

This craving for risk was odd, he commented; for he funked the physical hazards of the gymnasium with horror and then returned later and alone to vault the horse, to his grim and perverse satisfaction. It was a dismal round and far from the nerve cure he had sought, unless the cure was a calculated destruction of mind and nerve until nothing was left but a dull, unfeeling husk. But there was still another aspect; the justification for his suffering and the only solvent, if mercifully it is present, for those who must go down into the pit.

> You say my friends feel the absence of me [he wrote, for Lionel Curtis had been trying to persuade him to return and give up his mad experiment]; but personality (which it is my gift to you to exhibit) is of a short range, and in my experience has not touched more than ten or twelve friends at a time: and here I live with twenty very barren men who feel

[17] *The Seven Pillars of Wisdom.*

> my being with them. The hut is changed from what it used to be, and unlike what it would be (will be?) if I left. This isn't conceit, but a plain statement; for there would be a change if any one of us twenty was taken away: and I am richer and wider and more experienced than any of the others here. More of the world has passed over me in 35 years than over all their twenties put together: and your gain, if you did gain by my return, would be their loss. [*Letters*, No. 208.]

That was his mood at the end of May, when the heath was ablaze with rhododendrons. It would not hold constant; but neither would it be entirely dissipated. There follows a scene played out in the shadow of a cathedral—Wells, apt setting for a modern miracle play; with the strange and tortured Everyman being led around by an aging priest who, in his insular cloister, had lost all contact with the world as it is and would doubtless have in some manner to re-establish it before he could attain to the Beatific Vision. The priest was gently skeptical of the man-at-arms—khaki being presumed to cover a multitude of sins, and gently astonished to find that khaki in this case covered also a mind. The mind pleased him greatly with the intellectual *hors d'oeuvres* it offered. Of souls or the sickness of souls he said and probably thought nothing. One does not talk of such things except from a pulpit, and only then with a proper discretion. They ended by watching together the fish as they swam about the moat, and T. E. Shaw, if he could have had his miracle then, would have chosen one of the simpler variety and exchanged his identity with that of the fish: a new life, a new dimension, a real brain sleep, for in their cool and silver detachment they seemed to him to have reached nirvana: the perfect equilibrium beyond the attainment of human philosophy.

In September Private Shaw met the poet of Wessex through prearrangement with Robert Graves, himself a poet. It was not the last time the "anonymous" soldier in khaki was to cross the threshold of Max Gate, for the presence close by of Thomas Hardy was one of the rare pleasures that made Bovington tolerable, and he returned again and again to savor its haunting flavor and the air of remoteness and peace that enveloped it.

His impressions were hard for him to describe and crystallized slowly. Hardy he found "so pale, so quiet, so refined into an essence . . . waiting so tranquilly for death, without a desire or ambition left in his spirit." And he continued to cherish so many illusions—or what T. E. Lawrence, formed in a harder school, considered illusions. The truth was, Hardy was living in the past as old men often do, and the contemporary scene with its demands, its denials and restatements, left no mark on him. Napoleon was more concrete than the Hohenzollern and Waterloo more significant than the Marne. The peace of Max Gate was already the peace of the grave, though the teacups rattled, the silver chimed under Mrs. Hardy's hands, and subdued voices spoke of Homer and of Scott, or fell silent while the poet in his tranquil but dessicated voice meditated out loud. It was an experience so precious, Lawrence told Robert Graves, that he grudged even the writing about it. His worship of Hardy, like his worship of Doughty, was the worship of an essence, an ideal made fragilely manifest.

Under the influence of Hardy's spirit, he found a ruined cottage one and a half miles away from the camp where the scarring of tank town's hutments and firing ranges did not reach, and the heath came into its own again. "Mistover Knap" was what Hardy had called the place in *Return of the Native*, and it pleased Lawrence to think of the two-hundred-year-old cottage with its shattered roof as the one where Eustacia Vye had lived with the Captain, her father. The land on which it stood belonged to his father's kinsmen from one of whom he leased the five acres surrounding the ruin. This is seemingly the only instance of his father's family ever being aware of the Lawrence sons, and in particular, of the one who had brought so much luster, if not to their name, then to their blood. Pioneer Sergeant Knowles helped him to rebuild the cottage and reroof it with nine thousand slates. It was the closest thing to the Morrisonian Hall he had been able to achieve, and he was prepared to lavish on it all his imagination and ingenuity. There he stored his books and belongings retrieved from Pole Hill, his Columbia gramophone, and the records of Mozart and Beethoven he had acquired; and he bestowed on it all the reluctant affection of one who had not known a settled home since childhood. Not that it was a home in any real sense of the word, but only as E. M. Forster has said, "the place where his feet touched the earth for a moment, and found rest." He was hardly ever to sleep there throughout his tenancy and, while at Bovington Camp, used it only as a temporary refuge from barrack life: to sit by the fire reading on a winter's evening or to lie under the skylight of the upstairs room in the long summer twilight watching an aerial sea of oak and ilex in continual motion. But it was important in still another sense, for it provided him with a sanctuary quiet enough for writing, for the translation of French books into English which he was undertaking for Jonathan Cape, and for the last revision of his war history —for it was becoming apparent that he could not withhold publication, either of the private or the public versions, much longer. Friends, among them Gertrude Bell, were pressing for the private version by volunteering to find subscribers at thirty pounds a copy; while the rumor of a book on him by Lowell Thomas made it imperative that he tell at least some truths about himself in the Arab Campaign.

Between them, he and Edward Garnett had produced an abridgment which reduced the original three hundred and fifty thousand words to about one hundred and fifty thousand, by omitting all the personal reflection, all the intimate and private agonies of the author, and much of the historical background. The result, said Lawrence, resembled "one of those most genial trees of a bird-shape"—objects he had always laughed at but secretly longed to possess. This mutilation was not *The Seven Pillars of Wisdom* which was the summation of all that he had become up to the age of thirty; it was a factual and descriptive account of his part in the Arab Campaign, and it was all he could bear to expose to public gaze. Even so, another three years were to pass before publication became a reality. Meanwhile, his consent to the private edition was won at last, and from December on he was absorbed with preparations to print, edit, and finance the voluminous text with its accompanying portraits and drawings, now numbering well over fifty. A hundred copies were to be produced based on an estimated total cost of three thousand pounds, with a ten per cent margin for extras. That the cost went far beyond the estimate was due to his exacting and extravagant standards as a lifelong connoisseur of typography, and when it came to the actual printing and binding, to the mathematical exactitude in his arrangement of paragraphs and chapters so that they should conform to an aesthetic pattern. The lavish reproductions of portraits and drawings of the Arabs and Britons who were the supporting cast in this epic drama of desert warfare and personal conflict brought the cost to the level of a fine folly. This last extravagance was an important factor, for in his mind the sole justification for yielding to the demands for the private edition was to publish the collection of drawings and portraits which he had commissioned from so many artists. With the combined help of Manning Pike and H. J. Hodgson who printed the book, Sangorski and Sutcliffe who bound it, of Hogarth who edited the proofs and Eric Kennington who acted as art editor, the subscribers' edition came into being. And his erstwhile Camel Corps comrade, Colonel R. V. Buxton, in his capacity as banker, arranged to carry the overdraft which inevitably developed.

In May George Bernard Shaw with Hogarth's knowledge had addressed a private memorandum to the Prime Minister, the Right Honorable Stanley (later Lord) Baldwin, deploring Lawrence's poverty. Quite aside from the part the eccentricity of his own behavior played in his state, the fact remained, Shaw said, that his position was a national scandal and steps ought to be taken, in the form of a pension, to bring it to an end. The pension was not offered, though the subject of this memorandum, gratefully acknowledging the efforts in his behalf, indicated that he would have accepted it had it been offered. But would he have done so? He was to tell Liddell Hart that his optimum was three hundred pounds a year which he could augment as he pleased with translations or other labors, and it was such a small amount that the astonishing thing is that no one came forward with an offer of it. It was a time when his father's family might perhaps have made a magnanimous gesture toward him. So far as is known, no such gesture was made, and there is no reason to believe he would have accepted it if it had been made, despite his occasional wistful longing for the easement of financial independence.

> You suggest that I'm not genuine in the ranks [Shaw in the memorandum to the Prime Minister had called his soldiering in the ranks "a shocking tomfoolery"]: but I am: just as good, now, as the others. Not very good, I'm afraid (I will be if I can) since I'm slow, having to learn to do all the daily trifles which others used to do for me . . . Your picture of my ending up to find that I am a soldier, by dint of much playing at it, comforts me; for it's the end I want, and am wanting with deadly seriousness. The peace of finding that my horizon was grown so near! If I could be happy drunk I'd drink: but so to take the control off myself might be to loose myself out again: and I want not to be big any more. [*Letters*, No. 235.]

Even the army was a refuge of sorts.

> People come into the army often [he told Shaw in that same July letter], not because it is brutal and licentious, but because they haven't done very well in the fight of daily living, and want to be spared the responsibility of ordering for themselves their homes and food and clothes and work—or even the intensity of their work. Regard it as an asylum for the little-spirited.

There are no published photographs of him in the khaki and beret of the tank corps—perhaps because it was a livery he so consciously hated. He served the army correctly, though without enthusiasm, being described by authority as "exceptionally intelligent, very reliable and works well"; but all the while he languished for the air force into which there seemed no hope of his ever being reinstated. In dismissing him with one hand, Lord Trenchard had offered him a commission with the other. This he refused, and if it seems like perverted obstinacy, it should be remembered what were his intentions in enlisting in the ranks. As an officer, his tight little shell of security, fabricated with such pain at Uxbridge, would be broken; he would have had to wear again the mantel of authority, to live in amity with his reputation and assume responsibilities commensurate with his powers of mind. The paradox of the ranks—a view which few of his friends could understand—was that while they deprived him of personal comfort and privacy, they did free him from himself and from the burden of being a celebrity, and afforded him that blank anonymity in which his hurt and exhausted nerves could slowly heal.

From six to six the army ordered all his down-sitting and up-rising, and he performed all the duties, from the inevitable "square bashing" to ditch-digging, of a private soldier. Only in the hours from six to nine was his time his own to do with as he pleased. Thinking came after midnight when the current of other men's thoughts had been turned off. The terror of nightmare dreams which had been the unconscious legacy of Der'a lessened; the daytime nightmare continued.

Christmas came with its dedication to orgy, and the camp was awash with the noisome ooze of an overflowed cesspool. It was like a ship in a heavy sea, he confided to Lord Wavell, with all inmates in need of slop jars. "The old army, in my recollection, did at least carry its drink," he remarked. The strain of this rife debauchery on a man who did not himself drink, even wine, is to be imagined. It seemed to shatter his last and lingering hope that man was more than an animal grown clever by artificial forcing. The roar and snarl of the beast would always be heard above (or below) the wit, he told Harley Granville-Barker whose play, *The Secret Life*, he read early in 1924.

> Here in camp it's the lesson stamped into me with nailed feet hour after hour: that at bottom we are carnal: that our appetites and tastes and hopes and ideals are beast-qualities, coloured or shaped somewhat fancifully, but material always, things you can cut with a knife: and you have hidden that, out of shame perhaps: out of fear perhaps: or, like Shaw, in revenge. [*Letters*, No. 241.]

The year lengthened; the Jazz Age began—the age of the Brave New World and the "It" girl; of *The Great Gatsby*, the Charleston, the shingle, of ukelele ladies, mahjong parties, and the Bright Young Things of Mayfair—all violently infantile reactions to war from which, in some measure at least in a later era, the chilling sobriety of the Atom Bomb and the exasperating paradox of "cold war" saved another postwar world.

In March Lawrence wrote asking to be taken back into the R.A.F., but his request was refused, and the army seemed his permanent penance. There were letters and visits: Clouds Hill was becoming a way-station for the great and near-great in the world of art and letters, H. M. Tomlinson, Siegfried Sassoon, George Bernard Shaw, Augustus John, among others; and in June E. M. Forster arrived for a week end to "sojourn among the beetles and the fallen rhododendron bloom." The Hardys called sometimes at Clouds Hill that summer for tea, its most cherished visitors. In all these incredible hours of conviviality, writers, artists, and soldiers mingled, brought together by their host who cared nothing for honors or reputations; and there were casual feasts of tea, bread, and cheese and tinned beans at which no one sat still for long at a time, and self-appointed guardians tended fire, kettle, and gramophone. There was talk, books, music, even laughter, and all the while the inner core of his being fretted slowly away in this terrible effort to blunt his faculties and brutalize himself.

One by one like giants of the forest stricken with age or sudden catastrophe, the titans were falling around him: W. H. Hudson in 1922; Conrad in 1924, while Doughty was already past eighty and Hardy visibly waxing more frail. For himself, the years seemed to stretch out interminably, though he dared to hope that his physical excesses in Arabia and after, would guarantee him not too long a course. "The army is dyeing me khaki by degrees, and I don't know that I'm any longer much company for real people," he had told Sir Sidney Cockrell in the previous October, excusing himself for not going lately to Max Gate. He had done over a year in the army and had nearly six to go if he was to complete his seven years with the Colors; then he would try for a job nearby as a garage hand.

Time walked in fetters, dragging its feet, though what H. M. Tomlinson called "this trampled planet, this muddy star" ground through the early part of the Roaring Twenties like a juggernaut. That May Lawrence wrote to D. G. Hogarth: "Here at Bovington I seem to sit still: so still that often I fancy the slow passing of time about me can be *heard.*" [*Letters*, No. 246.] In 1940, if he lived that long, how would his war history read, he wondered? In 1940 indeed: it was 1924 and Christmas again, with God resting merry all the King's gentlemen on their way, if they could manage it, to the latrines to be sick.

Then it was 1925 and February, "supplication month" he called it, writing again to Lord Trenchard to plead for reinstatement in the air force. His record in the army had been good; there had been no scandals, no disturbing outcries in the press, and in the face of it, it seemed absurd for the Air Ministry to withhold from him what the War Office granted without any obvious injury to itself. Lord Trenchard was finally willing. There were others who were not willing, however. The chief voice of dissent was that of the Air Minister himself, Sir Samuel Hoare (Lord Templewood) who so disapproved of Colonel Lawrence degrading himself in the ranks that he would take no action whatever to encourage him in his course.

This longing of Lawrence for the air force was a curious, impassioned longing, like the languishing desire of a man for a woman; or perhaps more appositely, like that of a postulant for the Order in which he desires to dedicate himself. It could not be assuaged; when he thought it quiescent or withered, it rose up again and gripped him: a sudden tightening of emotion at the sight of an airman in blue, the winged badge, the eagle on a sleeve. Was there really so much discrepancy between the two arms he served? Were the men at Uxbridge so differently formed from those at Bovington? No one reading *The Mint* will believe that they were. The difference perhaps was that of outlook and lay in their hope of the future.

"The difference between Army and Air is that between earth and air: no less," he told John Buchan, after running into him in London on a quiet Sunday afternoon and opening his heart. [*Letters*, No. 265.] That perhaps was the quintessential answer. His imagination had been touched by the air and its exhilarating challenge, and no substitute, however worthy, would suffice.

"There is a faint chance, they say, of my return to the R.A.F. in May next," he had written Edward Garnett early in April. [*Letters*, No. 262.] "I've been deceived too often to dare hope now till the fulfilment—and then it will be too late to hope, probably: sad, because the hope is usually the only happy part of an achievement." By May it was apparent that his "supplication" had failed again, and because in spite of himself he had dared to hope for two weeks, the disappointment was crushing. He was correcting the text of Book VI of his history, *The Raid Upon the Bridges*, at the time, readying it for Manning Pike, the printer; and it seemed to him flat, dull "muck, irredeemable, irremediable." He had failed as a writer, he had failed in his effort to redeem himself by service to an ideal greater than himself, and in June the effervescent spring of his humor seemed to dry up.

> I'm no bloody good on earth [he wrote Edward Garnett], "so I'm going to quit: but in my usual comic fashion I'm going to finish the reprint and square up with Cape before I hop it! There is nothing like deliberation, order and regularity in these things. I shall bequeath you my notes on life in the R.A.F. They will disappoint you. [*Letters*, No. 266.]

There is something almost artificial in this veiled threat of suicide; a discordant chime in the harmony of thought, even despondent thought, which had gone before. Yet the dejection that prompted it was real enough. "It's a failure to kill them (our bodies) out of misery," he had written Lionel Curtis in 1923; "for if there isn't any good or evil but only activity, and no pain or joy, only sensation: then we can't kill ourselves while we yet feel." The despondency then had been real too, but despair had not yet sharpened into the final agony; feeling was still present, and failure was a sword thrust to be parried by some counterstroke, if only with bitter irony.

Perhaps he would have killed his body in 1925—in the legal phrase: while the balance of his mind was disturbed. His friends feared so, at any rate, and this veiled threat, real or unreal, was destined to persuade where reason had failed. It galvanized that fiery Fabian, the author of *St. Joan* and of *Man and Superman*, into action once more. He sent Edward Garnett's message of alarm on to the Prime Minister with a caustic suggestion that in view of the scandal which most certainly would accompany Lawrence's death by suicide—after the appearance of Mr. Lowell Thomas' book especially—some action ought perhaps to be taken to forestall it. John Buchan also appealed, the Prime Minister moved, and the Air Minister's reluctance was hurriedly overcome. In the midst of a course in revolver-shooting—an odd exercise for a crack marksman—Private Shaw was sent for by Lord Trenchard who told him of his acceptance. He ran down from London to Bovington in a state of quiet but heady joy, touching off 108 miles an hour on the mighty "Boanerges." It was his champagne cocktail downed to success and the achievement of his heart's desire.

> My sense is of something ineffable: like the ship *Argo* when Jason at last drew her up upon the beach [he told Edward Garnett]. Surely nothing but time and physical decay will uproot me now . . . I've got the only thing I care about—or cared about: for in getting it the care is over. [*Letters*, No. 269.]

The transfer was effected on July 16; in August he was processed at West Drayton, and Clouds Hill and his Bovington friends suddenly became poignant memories pulling at his heartstrings. Private Shaw in another metamorphosis became Aircraftman Shaw; his identity now for the rest of life. Uxbridge came briefly into his experience again, its rule as iron-clad as ever, and he was threatened there with summary punishment when he demurred against the unwieldy gear which regulations decreed, even in summer, for airmen posting from one station to another: a greatcoat worn buttoned to the neck, a full pack, iron rations, a water bottle, and a bayonet. But the livery was blue, not khaki, and he was content to endure its discomforts. He catalogued his experiences for his friend "Posh" in a terse, racy letter and afterward expanded them into a new Uxbridge chapter for *The Mint*.

The descent to the pit was completed and he came forth, but time alone would show what mutations his season in hell had wrought in him.

7

THE WAY OF AN EAGLE

In the sharp morning air of Waziristan on the northern horn of the Sulaiman Range in the Northwest Frontier Province of what was then British India, an aircraft from Peshawar circled the plateau to land. To the west lay Afghanistan; below, as diminutive as a child's toy set out on the floor with a brown, blue, and white carpet humped up around it, was Fort Miramshah girded by its chain of saw-toothed peaks. Incredibly small though the plateau, and still more the fort, seemed, it was there they were to land—the only landing ground for miles around of bleak mountainous terrain. The encircling peaks loomed larger, the plateau grew more creditable, and the aircraft touched down on the dusty runway.

Leading Aircraftman B. V. Jones, leaping out of the plane, saw a small fair-haired airman in shorts and open-necked shirt with paper and pencil in hand, calmly checking off bombs as they were loaded into the bomb racks of ten De Havilland 9A's lined up before the fort. And Leading Aircraftman Jones shivered at the sight, for it was bitter cold on the plateau and other airmen were swaddled heavily in "blues" and greatcoats. Was he not cold? asked Leading Aircraftman Jones. No; not by day—only the nights were cold. Aircraftman Shaw then told Jones he was in charge of stores at Miramshah and had given two of his own three blankets away to comrades who could not keep warm with their own three. Would L.A.C. Jones therefore bring him an extra blanket from Peshawar next time he flew in?

Here in this outpost of Empire, this remote, high-walled frontier fort, Aircraftman T. E. Shaw had come to rest. It was not paradise, for all its nearness to the stars which overhung it like pendants of fire. Its frosty days and bitter nights were not the joyous dedication he had dreamed of giving to the R.A.F., but it was a refuge, a place, he said, of magnificent silence and great peace. More important, he was out of the way, inaccessible to "lion-hunters," well-meaning admirers, and those stubborn romanticists who would never be able to see him in anything but white silk and gold head-ropes, charging about on a racing camel. And his very future in the R.A.F. hung upon preserving his anonymity, of being content to lie low for the time being at any rate, for the long-postponed abridgment of his war history had at last been published, and the legend—his own version of it this time—was irrevocably public property.

From the Royal Tank Corps Lawrence had gone, in 1925, to Cranwell to serve the officer-cadets at the R.A.F. College, and at Cranwell, the air force came into its rightful heritage and was all he had hoped for. In B Flight, his job was to pull the training machines —Bristol Fighters and De Havilland 9A's—in and out of the hangars, groom and refuel them, and "spin" the props for the eager cadets. It was, he said, "posh" work with an abundance of hot water for bathing afterward, and he reveled in it. It was true, the green flats of Lincolnshire could not compare with the wild beauty of the Dorset heath; and he missed his Bovington friends, Sergeant Knowles and his sons, Private Palmer, and Sergeant Banbury. But he became tranquil, almost happy, at Cranwell, and for the first time since the end of the war, his burden of strain and overwrought nerves fell from him. This tranquility is reflected in his letters of 1925–26 and in that appended section of *The Mint* which comes close to marring the grim wholeness of the Uxbridge chapters which precede it. It was not Dorset, yet as he lay in the grass at Lincolnshire on Sunday afternoons and watched it turn slowly from green to yellow in the dry, hot summer of 1926—a county of extremes and suddenness he said of Lincolnshire: of severe winters and severe summers—Lawrence was well content.

He had thought to remain at Cranwell for many years, but in 1926 the certainty that a book by Lowell Thomas about his Arabian exploits would appear nerved him to bring out his abridgment; and with two books pending on Colonel Lawrence, alias John Hume Ross, alias T. E. Shaw, the Air Ministry prudently set him down for the winter draft of overseas troop replacements. He was then thirty-eight, an age which generally dislikes change and dreads uprooting with all its entailed adjustments. Eric Kennington has described his condition on that last day of grace in England. He had come to sit—for the last time—as model for the head Kennington was sculpting and which, cast in bronze, now rests in the crypt of St. Paul's Cathedral.

> From that night he was to be confined to barracks, and perhaps tomorrow sailing. His eyes began to show turmoil. Their usual outward glide was repeatedly stopped and they would suddenly turn aside. I noticed a vibration of the head. Was he cold? I asked. I thought he shivered. "No, it is not cold." He shivered again worse, from head to foot. "No, I'm not cold. I'm always like this before a crisis."

Kennington drove him back to Uxbridge and was allowed to take his car through the gates. He pulled up, he says, against a double line of men standing easy, and Lawrence joined the rear rank without saying good-by. "He did not see me or the car. For a few minutes I watched him shifting, chin thrust forward, turning blindly left and right." So he was to write later in *T. E. Lawrence by His Friends.*

The troopship *Derbyshire* carried him to India. At Port Said, Colonel Newcombe, who was then in Egypt, tried to get permission from the authorities for Aircraftman Shaw to disembark for a few hours, and was informed that in no circumstances were troops permitted to leave ship while in port. Shortly afterward, even as he stood on the dock looking up at the troopship to see if he could recognize Lawrence among the garlands of faces wreathed about the decks, Aircraftman Shaw came stepping nimbly down the gangplank, obviously delighted at his friend's surprise. How he managed it Newcombe never found out.

It had been a brutal voyage out to Suez, as the few odd pages of a manuscript called "Leaves in the Wind" indicate. His description of pitching decks, seasick women, and stopped-up lavatories in the married quarters where he did a tour of guards' duty is in the style of *The Mint*, and it is thought he may originally have intended to add them to *The Mint*. The rest of the voyage to India was uneventful however, and by January 11, he was installed at the R.A.F. Depot, Drigh Road, Karachi. Leading Aircraftman B. V. Jones described how, after their arrival at Karachi, Aircraftman Shaw lay on the bed next to his own with eyes half closed, his kit bag turned toward the wall so that the name and number should be obscured. Then suddenly he took pencil and pad from kit bag and, propped against a bolster, began to write slowly and precisely, oblivious to the babble of voices around him.

At Karachi the work was not arduous, discipline was light, and hours of leisure were long—oppressively so at times.

> He was posted to the Engine Repair Section for employment in the workshops, but it was immediately apparent that he was above the run of ordinary handymen and he drifted naturally to the section office where he was a little gift from Providence to the paper-laden officer in charge.

So wrote W. M. M. Hurley, squadron leader of the Royal Air Force and Adjutant of the Drigh Road Depot.[1] The officer in charge, Flight Lieutenant Boswell, it appeared was a plain and capable engineer without any particular literary gifts, and it was with delight therefore that the adjutant began to receive erudite little minutes, impeccably phrased, whose hand he at once traced as being that of the new airman-clerk. The correspondence, he said, was often prolonged for its own sake rather than for its importance; curiosity was joined to delight and the adjutant wondered. Then he discovered who the new airman-clerk was. Thereafter, he tried within the limits of air force propriety, to put this odd, shy, but undeniably forceful man

---

[1] *T. E. Lawrence by His Friends.*

at ease and to make his life at Karachi as unburdened as possible.

The chiming of camel bells and the bright corruscations of stars by night set the mood of this dusty wasteland of the Sind Desert tufted with cactus and seven miles removed from the town proper, but Aircraftman Shaw rarely left the camp to see what lay beyond. Reveille sounded at six when the working airmen paraded in overalls; breakfast and the color-hoisting ceremony over, duty began at seven-thirty, and by an hour past noon the day's work was finished. They drilled only once every week or two except on patriotic festivals, or if lofty personages like the Viceroy were in the vicinity and must be suitably propitiated. Guards' duty with its rifle-juggling which he so loathed fell to his lot only once in two months. It was a camp with few comforts; hot water was nonexistent until his ingenuity devised a heating system with an oversized blowtorch and an empty five-gallon oil drum. There were no roads and therefore no motorcycle; nothing but time *ad nauseam*, and the camel bells sounding "like a water tap dripping, drop, drop, drop into a deep cistern" chimed out the sterile hours of his lonely exile ever so slowly. There was ample leisure to reflect, if he would, on the birthright he had forfeited for this mess of pottage. He might have enjoyed the dignity and honor of high office; better still, he might have been a private citizen, Thomas Edward Lawrence, T. E. Shaw, or what he would, living out his life span quietly with books, a printing press, music, beholden to none, claimed by none, in blissful nonentity. This humbler fulfillment would certainly have been his if the obstinate desire, too delicately formed to be confused with crude ambition, had not thrust him headlong into Arab affairs, and his conscience ever after lamented what he had become as a result of it. But this was remorse most futile: to metamorphose one's life it is necessary to alter or negate a hundred little events in all their ramifications from birth onward. Lawrence was living out the long hours at Karachi as an obscure airman because, a ruthless self-inquisitor, he had set by a well in northern Arabia on his thirtieth birthday and condemned himself to penal servitude; because mischance had revealed most horribly the bestiality which runs secretly like a putrescent stream beneath that most imperfect of animals and unregenerate of spirits, Man; because, as a young man at Carchemish he had discovered his inherent power to mold men; because as a boy he had dared to dream of making history as he paced out the length of a machicolation in Wales and France. The skein was drawn too tight to be unraveled. Life and conscience lodged him where he was, and he had written Lionel Curtis in May, 1923:

> Conscience in healthy men makes more tasteful the ordinary sweets of life: and in sick stomachs the desire of condiment becomes a craving, till what is hateful feels therefore wholesome, and what is repugnant to the moral sense becomes (to the mind) therefore pure and righteous and to be pursued. [*Letters*, No. 208.]

Dislodgment therefore was hopeless.

England was withdrawn; Clouds Hill, his Dorset sanctuary, was hired out to tenants at twelve shillings a week, and all for the sake of "a dishonest little sweep of a book" stripped of all that gave it, in his view, substance and virtue, a book which Jonathan Cape would publish under the eye- and mind-catching title of *Revolt in the Desert* and which innocent, uninformed people would confuse with Mrs. Hull's fulsome novel *The Sheik*, thinking the one a sequel to the other. In the dust of Karachi between composing ornate memoranda and reports for the delight of the adjutant, fighting an infestation of bugs with a blowtorch, and living through the tedium of the long, drowsy Indian afternoons, it came to him forcibly that the book was the root of the immediate if not all the evil—not the truncated *Revolt* but *The Seven Pillars of Wisdom* on which he had lavished his love and now expended his hate. A copy of the 330,000-word Oxford text resided in a tin box under his bed during his sojourn at Karachi; the the subscribers' copies meanwhile, all with their illustrations variously arranged to defeat bibliophiles, and their expensive Morocco bindings running through a gamut of color from moss green to tomato red, were in their owners' hands at last. A few incomplete copies he had presented to friends, advising the more impecunious to sell them for profit as quickly as possible. With eager readers offering up to twenty pounds for the loan of a copy through the "Personal" columns of

The Times, it was indeed a seller's market. Private Palmer was able to raise four hundred pounds for a set of proof sheets bought by Colonel Ralph H. Isham, and Robert Graves sold his copy for three hundred and thirty pounds. This ability of his friends to make money out of him was the only aspect of his reputation upon which he could look with any favor.

In March 1927, *Revolt in the Desert* was published simultaneously by Cape in England and by Doubleday, Doran in America. Reviews were mixed, moving from unmitigated enthusiasm through cautious praise to outright condemnation. In the eyes of his critics he was gnarled and twisted; he was effortless and artless; he was obscure; he was lucid; he was affected; he was simple; he parodied Doughty; he skillfully avoided Doughty's anachronisms. In short he was whatever the reader wanted him to be, and his epic aroused admiration or hostility according to whether the reader felt sympathy or antipathy to its style or to its author. This is true of the best and the worst of books, for that precious rapport between reader and author depends in part on what the reader brings to his reading out of the sum total of all his experience and the aggregate of his emotions. *Revolt in the Desert* was to pay off Lawrence's overdraft and contribute fourteen thousand pounds to the Royal Air Force Benevolent Fund before it was withdrawn by the author under an escape clause in his contract with the publishers. For the author himself it netted no profits, for he would accept none. So much for his earlier thought of buying with it his freedom from servitude. He did not now desire freedom; servitude was become a habit.

"Penance, promise, obstinacy, a vow, self-hypnotization —— you catalogue my motives. Isn't it possible that I like being in the R.A.F.?" he was to write Edward Garnett in September, 1927. [*Letters*, No. 324.] Later he was to tell George Bernard Shaw: "You see I'm all smash, inside: and I don't want to look prosperous or be prosperous, while I know that. And on the easy level of the other fellows in the R.A.F. I feel safe: and often forget that I've ever been different." [*Letters*, No. 363.] Barracks life was hard, but it was safe and it was safety he craved still, and the circumscribed but comforting freedom from making choices. "It's better to rust out than to go on grinding other men's lives through the mills of your own political ideas," he had written Lady Sandwich in 1924. "A leader who sees two sides cannot lead—cheaply at any rate." [*Letters*, No. 251.]

Yet he knew he was the loser, in color, in abstract talk, in all those little adjuncts of gracious living which, schooled hardily as he was, he recognized as intrinsically desirable, which he had forfeited and must now learn to shun. "I'm a funny card really," he wrote Robert Graves from Karachi. "I'd have been all right, apparently, if I'd never tried to do any of the things I have probably done well: or if I'd failed to do them." [2]

But he rejected violently the suggestion that he was different in any way from other men.

> Nobody could live, as I do, inside myself for year after year, and preserve any illusion of unlikeness," he told Robert Graves. "During the Revolt I had a motive, within me, for activity, and therefore became capable of imposing my will on others. The very accident that normally I am empty of motive, helped make the rare motive, when it finally came, overpowering. Now that is over, and the only sense in which I am now remarkable is that I am, compared with other men, an empty room. They like all manner of things and want all manner of things. I often think that there is nothing in the world I care of, or for: and nothing of which I could say "I know" or "I do not know." [3]

All this is close to what Richard Usborne in his unique and fascinating book, *Clubland Heroes*, has suggested are the John Buchan motifs: the courageous man who has grave doubts about his own worth and courage, and the man of action who feels he would rather obey orders than be himself in a position of authority. To those brought up on Buchan and Sapper and Dornford Yates, Lawrence seems a hero made to order whose real ardors and al fresco adventure with violent political repercussions rival the most chimerical derring-do of thriller fiction. But there is an important difference: Lawrence despised the clubs, the honors and trappings of success, the Rolls-

[2] *T. E. Lawrence to His Biographers.*

[3] *Ibid.*

Royces, and the beautiful girls that were the reward of Messrs. Hannay, Drummond, and Mansel. And he had no special reverence for white skin or undiluted British blood.

"This place, Karachi, is a colourless, unrelieved desert, without any of the beauty of clean emptiness, for it is all spotted over with odd military and air force magazines or barracks," he wrote Edward Garnett on the first day of March, 1927 [*Letters*, No. 299]—and who should be a greater connoisseur of deserts than himself? If, he said, his mind took on the likeness and tone of its surroundings, then he would indeed have achieved that nirvana he craved. Meanwhile, he commenced at Karachi the task of copying out his Uxbridge notes as a present for Edward Garnett, to convince him that the roots of writing were not there. The laconic dedication was to read: "You dreamed I came one night with this book, crying: 'Here's a masterpiece. Burn it!' Well, *as you please*." It was still another hope foiled and frustrated. The work proceeded slowly and tried his eyes and his patience both. Between it and his air force duties he sandwiched his mammoth correspondence (rationed eventually to fifteen letters a week) which grew defeatingly large as his exile progressed. And there were books sent out from England, and music: the Siegfried Funeral March, the Beethoven Choral Symphony, the Jupitor Symphony ("not perhaps the greatest bit of music, but assuredly one of the most beautiful"), some Bach, and for lighter relief a champagne sparkle of Boccherini, all of which was strange meat for most of the inmates of Room 2 in the engine repair section. As at Bovington and Cranwell, his intellect and his extraordinary store of correlated knowledge were at the disposal of any man who wanted to make use of them. He genially acted as a handy perambulating encyclopedia for the crossword-puzzle addicts, willing to answer to the question: "What's an iconoclast, Shaw?" to launch into a masterly and precise exposition of historical iconoclasm in Byzantium.

"Often while darning socks (*sic*) he would discourse brilliantly on subjects as remote as Woolley's finds at Ur, or the exploits of Charles of Sweden," said Leading Aircraftman Jones.[4] Indeed: "Shaw's advent among us did much to awaken an interest in literature; an airman who had been accustomed to read penny-dreadfuls could be seen struggling with such a book as Churchill's history of the Great War." Here the picture of Aircraftman Shaw darning socks vies for delicious incongruity with that of the airmen under his influence manfully struggling with Churchillian prose for the sake of self-improvement. But this loving willingness on Lawrence's part to share the fruits of his vast knowledge and superior education with those less fortunate, without any suggestion of condescension or parade, accounts in part for the sense of loyalty which ordinary airmen and soldiers felt toward him. It explains why he was defended by them at Farnborough and deferred to by them at Bovington. At Karachi none of the morbid curiosity-seekers outside the bounds of the camp was successful in eliciting information about his habits from the airmen they questioned. He was among them, he was one of them, and not for anything would they betray him or let others trespass on his privacy.

Even in the exile of the Sind Desert his puckish humor found an outlet and enlivened the monotony of the days for his fellows as well as for himself. An official ban on homemade lamps which, following his example, had blossomed over each airman's bed in Room 2, found him at inspection standing rigidly at attention in the presence of his commanding officer and his adjutant, while an irate sergeant major on hands and knees attempted to trace the suspected source of power. For Aircraftman Shaw's lamp burned like that of an impish jinni in brazen contravention of orders that no airman's lamp was to be connected to the main switchbox, and the worst seemed certain: a charge and punishment. But to the relief certainly of the adjutant, Aircraftman Shaw's lamp was found to be connected to a large battery underneath the bed. The truth, of course, was that the sergeant major had been properly tricked without so much as a flicker of a muscle to betray it: the battery was a dummy and concealed wires

---

[4] *T. E. Lawrence by His Friends.*

passed from the offending lamp into the forbidden switchbox. Again, the schoolboy prank which every serving airman could enjoy whether or not Churchillian history or Beethoven symphonies were beyond him.

While at Karachi, Aircraftman Shaw learned to use a typewriter and spent the Thursday holiday writing in the orderly room at the invitation of Squadron Leader Hurley. Officer and airman worked quietly together at their separate tasks, but occasionally there was conversation between them at which the adjutant was a most willing listener, though wise enough not to press his companion to speak of his own peculiar history unless he chose. Yet if the events themselves remained unspoken, the outward signs of identity were often unmistakable. On the pistol range at Karachi one day where a group of officers were firing their annual course and Aircraftman Shaw was acting as range orderly, he quietly picked up the pistol when only the adjutant, the armament N.C.O. and himself remained, and unerringly put six "bulls" on the target. Hurley was to go on to Transjordan, scene of his clerk's later wartime exploits, and to find it even more difficult to write of the events than to speak of them, but he saw him again with pleasure in Felixstowe in 1932 when T. E. Shaw, on his way to Bridlington, brought in one of the new target boats he was testing.

As exiles go, Karachi was fair enough, and less unpleasant than it might have been. Yet before the year was out his endurance was wearing thin.

> This place induces softening of the brain [he told Lionel Curtis in December]. I notice an incredible shabbiness and second-rating in all our effort here. We talk much of the climate . . . It has never been hot in the sense that Baghdad and Cairo are hot. There is no sunlight, no direct glare to hurt men's brains. [*Letters*, No. 331.]

The climate was like St. Raphael in summer, he said, and yet everyone complained of hardship, excused themselves from work, wore sun helmets, and indulged in laxity and liverish temper. "We could work exactly as men do in England, and be all the better for it, for we would then not have time to remember and cultivate all these fancies of fever and disease," he continued. He was ashamed of his race in Karachi; they deserved, he felt, to lose ground for their frivolous ineptitude.

There is an odd demureness about Lawrence's submission to this sterile existence at Karachi and later at Miramshah, and it is impossible not to suspect the coursing of strong feeling far below the surface which rarely comes out into the open. Was he really as impassive as he appeared? "This travel, or rather this residence in the East, is one perpetual temptation to me to cut loose again on some further project of my own," he told Dick Knowles in December; "and I do not want to take off. Taxying is quite fast enough for so wing-crippled a duck." [*Letters*, No. 329.] Beyond Karachi was the Arabian Sea; beyond that, the Arabian peninsula where he had wrought much, suffered much, and made history. He professed to have emptied his mind of it and its adventure, but as late as 1930 he was to write:

> I wake up now, often, in Arabia; the place has stayed with me much more than the men and the deeds. Whenever a landscape or colour in England gets into me deeply, more often than not it is because something of it recalls Arabia. It was a tremendous country, and I cared for it more than I admired my role as a man of action. [*Letters*, No. 416.]

In 1922 at Uxbridge he had been sick in mind and body; by 1927 he had recovered sufficiently to toy with the idea of accepting the post of airman-clerk to the air attaché at the British Embassy in Kabul, Afghanistan. At that time, with Soviet Russia pressing to extend her influence in Central Asia, this would have meant a re-entry, however humble, into politics and at least the elemental practices of intelligence work. It is interesting to speculate how far he would have allowed himself to be drawn into intrigue, had he gone to Kabul, and how far for that matter the Air Ministry would have permitted him to be drawn. As it was, insufficient skill in typing disqualified him from applying, or so he was to claim.

An odd piece of prophecy appears in a letter written in June, 1927, to (Sir) Edward Marsh, then Sir Winston Churchill's private secretary, recording this close call.

> The clash [with Russia] is bound to come, I think. In modern Europe it was first Spain which tried to dominate: then France had two tries . . . Then Germany has her go. It works from West to East, doesn't it? And England has been the main obstacle each time. Usually there has been about a hundred years between each effort: but the tempo of life has grown so much faster since the age of machines opened, that it's quite on the cards Russia may have her go in our time. [*Letters*, No. 311.]

The German "go" was not finished, quite, and the obstacle to Russia was destined to be not England but the United States which, by the time the clash came, had assumed in riches and power the historic role of Britain. Yet the essential elements of the prophecy remain. "Russia to these people (Asiatics) seems the new and growing idea: whereas there is more promise and capacity in our structure than she will contain in the next thousand years," he concluded—a reflection that should gladden the hearts of contemporary Western statesmen.

But Lawrence was still a celebrated figure in Eastern affairs despite his insistence on obscurity and poverty, and when in 1927 British Imperial Airways was seeking an alternative landing ground on the eastern coast of Arabia, pending confirmation of an agreement with Persia, he was called into private conference with the Political Resident of the Persian Gulf to give information on, and an assessment of, the character and influence of the Arab chiefs in the affected area. This is all the more interesting, since there is no direct evidence that he had ever gone into the eastern corner of Arabia, though he had most certainly encountered tribesmen who were indigenous to it. There is a piquancy in this summoning, as related by Squadron Leader Hurley, of an airman-clerk in overalls for a political conference with diplomats; it is not unlike the situation which George Bernard Shaw was later frivolously to exploit in the play, *Too True to Be Good* which is in part a sly lampooning of Lawrence. Private Meek in the play is "an insignificant-looking private soldier, dusty as to his clothes and a bit gritty as to his windbeaten face." He is meticulously correct in dress and manner, however, yet withal there is something inexplicably wrong about him.

"His figure is that of a boy of seventeen; but he seems to have borrowed a long head and a Wellingtonian nose and chin from somebody else for the express purpose of annoying the colonel . . ."

Meek's most effective goad is his knowledge—of everything and everyone in the country, and of every military expedient that can or ought to be taken in a crisis. He is intelligence officer, code clerk, interpreter, and dispatch runner combined, and his ready answers, while outwardly correct and modest, are exactly calculated to throw his superior into an exasperated rage. Allowing for the preposterousness of Shaw's situation, they are very much the sort of answers Lawrence was likely to give unsympathetic officers who tried to needle him about his superior knowledge and his inferior rank.

> And why, with all these accomplishments, are you not at least a corporal? asks Colonel Tallboys.
> *Meek:* Not educationally qualified, sir.
> *Tallboys:* Illiterate! Are you not ashamed?
> *Meek:* No, sir.
> *Tallboys:* Proud of it, eh?
> *Meek:* Can't help it, sir.
> *Tallboys:* Where did you pick up your knowledge of the country?
> *Meek:* I was mostly a sort of tramp before I enlisted, sir.

There is no record of how the Political Resident of the Persian Gulf reacted to having an airman called in for consultation; but he knew to whom he spoke, and aircraftman or no, the voice and the recommendations, whatever their character, were those of the man whom the world knew as Colonel T. E. Lawrence, whether he would acknowledge it himself or not.

In 1928 a glimmer of the old fire flashed out suddenly in a letter he sent to Lord Trenchard who had written him on the question of Wahabi raiding in Iraq. He would, he said, if he were in Iraq, walk unarmed and unannounced into the camp of the Arab chief behind the raiders, and in two days of guesting give him a wider perspective than the Puritan Brethren could. Such performances, he cautioned, required a manner to carry them off. He had done it before—could he again? He was not disposed to try. "I do wish hourly," he had written to Dick Knowles in February, "that our great Imperial heritage of the East would go the way of my private property." [*Letters*, No. 296.] (At another period he had written: "It will be a sorry day when our estate stops growing," but as to this, as Robert Graves was to point out, Lawrence the imperialist and Lawrence the nihilist are two aspects of the same mind: you take your choice between them.)

The better portion of his remaining years was ebbing away and there seemed no end in sight to the exile. In June, in view of the interest aroused by *Revolt in the Desert*, Robert Graves was approached by both Cape and Doubleday to produce a popular biography of Lawrence which was to be completed in July, and after securing Lawrence's reluctant consent, he set to work. The result was *Lawrence and the Arabs*, published in America as *Lawrence and the Arabian Adventure*, a great proportion of which seems to have been suggested, if not actually written, by the subject himself. Again, it is an instance of Lawrence's willingness to let his friends profit by his legend, though he would not himself profit by it. Critics may call this rank sophistry and insist that there is no discernible difference between a book written by Lawrence about himself and a book written by Graves, dictated largely by Lawrence, and published under Graves' name. But there is a difference; to Graves accrued the profits, while the book was ever after a source of embarrassment to its subject.

Though produced under great pressure which made for an inevitable unevenness in places, it was a sincere, workmanlike job in spite of the speed at which it was written. To Lawrence, it appears to have been something less than satisfying. In July he wrote to Lionel Curtis:

> Robert Graves is writing a life of me for Doran who ramped about England asking many of the worst people to do it. Said he wanted something true. Apparently *Revolt in the Desert* isn't finally convincing to all tastes. On the whole better Robert Graves than another. He is a decent fellow, does not know too much about me: will think out some psychologically plausible explanation of my spiritual divagations and will therefore help to lay at rest the uneasy ghost which seems to have stayed in England when I went abroad. [*Letters*, No. 317.]

But Graves was a poet; and with his unreasonable admiration of the poet's craft, Lawrence, in spite of his skepticism, seems secretly to have anticipated a rather more transcendental exposition than Graves, with the limiting handicaps of time and his friendship for Lawrence, could possibly have produced. And secretly Lawrence was disappointed. This and the knowledge of his own extensive participation in the book accounts for his disparagement of it. "Graves has worked too quickly," he told Edward Garnett. "His book is only milk and water. Which of us, he or I, is milk?" [*Letters*, No. 319.]

At the end of August, 1927, Lawrence took the long-considered step and changed his name by deed poll to Thomas Edward Shaw, but it was a legal form only: he was Colonel T. E. Lawrence of Arabia now to thousands who had read Lowell Thomas, *Revolt in the Desert* and *Lawrence and the Arabian Adventure;* he could no longer hope to preserve entirely his incognito as Aircraftman Shaw. (At Cranwell by way of experiment he had told everyone on arrival who he used to be and spent an uncomfortable month with every airman alerted and breathless in the canteen whenever he entered, waiting, he said, for a sign until their strained lungs expired under the effort.) Both he and those who shared his life in the R.A.F. at Karachi, at Miramshah, and elsewhere had to accept the fact of his dual existence and make the best of it. Later, at Miramshah, the fellows were to sit around on their beds reading bits of Graves' book out loud to tease him. "They regard my legend as a huge joke: if it wasn't *my* legend, I'd do ditto," he wrote H. S. Ede in the following summer. [*Letters*, No. 362.] But Graves' book would, he felt, serve a useful purpose: "to turn the public stomach, and make it spew when it thinks of me!" [*Letters*, No. 324.] So this premature "life" coming on the heels of *Revolt in the Desert* would satiate taste for his legend and bring about his release sooner. By 1930 he hoped to be able to return to England, being assured that the trustees of the *Revolt in the Desert* fund would soon withdraw his own book from publication.

Quando io udi questa profferta, degna
Di tanto grado, che mai non si estingue
Del libro.[5]

So he wrote jubilantly on hearing the news.

Suddenly, early in November, Hogarth died, and his passing left Lawrence, whose dynamic youth and potentialities he had recognized and guided, with a sense of loss such as he had not before endured. The emptiness of it yawned deep and wide, yet his attitude toward death was more serene than most.

> . . . to sorrow too much at others' deaths is to contradict ourselves. Which of us would give anything for a generous extension of our own [life]? The thought that the job will end somewhere, may end soon, is an abiding comfort to 99 percent of the people over thirty. [*Letters*, No. 324.]

So he had written Edward Garnett on the death of his brother by drowning. But Hogarth's death was a sorrow with ever-widening rings of desolation.

> The shadow of Hogarth's going is still always there whenever I turn around to think [he was to write Edward Garnett in December]. He was really to me the parent I could trust, without qualification, to understand what bothered me. And I had grown to lean on his knowledge of my motives not a little. [*Letters*, No. 347.]

At the same time he told Sir William Rothenstein, the artist: "The death of Hogarth hit me very hard. Oxford was to me a beautiful place, and a home, because he lived there, for me to see for a few minutes whenever I passed. I did not want to delay there: but I did like to see and hear him just for a moment." [*Letters*, No. 330.] And again in March of 1928 he wrote to Sir William Rothenstein: "Hogarth *shone* in Oxford, because he was humane, and knew the length and breadth of human nature, and understood always without judging." [*Letters*, No. 347.]

To Lionel Curtis he said that Hogarth was his background, the only person to whom he never had to explain the "why" of what he

[5] Dante, *Paradiso*, Canto XXIII, ll. 52–54.

was doing. It was no less than the truth: at every level of his existence—in the eager, sanguinary period of his Oxford youth; in the enchanted, golden days of Jerablus; in the dust and heat of Arabia; in his martyrdom at Uxbridge and Bovington—Hogarth had touched his life's infinite radiations and influenced him, always to the good ultimately. He was to tell Liddell Hart afterward that Hogarth was the best friend he ever had, but the bond between them transcended friendship wholly, being genuinely paternal on the one side and filial on the other. "He was like a parent who had never stopped growing," he told E. M. Forster. The death of his own father in 1919 did not affect Lawrence so strongly, perhaps because at the time he was harassingly preoccupied—though the telegram announcing it was discovered preserved among his papers after his own death. Hogarth's death came when he had more than ample time to reflect, and the wound of it cleft deeply into his spirit and left him grieving.

The days at Karachi passed in clerical jobbing, in the performance of guards' duty on holidays when no other airman wanted to be on "guards"; in reading, in being occupied by "the amazing convolutions" of his mind, with only a ripple raised by a fulsome and foolish article which appeared early in 1928 in *The Daily Express*, revealing to the public the whereabouts of the elusive Colonel T. E. Lawrence—the "boyish-looking blue-eyed dreamer" who at Karachi went off to the edge of the desert with a pocketful of cigarettes to chat with the villagers and join in their profound meditations. "Only unluckily," commented T. E. Shaw in the margin of the paper sent on to him, "I have never smoked!" As for the villagers of all countries, East or West, their thoughts were centered on those parts of their anatomies which lay between the navel and the knee: food and sex; and, he said, he did not meditate, not even profoundly, about either.

Halfway through 1928 Lawrence's sojourn at Karachi came abruptly to an end. On May 26 he was posted to No. 20 Squadron at Peshawar and from there, at his own request, to the isolated frontier station of Miramshah.

> Moving is no fun [he wrote Colonel R. V. Buxton, his banker]. For nearly a month the new camp gapes at me, expecting me to belie my ordinary shape by doing something extraordinary: and I grow red all over, and my spine trickles damply. I know it is silly: but other people's eye-sight tickles ones skin nearly as perceptibly as their fingers or their breath would tickle. And scrutiny at such defencelessly close quarters as our barrack-life imposes, hurts a good deal. [*Letters*, No. 358.]

He had exchanged one "dust hole" for another, he told David Garnett, but the new dust hole was an improvement both of scene and atmosphere. The Northwest Frontier was at least definite: it was cold. Karachi had blown neither cold nor hot; and Waziristan was a region of blood and tension where twenty-five airmen lived alerted for trouble in their mud fort. The burden of Empire here was the hazard of keeping order in a lawless tribal area between India and Afghanistan where high ambush rocks overshadowed the roads, and homemade firearms in the hands of hostile tribesmen took a swift toll of any but the strongest caravans. The stony ridge of the line established optimistically in 1893 by Lord Durand's mission was a no-man's-land, full of hidden perils and sudden deaths over which Pathans and Afghans made armed sorties in search of foemen or booty or both. The justice which the air force meted out in this region of strong-armed law was summary and tough: punitive bombing of offending villages after due warning for the women, children, cattle, and other valuables—including roof timbers—to be removed.

There is nothing of this in Lawrence's letters from Miramshah; yet the game of strike and run played out in the hills by strong sheepskin-coated and fiercely handsome men was the sort of game he would once have relished. In this turbulent, barren, yet beautiful country of northern India,[6] where the mountains lay like a necklace of agate under a pale and frosty sky, he showed not the slightest interest, nor in the peoples who inhabited it. A hundred odd miles to the north, in Peshawar, the rendezvous of Asiatic caravans, Uzbeks, Tejeks,

---

[6] In the geographical sense, for of course this region is now politically a province of Pakistan.

Kabulis, Chilzais, Pavindahs, Jews, and Hindus—all the cross strains and high blood of Central Asia—met and mingled to trade in Bokhara silks, Turkestan carpets, lambskins, and spices; to trade and to gossip, and to cast wagers on the fighting quail hung above the market stalls in their wooden cages. It tempted him not at all. That his motives would have been suspect and his incognito jeopardized had he shown any interest in the local tribes goes without saying. And yet the fact remains: so far as can be known, Lawrence had no interest in them. In all the vast, rich, and teeming regions of the Asiatic East, only the Arabian peninsula and its Fertile Crescent seems to have called forth in him any response. Is this evidence of a limited faculty, a thwarted vision? Or is it certain if oblique confirmation that he was a man called up by history, or whatever obscure spring lies coiled under the sequence of eventualities called history, to play a solitary role which, having been played, left him spent and empty? This is one of a number of speculative theories that have been offered to explain Lawrence's failure to follow the Arabian venture with other ventures, as well as his lack of interest in all but a few selective spots on earth. But as a theory it should not be pressed too far.

Miramshah brought about an improvement in his health. At Karachi he had been bothered several times with a recurrence of his old complaints, dysentery and malaria.

> Do not take my illnesses seriously [he had written E. M. Forster who was concerned about him]. They are only indispositions: and may be partly due to my refusal to see that I'm too old to lead a boy's life much longer. They do not allow, in the Services, for grownups —— the whole treatment and regimen is designed for the immature: and physically I'm in decay, however half-baked my mind may be. [*Letters*, No. 352.]

Perhaps the mountain air was more salutary; the fort was certainly more picturesque in its mountain basin, the nightly stars plucked and scattered across celestial ways: the shimmering cluster of the Pleiades sunk in a pool of brilliant indigo; Cassiopeia's chair aslant on the cosmic crossroads. It was romantic, but it was not peaceful—not at all times. Christmas of 1928 saw the commencement of what was the first major airlift in aviation history, when beginning with the women and children from the British Legation, the Europeans of Kabul were flown out to Peshawar. A rebellion in November of the Shinwari tribe against the reforms instituted by the Amir Amanullah touched off a confused and chaotic civil war in Afghanistan which, before it ended, was to see four amirs on the throne, a welter of bloodshed and license, a stir in all the Chancelleries of Europe and the Middle East, and the recall of Aircraftman Shaw from India. Not only was Fort Miramshah the sole landing field between Kabul and Peshawar in miles of wild and mountainous country, but it had a stern duty to keep the peace on the frontier and to prevent the hot-blooded border tribes from participating in the Afghan fighting. By the end of February nearly six hundred persons had been flown out of Kabul in Royal Air Force planes which in all made eighty-six flights and covered over twenty-eight thousand miles. This difficult flying operation carried out under the hazard of severe winter weather might have gladdened Aircraftman Shaw's heart by its vindication of his belief in the role of air power, but by the time it was completed, the events which made it necessary had already overtaken him.

Just before leaving Karachi his "fair" copy of *The Mint* written in India ink and bound in air force blue Morocco had been sent off to Edward Garnett. The original was burned with paraffin in the Sind Desert to insure that no two versions survived. It was, he said, a new note, a note for Edward Garnett's private eye; a swollen letter, but he thought it was well written as prose went. Its subject: "our dull clothed selves; our humdrum, slightly oppressed lives; our tight uniforms: the constriction, the limits, the artificial conduct, of our bodies and minds and spirits, in the great machine which the R.A.F. is becoming." [*Letters*, No. 353.] He had, he said, to hold himself down on each page with both hands. But Garnett was not to let his enthusiasm for new notes in writing carry him away.

> Regard it [he said], as a notebook of mine, given to you because you like my *Seven Pillars*, and because I had no further room or reason for it. I won't tell you it's rubbish: for I wouldn't have given you what I believe to be rubbish, but it's pretty second-rate, like me and my works: it's the

> end of my attempts to write, anyhow: but please believe that this inner conviction of the thing's not being good enough only increases the momentary pleasure which I obtain from having you praise it. I'd so like something of my creating to be very good: and I bask for the moment in the illusion of your praise.

It was the old unredeemed longing: to create and to create well, and the old bedeviling certainty that fit creation was beyond him, a tortured and torturing perplexity impossible of resolution: could a man burn with all the passion of heart and mind to create, and yet be unable to rise above mediocrity in his creation? But he was fonder of this younger child than he was of the elder. It was clearer formed, more coherent, in spite of its brevity as notes for a book and not, he insisted, the book itself, and there was less of himself in it—though Edward Garnett felt there was more. Its terseness seemed to him superior to the pretentious ornamentation, the contrapuntal fullness, the artfully contrived cadences of *The Seven Pillars of Wisdom.* Yet there was a difference in tempo as well as style, in texture as well as in quality.

> They worked us too hard at Uxbridge (where I was weary after 1½ years with Winston, with the 3rd version of *The S.P.* to write meanwhile) for me to have proper leisure to see it with untroubled eyes [he told Edward Garnett]; "the rewriting here, done carefully and arduously over six months, every day, and all my spare hours from 2 P.M. till bedtime at 10 o'clock: even that was not untroubled. So do not imagine that you have in *The Mint* my full strength, as it was lavished on *The S.P.* You have me six or seven years older: that is it. [*Letters*, No. 359.]

Earlier he had warned Garnett:

> You understand, they are not emotions remembered in tranquility: but the actual fighting stuff. Photographic, not artistic . . . It's better than *The Seven Pillars*, in its class, as like as butter and cheese: that is, not like at all: but equally rotten. *The S.P.* showed that I could not ratiocinate: this that I can't observe. [*Letters*, No. 319.]

In fact, *The Mint's* eighty thousand words is an assemblage of moods, of conditions, and of men, ascerbent and unforgettable, but it is what he said it would be: "an iron, rectangular abhorrent book"; and being less oblique than *The Seven Pillars*, it reveals far more of himself than perhaps he realized, more, certainly, than he permitted to be revealed in *The Seven Pillars*.

"I want the existence of these notes kept dark; otherwise asses will want to print them," he had told E. M. Forster whom he invited to read them in return for the privilege of having been permitted to read some of Forster's unpublished "imperfections." [*Letters*, No. 352.] And his terms to publishers, Jonathan Cape, or any others interested—one million pounds in advance of a ninety per cent royalty—were calculated to place it beyond the reach economically of any publisher. Yet there were occasions when he seemed not averse to its appearing in his lifetime, had the Air Ministry sanctioned it, and except for the betrayal it would have seemed to all who served with him at Uxbridge. "To be photographed, they put on what they call 'best clothes,' and brush their hair, and wash. To be portrayed, as in my book, unadorned would break their hearts," he told E. M. Forster. [*Letters*, No. 365.] *The Mint* was photographically exact and penetratingly clear; many of its personalities were called by their own names, and to turn informer of their private agonies and unbuttoned moments would have been rank disloyalty. So *The Mint* was to remain unpublished until 1950. (Edward Garnett meanwhile aroused his misgivings by having a number of typescripts made.) By that time he would be sixty-two or dead, and personalities would have ceased to matter. ("Stiffy," fat drill master of the old Guards' school and one of the saltiest characters in *The Mint's* gallery, already by 1928 was retired and running a hotel in Essex.) And, he remarked: "What a quaint performance *The Mint* will seem to a white-beard of sixty-two!"

Neither Edward Garnett nor George Bernard Shaw were content with this; both urged on him his duty to publish another book, and Shaw was particularly persistent in his urgings. Lawrence could have twenty copies run off and deposited in special libraries like that of the War Office; or he could revise for general publication. He should not let reticence or self-consciousness stand in his way, and certainly not his desire to conceal himself. Lawrence's comment: "that from the old fox (pardon the metaphor) who throws a red herring in the pack's face at ever twist of the chase!" [*Letters*, No. 357.] And he continued: "Your advice would sink my ship: would sink any ship which had less than your speed and power of manoeuvre, and hitting power." General publication would in any case have been impossible unless he had been prepared to edit out of it all the pain and suffering and to make of it something other than what he had intended in order to overcome the Air Ministry's reluctance. Without that editing, the embarrassment to the organization which sheltered him, and would, he hoped, continue to shelter him until 1935, would be the worst kind of ingratitude and would probably result in a second dismissal. It was a course he felt he could not afford to follow. ". . . the R.A.F. is my home, of which I am very fond. I am like Charles II, too old to go wandering again." [*Letters*, No. 357.] So he wrote Shaw from Karachi just before his transfer to Peshawar. *The Mint* was too frail a product to jeopardize his future; it could give him no comfort, no warrant that he was leading a useful life. The R.A.F. might still do that for him.

But Lawrence recognized clearly the grim futility of this life without adventure, without aim.

> . . . when I travel [he told Lionel Curtis], I carry the R.A.F. with me. I move from one service bed to another service bed, from one standard barrack to another standard barrack: from one ration meal to another ration meal. Uniformity is my bedfellow. Your life is chaos. Chaos breeds life: whereas by habit and regularity comes death, quickly. [*Letters*, No. 317.]

As for another book, he was about to undertake at a high fee an anonymous translation of *The Odyssey* of Homer for the American typographist, Bruce Rogers, following the example of his old exemplar, William Morris, who had put the poem into English verse in 1887. As in other decisions, this was not his final word on *The Mint*. There is adequate proof that six years later he was contemplating printing it himself on a hand press with a drawing of himself in uniform by Augustus John as frontispiece.

At Miramshah a small complement of thirty-one officers and men of the Royal Air Force and seven hundred India Scouts lived in the fort behind barbed-wire entanglements, the two groups occupying separate quarters and living out the fiction of East–West incompatibility by seldom if ever meeting. By day airmen were not permitted to venture beyond the barbed-wire barrier, and at night were confined still closer within the walls of the fort. Ringed, crowned, and doubly defended by its bare mountains and barbed wire, as inaccessible within its machine-gun and searchlight screen as a Tibetan monastery, Fort Miramshah seemed poised on the edge of infinity, wondrously still, untouched, and unspotted by the world. Its high walls, sparse trees, and cloistered walks gave to it the secluded air of a spiritual rather than a military outpost.

"It's the station of a dream," he wrote H. S. Ede soon after his arrival: "as though one had fallen right over the world, and had lost one's memory of its troubles. And the quietness is so intense that I rub my ears, wondering if I am going deaf." [*Letters*, No. 362.] That silence was interrupted only for five minutes each night when the searchlights went into play, crisscrossing the sky and the empty plain beyond the fort with their brilliant trajectories, and the beams startled a chorus of jackals into ecstatic baying. It was the one persuasive sign of breathing, striving, propagating life in a world given up wholly to contemplation.

As the only airman on the station who could use a typewriter, Aircraftman Shaw's duty was to type out all the Daily Routine Orders and the correspondence. "No, I am not adjutant to this camp. Just typist and i/c files, and duty rolls. I do what I am told to do and re-write the drafts given to me, meekly," he told George Bernard Shaw. [*Letters*, No. 363.] He also acted as postman, pay clerk, and, he said, "bottle-washer in ordinary"—the shade of Private Meek again! But he left his own peculiar mark on air force life at Miramshah: all airmen were persuaded by him to ignore the rules for wearing topees, and an old officer-friend visiting the fort telephoned through to him to inquire with ironic humility: "Please, Shaw, may I wear my topee?"[7] Like his erudite memoranda at Karachi, these humble little skills of clerking seemed hardly sufficient justification

[7] *T. E. Lawrence by His Friends*. Flight Lieutenant R. G. Sims.

for his continuing exile. And cut off from the society of friends who could occasionally have consoled him, loneliness and apartness haunted him still unremittingly.

> I've lived now five years in barracks [he told Dick Knowles, himself an airman], and can honestly confess that I have never been really one with my fellows. I have sometimes, for a moment, imagined myself into a unity with them: and before I could seize it and settle down into it, like a rabbit into a burrow, I'd be whisked off to another existence, incontinent. This may be my solitary misfortune (Graves suggests that I'm a unicorn) or it may be the common fate of man . . . Do you ever feel like a unicorn strayed amongst sheep? I fancy so from your letter. If so, you must prepare yourself for not ever becoming quite a part of the earth—or quite unconsciously happy. [*Letters*, No. 329.]

So much scope for meditation and so dangerously little active stimulus, both intellectual and physical, exposed him to a Daruma-like dissolution. A few more years of this and his lower members would atrophy: he would be all introspective head and nothing else.[8] It was partly to counteract this dissolution that he undertook to translate *The Odyssey*, an exercise for the brain lest it forget the mechanics of ordinary intellectual effort, as his typing was an exercise of coordination of brain and hands. What he could not do at Miramshah was refresh the spirit lest with all this dryness it fall into the unforgivable sin, despair.

On August 16 his birthday came around again. "I am forty now, and six years may be enough to see me out," he wrote prophetically to his architect-friend, Sir Herbert Baker.[9] This bleak, empty, and in many ways hard life, so lacking in grace and refreshment, was scarcely a fitting or an auspicious entry into middle age. Forty is a notoriously critical age, the age at which men who have led a full, active, and adventurous life often succumb to marriage. It is in any

[8] Daruma: a Buddhist monk who, according to legend, sat in contemplation until his body atrophied leaving only his head alive.

[9] *T. E. Lawrence by His Friends.*

case the threshold, at least, of change: it marks an orientation toward philosophic reflection as opposed to action, a yielding to the desire for quiet living, of garnering the fruits of success. "*Wer jetzt kein Haus hat, baut sich keines mehr. Wer jetzt allein ist, wird es lange bleiben*" says Rilke. The heroes of John Buchan's thrillers, confirmed bachelors all and quite unfamiliar with the ways of women—having always shied off them with minds and hands full of other things—usually, at forty, reconciled themselves to the inevitable and took wives. But Lawrence, having rejected success, also rejected marriage with equal vehemence. To E. M. Forster who appears about this time to have suggested that he might now care to explore the possibility of women, he replied: "There are no women free in Waziristan to explore: so that point does not yet arise." [*Letters*, No. 364.] In his heart he must have doubted if it would ever arise. That many of his friends, some of them certainly as odd in their own way as he in his, had married, did not alter his opinion that marriage was "prostitution *à la carte*." He obstinately refused in his mind to make the distinction between carnal love sanctified of the spirit and the "jobbing" of a woman's body to satisfy lust, and certainly his prolonged life in barracks did nothing to militate against this view.

In the apartness and the consanguinity of male and female is mirrored not only the mystery of creation but the more profound mystery of love. Their coming together is a power and a promise of fulfillment to come which is foreshadowed by it and in which it is imperfectly conceived. In this it is a means, not the end of life. But to Lawrence the creative urge, whether sexual or aesthetic, was not an attribute of the divine, though he might make an exception in the case of poetry or sculpture. Perfect creation, if it existed, might indeed hope to touch the outer fringes of divinity, but the physical act of love seemed to him too crude, too grotesque, to be anything but a degradation, an animal posturing, the sole end of which was to bring into being a blind and bloody thing endowed with a life it had not sought. It was to this that his blighting in adolescence and the shocking of his senses in Arabia had brought him.

Yet he was neither a boor nor a misanthrope where women were concerned, and his treatment of them was always correct, if uninspiring. His hatred for sex should not be misconstrued, as it often has been, into a hatred of women. Certainly, he was able to protect himself from feminine ebullience and curiosity by an enigmatic reserve or by a flippancy calculated to repel the most enthusiastic efforts; while for what he called the "whetstone woman," who came to sharpen her opinions on him, he reserved an even stronger distaste and a more drastic treatment. Yet he could be at his ease with women if they proved themselves sensible about him or mundane enough not to be bothered by his legend; and significantly, it was to a woman, Mrs. Shaw, that he revealed the ghastly culmination of his Der'a capture. Only a woman perhaps could bear to hear it, in compassion, without recoiling.

"I try and talk to a woman as I would talk to another man, or to myself: and if she does not return the compliment, I leave her," he told Robert Graves.[10] But even women like Gertrude Bell—"a woman of enormous heart and whirling head"—who did return the compliment, could not quite achieve that freedom of association with him which his male friends enjoyed. It is impossible, for instance, to think of his writing to any woman in the way he wrote to Lionel Curtis or to Edward Garnett. He was to claim later to Ernest Thurtle that there was no difference that he could feel between a woman and a man; but the physical functions of Woman affect her emotions and make her different, in feeling if not in intellect, from Man; and unconsciously that difference regulated Lawrence's attitude toward women. Even consciously he was not always steadfast in his claim of parity.

"These women wound one another more cruelly than they can wound us or we each other," he wrote Robert Graves in 1927.[11] And again on another occasion he told Graves that with women dishonesty was innate, a sort of congenital sickness which by nature they could not avoid or help. In later life he was to say that he liked American

---

[10] *T. E. Lawrence to His Biographers.*

[11] *Ibid.*

women, which is in itself a revealing admission. American women are intelligent, eminently capable and attractive, but not feminine in the way that French and even English women are feminine. The inference is clear enough. That Lawrence did find the few American women he met congenial is certainly true, but they were too few to constitute a decisive factor in his judgment, and whatever their nationality, he was not an easy man for women to meet and know.

"It is fun," he says of Homer in his introduction to *The Odyssey*, "to compare his infuriating male condescension towards inglorious woman with his tender charity of head and heart for serving men." It was fun—for a man of kindred instincts who did not however condescend to inglorious woman, but simply ignored her. And that most tender charity he felt for the fellows of Hut 2 at Uxbridge and B Flight at Cranwell, what a prize it would have been if any woman could have won it for herself! Vyvyan Richards in his *Portrait of T. E. Lawrence* has said: ". . . it is a smiling thought to fancy what a lover he himself would have made with a vocabulary like Shakespeare's and a gift of phrase hardly less." It is indeed, but neither the tender charity nor the Shakespearean vocabulary and gift of phrase were ordained for a lover's trappings. As an example of the tenderness he could exhibit, to women among other creatures, Celandine Kennington, the wife of the artist, has told of his visiting her soon after a distressing miscarriage, and of his being able clearly to represent to her her own feelings: the sense of failure and despair from her own feminine point of view; of his being able to give back to her a confidence she had lost and recreate a warmth of feeling which had become numbed. But this was the wife of a friend, and while it is easy to feel that he might have been equally tender and sustaining as a husband, the difficulty lies in imagining him in the role of husband.

"I haven't got a heart: only the former site of one, with a monument there to say that it has been removed and the area it occupied turned into a public garden, in pursuance of the slum-clearance scheme," he told Lady Astor in 1930. [*Letters*, No. 403.] And again in 1933 he was to write her a quasi-humorous, quasi-serious plaint:

> Probably it would be wholesome for me to lose my heart—if that monstrous piece of machinery is capable of losing itself, for till now it has never cared for anyone, though much for places and things. Indeed I doubt these words of "hearts." People seem to my judgment to lose their heads rather than their hearts. Over the Christmas season two men and four women have sent me fervent messages of love. Love carnal, not love rarefied, you know: and I am uncomfortable towards six more of the people I meet, therefore. [*Letters*, No. 508.]

This, of course, was an unhappy anomaly—the wages of his inflated reputation. Yet the truth is it was impossible for him to give himself to another or to claim another for himself: the first because of his unshakable conviction of his own awkwardness, both of body and mind, the second because of his shrinking from the sin of violating another's freedom when his own stood so precious in his sight. In love, freedom is always violated, is surrendered, but willingly and joyously in order to experience the larger freedom that comes with completion in and through the personality of the beloved. Lawrence could be a warm and most considerate friend: he could experience a deep compassion for his fellows, and often a very tender affection for another being, but he could not love—at least, not after his first youth was spent. Women—and men—would continue to butt their heads against this wall of numbness; it could not be broken down. There were times when he would have been glad to have it broken down. "All visitors there intrude, as yet, I think," he wrote of the poet Siegfried Sassoon and his wife. "He and she are like children alone in the world." [*Letters*, No. 530.] The beneficence to himself of such a state was clear: his instinct perceived it, if his mind rejected it; and a cadence of unuttered longing breathes through his words. Though there were moments when he desired the beneficence of the married state, he would not, could not, bring himself to beget on a woman's body children who should perpetuate all his own (and his parents') cross-grains and morbidities. To do so would be as unforgivable a sin as it had been for his parents to produce him and his brothers out of their illicit union. To Arnold, upon the announcement of his marriage, he wrote half-teasing, half-reproving: "If there is no insanity in the family there will soon be!"

There have been some few mischievous or diseased persons who laid claim quite boldly to carnal relations with the man to whom carnal love bore such an insuperable stigma. It is easier to forgive these victims of their own illusions than it is to forgive those who have accepted their claims as genuine, on hearsay, upon the conviction that no man can ever succeed in holding himself aloof from the febrile demands of the flesh. And the ranks, as Lawrence himself remarked, are ever suspect as the breeding ground of sodomy. It is on this level of suspicion and scandalous incredulity, as well as on the evidence of his compassion in *The Seven Pillars* for the boy-lovers, Farraj and Daud, that the myth of overt homosexuality has been raised.

Much has been said and written about his apparent sympathy to the male relationship as exemplified by those passages in the first chapter of *The Seven Pillars* where he writes of Arab youths slaking one another's needs in their own clean bodies, and of friends quivering together in the sand. But these passages should be read whole and in context, not lifted from the body of the text. Moreover, they are poetic figures, Greek in sympathy, only in part sincere and partly a striving for elaborate effect. The introductory chapter which precedes this paean of continence and cold convenience speaks of the Devon Territorials one hundred strong, "clean, delightful, full of the power of happiness and of making women and children glad." A man makes glad a woman by taking her to himself and giving her children, and if Lawrence frequently inveighs against this normal act, it can surely be recognized properly as the corollary of his violent execration of his own birth.

Lawrence's own word that he never experienced the carnal intimacies with another person [12] has been discounted and his continence set down as fraud by those who hold the myth of overt homosexuality. This is a sad commentary, not only on the woolly-mindedness of psychology in its popular diluted form, but on the moral temper of the age which, though less licentious by far than earlier ages, is strangely inhibited to either the worth or the validity of chastity. That

[12] The Der'a experience would technically disqualify this claim, but Der'a was scarcely a voluntary act.

Lawrence was more at his ease with men than with women is certain; that he found in his friendships, as his brother, A. W. Lawrence has said, a satisfaction akin to that of sexual love is also true, but it was an emotional not a physical compensation he sought, and that is as far as it went. Had he not hated sex so violently and deplored it as a betrayal of the mind, it might have been otherwise; he might then conceivably have followed, in his despair, the line of least resistance. But this is to enter the realm of speculation which is unprofitable.

"Very 'repressed-sexy,' I feel. Celibacy has its dangers!" he wrote of Gerard Manley Hopkins in 1932 [*Letters*, No. 474.], and, with the queried "homo" in a footnote, cast the same doubts on the Jesuit that were to be cast upon himself: suspicion *à la mode*. But priest and airman were victims of their own implacable self-doubt, their own secret burden of guilt and shame, and both brought their bodies and their desires into subjection by the same means: fasting and denial—that abstinence which "sows sand all over the ruddy limbs and flaming hair" but which when espoused in love and not in bitterness sows its own harvest of joy and beauty even as desire gratified. Lawrence had quoted the Blake lines once in 1908 to reassure his anxious mother that he was looking after himself properly. And if the paradox between austerity and hedonism in his nature made him curiously susceptible to Blake's desire gratified, with him it meant always desire of mind: the freedom of spirit which transcends any seductiveness of flesh.

Snow and ice encrusted the mountains of Waziristan like a dazzling armor, four thousand feet thick, Lawrence told E. M. Forster. The Amir Amanullah having beaten off the forces of the brigand Bacha-i-Saquao just before Christmas, succumbed to their threat in mid-January and fled his capital. The abdicated throne passed immediately to his brother, Inayatullah Khan, who kept it for three days only and then gave way to the usurper Bacha-i-Saquao. But Amanullah was now hotly persuaded by his supporters to rescind his rash abdication, and so there were two amirs and eventually the added complication of a third and later a fourth claimant to the throne. The situation was worse than it had been in December, 1928, at the beginning of the airlift, and anarchy was now assured. These disorderly events had two not wholly unrelated results: a flurry of outraged and unfounded charges emanating from Germany and Soviet Russia that Britain was skillfully fomenting strife in Afghanistan for her own ends (Russian airmen had in fact helped Amanullah to resist the first of Bacha-i-Saquao's attacks in January), and the sudden termination of Aircraftman Shaw's Indian exile. They gave certain proof that no R.A.F. station was too remote for the long arm of sensational journalism, and that the brick and mud fort of Miramshah only ten miles removed from Afghanistan was as vulnerable as Farnborough, given the right provocation.

As early as July, 1927, an imaginative American journalist reported seeing Colonel Lawrence in Peshawar from which he had gone, disguised as an Arab sheik, into Persia to treat secretly with Riza Khan, and from Persia into Arabia again to settle with Ibn Saud who, the report said, was becoming troublesome. This lurid article was happily suppressed by the newspaper which received it, but early in January *The Daily Herald* was publishing reports of an order by the government of Afghanistan for the arrest of Colonel Lawrence for his part in assisting the rebels. His movements, always mysterious, were said to have ended in a secret mission to Afghanistan, though he was also reported as being in Amritsar posing as a Moslem saint. This latter fable had unfortunate repercussions; in Lahore one Syed Pir Karem Shah, a hapless and pathetic scapegoat, was mobbed and nearly torn limb from limb by a hysterical crowd under the delusion that he was the sinister, meddling Colonel Lawrence in disguise. The fantastic absurdity of these stories is apparent now; it was not so apparent in 1929 when, to uninformed people who knew nothing of Lawrence's life in the air force, it seemed quite reasonable to suspect his complicity in any Oriental embroglio.[13]

All this was too much for the government of India, which had been

[13] In 1930 Russian political prisoners were to "confess" to treasonable contact with Lawrence as principal British agent in London in 1927. That he had been in India at that time and accused by the same sources of espionage activities in Afghanistan seemed not at all irrelevant.

hostile to Lawrence since the old days of 1916 in Mesopotamia when he had consistently, and not without some obvious pleasure, rubbed its officials the wrong way. With haste and alarm that government now requested his immediate withdrawal from India by the Air Ministry, and he was whisked unceremoniously out of Waziristan by plane to Lahore—scene of the riot—and on to Karachi. On January 12 he was put aboard the P & O liner SS *Rajputana* at Bombay, in a state of high indignation at having had to leave behind most of his personal things. Yet it was less the loss of his possessions—in particular his cherished gramophone sent him by George Bernard Shaw, and the records—that irked him than the clumsy manner in which the affair had been handled. This harried and hasty dismissal from India seemed an imposition; it was in fact providential. He was really done with the East; England his last hope of refuge, the real "Well at the World's End," was within reach at last.

The exile ended a year before his expectation, but not a moment too soon. He felt tired and jaded, not from work but from the lack of it. His eyes had begun to trouble him even in Karachi when he was copying out his Uxbridge notes for Edward Garnett, and he had complained occasionally of deafness. He felt he had slipped into middle age and would just as suddenly fall into the decrepitude of age. White hairs already grew rampant among the gold, and the less wide a life span he could expect, he told Edward Garnett in 1927, the more he grudged having to spend it out of England. "Return to England might cheer me up to a few years of motor-cycle madness. Who knows?" he said. [*Letters*, No. 315.]

On the *Rajputana* he was given a second-class cabin to himself and spent the days of the voyage working on his Greek translation. In a borrowed civilian suit he was able to escape some attention on board, but the quayside at Port Said was picketed to prevent his going ashore, and he was warned by special signal that on arrival in England, he would be besieged by the press who would try to interview and photograph him—the first especially undesirable and to be avoided at all costs.

The voyage itself was uneventful: the Mediterranean, his Sea of

Destiny, and then the Channel—gray, damp, and penetratingly cold. The *Rajputana* anchored off Plymouth where a few passengers were disembarked by tender before the liner went on to Tilbury—long enough for Aircraftman Shaw to be met by his future commanding officer wearing mufti and smuggled away in an Admiralty pinnace before the press—which had got wind of the ruse and assembled some of its members at Plymouth—realized what had happened. Aircraftman Shaw himself was back in uniform, and one lucky press shot caught him in R.A.F. pantaloons, puttees, and greatcoat, hands thrust deep into pockets, stepping across the deck of the pinnace away from the *Rajputana*, inwardly amused now at all the fuss. From Plymouth to London the two men were tailed by irate and frustrated newsmen, and only after a mad taxi ride around London were they able to elude their pursuers. It was not a wise ruse, for the secrecy enjoined by the Air Ministry not only annoyed the press and aroused it to greater efforts of pursuit, it spurred on both press and certain Members of Parliament to believe that there must be something in the espionage stories after all—else why all this attempted smuggling away and hiding of the culprit if he had, as was claimed, only performed the ordinary duties of an airman while abroad. Indeed, it began to seem highly questionable whether the man disembarked from the *Rajputana* was Lawrence at all.

The Indian Member (Communist) for Battersea North, Mr. Saklatvala, was particularly insistent. After asking the Secretary of State for Foreign Affairs early in February whether the British government had not received representations from the government of Afghanistan prior to the temporary abdication of King Amanullah protesting against the activities of Colonel Lawrence, he said with more feeling than style:

> Does the Right Honourable Gentleman not agree that if Colonel Lawrence had returned quite openly it would have done much to drive away suspicion, and that this method of surreptitious landing and everything rather confirms the suspicion that it is a false man who is going about?[14]

---

[14] *Hansard's Parliamentary Debates*, February 6, 1929.

The Right Honourable Gentleman, Sir Austen Chamberlain, did not agree, but Ernest Thurtle, Socialist Member for Shoreditch, who had already crossed with His Majesty's Minister for Air—Sir Samuel Hoare again—on the question of Colonel Lawrence's enlistment under an assumed name, asked ironically whether the courtesy of an Admiralty launch would in future be extended to all aircraftmen returning from India.

It was an absurd situation; the Air Ministry's intentions in trying to quell the publicity were excellent, but the lack of candor and the resulting obfuscations led to a multiplication of the myths and legends instead of to their suppression. What was needed was the clear white light of a press conference decorously conducted in the presence of an Air Ministry press officer, with Aircraftman Shaw giving straightforward answers to straightforward questions. For the time being, however, Aircraftman Shaw had no choice but to "hole up" in his Barton Street attic waiting for the tumult to subside.

> I am being hunted, and do not like it [he wrote to E. M. Forster in February]. When the cry dies down I'll come out of my hole and see people—unless of course the cry doesn't die down, and the catchers get my skin. I have a terrible fear of getting the sack from the R.A.F. and can't rest or sit still. [*Letters*, No. 369.]

But unfavorable as the circumstances were, he was back in England, the desire of his heart, and that was much indeed. The Air Ministry admonished and cautioned but did not dismiss him—could not in the face of its own maladroit handling of the affair; and it was the beginning of a new and tranquil era in which his still-unrealized potentialities would be put to good use.

For all the atrophying effect of two years in India, his mental vigor was undiminished. Dullness had always been for him the sin for which no pardon was possible; yet he had never pursued intellectuality for its own sake. Intellectuals can be and often are duller than navvies or mechanics or farmers or sporting men, who are infinitely richer within the limits of their own particular knowledge. Dullness in his judgment meant a frozen attitude of mind, an incapacity for growth or development: a thickening of the spiritual arteries—and, at the end, the dead hand of complacency. For Lawrence such an attitude was tantamount to death in the midst of life; better physical death and, as he thought, annihilation, than the withering of the mind. He might feel, as he did in 1927, that quite likely by 1935 when he was due to retire he would require an occupation which was "slow and full of sitting down." It seemed reasonable to expect that his body, driven to the utmost during its years of maximum power, would all the quicker succumb to the ravages of time; but it is easier to fancy him making a first parachute drop in World War II than to imagine him immobile and phlegmatic, bound by the torpidity of blood to a life of comfort and ease.

In 1929, bright of eye, quick of step, he walked literally into a new life, and no one who saw him then could doubt that it was a life from which he intended to extract the last drop of interest and enthusiasm. Aircraftman Shaw had come home for good.

8

THE BURDEN OF GLORY

"*The least and most that can be said about Lawrence is that he is a* good man," Robert Graves wrote in *Lawrence and the Arabian Adventure*, but goodness is an attribute too vague, too ambiguous, for most people. Endurance, resourcefulness, bravery, are qualities easy to comprehend, but goodness is indefinite, a discomforting abstract, even a little discreditable for its popular association with piety and prudery. Yet properly understood, as an aspect of love, it is as stirring an attribute as bravery or endurance, for it is a pledge of man's future glory. There is in it also a measure of awe for those who exist chiefly in the lower levels and breathe a less rarefied atmosphere, yet there is an allurement in it too, and rightly so.

Did Lawrence recognize in himself this attribute of goodness? Time and again he says: I am not good enough—not good enough to exercise authority, to govern or to lead others. Not good enough to claim the rewards to which his exploits entitled him; not good enough even to enjoy the comforts and consolations of ordinary men. This self-disparagement would be offensive in many men, and suspect. Too often it is the counterfoil of an inner and secret pride, and the truth is

Lawrence was certainly not lacking in *amour propre*. He could reasonably assess his abilities, and when he excused his apartness, his peculiar bias, his rejection of fame and power, by attributing them to his inadequacy, it is clear he did not think himself really less capable than his peers of assuming responsibilities—of being a cabinet minister or a high commissioner—but that he could not meet his own severe standards of what was fitting for responsibility. All this is summed up in that very real and moving *cri de coeur:*

> One of the sorest things in life is to come to realise that one is just not good enough. Better perhaps than some, than many almost. But I do not care for relatives, for matching myself against my kind. There is an ideal standard somewhere, and only that matters, and I cannot find it. [*Letters*, No. 531.]

With St. Paul he could say truthfully: in labors more abundant, in stripes above measure, in prisons more frequent, in deaths oft; but he could not claim that vocation of the spirit to which all these things properly belong. Lawrence was a man without creed, and for the larger part of his adult life, without any formal religious faith. As he grew older his intolerance of formal religion increased.

"I regret Hardy's funeral service," he wrote in 1928 to Sir William Rothenstein. ". . . He would have smiled tolerantly at it all, but I grow indignant for him, knowing that these sleek Deans and Canons were acting a lie behind his name." [*Letters*, No. 347.] Neither Eastern nor Western philosophy touched him. So far as is known, he had no awareness of the perfection and wonder of divine providence, no sense of being overshadowed by the infinite. Meditation and theological speculation were, he told Liddell Hart, good as intellectual exercises but one could not "get anywhere" by such abstractions. Thought was material, as everything else within human limitation, and it was not possible, he felt, to conceive of thought apart from material being. This was a view very popular in the interwar period, but a view which is becoming outmoded. The purely materialistic, mechanistic world of cause and effect has been swept aside by the modern scientific postulation that behind all matter is an energy whose activities, in accordance with its law of being, produce the effects we see in material objects. In the theory of nuclear physics, in the awful and livid phenomenon of the atomic bomb, materialism has suffered its worst blow yet. In any case, as an expression of Lawrence's views, this statement to Liddell Hart, like many of his other expressions of opinion, should be accepted with extreme caution. Yet it would seem that he saw himself, as indeed he saw the whole of human life, as a stark and isolated reality, and that he concluded that the earth as an abstract and senseless creation would have been better off without either. This is a near approach to the "terrible freedom" of contemporary existentialism, which postulates that man is one fact and the universe another, and then proceeds by the fact of man's existence to arrive, not at any ultimate reality or solution of the universe, but at the cautious knowledge that man, moving from thought to action, may lay hold of the future and by so doing synthesize cause and effect.

For Lawrence the idea of physical propagation had become noxious early in life, and artistic creation was often equated by him with physical propagation in that he accepted the propagation of art, for himself at least, only if its creations were perfect. Better not to create anything at all than to create halt or blind. "On the whole I believe that not doing is better than doing, and I believe mankind will reach its zenith when it determines to propagate art no more," he had written in an unidentified letter sold at the Anderson Galleries in New York and copied down in part by Colonel Isham.

He never felt he had any message for mankind, and the suggestion by enthusiastic seekers after light and a modern prophet that he might have one, alternatively exasperated and amused him. "Nihilism is a chill creed whose first commandment is: Thou shalt not convert," he wrote Robert Graves. Few would have really cared to follow him, but although he called it nihilism it was something rather more than that. He had surrendered all the honor, all the comfort and pleasure which the world can afford, and had chosen instead a life of menial, often hard, labor. And this rejection of the world's standards is at the heart of all the great world religions: the hidden, gnarled, and unpromising root from which there springs like the budding of Aaron's rod, the fruits of the spirit—love, peace, freedom, and in whatever way it may be understood, life eternal. Intellectually, Lawrence rejected the fruits and did not subjectively experience them; but he saw in his actions the classic pattern of renunciation and of martyrdom even if he believed it to be without promise of redemption.

> Do you think there have been many lay monks of my persuasion? [he asked Lionel Curtis in 1922]. One used to think that such frames of mind would have perished with the age of religion: and yet here they rise up, purely secular. It's a lurid flash into the Nitrian desert: seems almost to strip the sainthood from Anthony. How about Teresa? [*Letters*, No. 207.]

This was not jocular or impious speculation; he was scarcely in a jocular or impious mood when he wrote from Bovington, and he recognized fully his own dilemma as a man without faith, giving himself up to a mortification of body and spirit as rigorous as any he could have found. Sir Lewis Namier who came to know him at All Souls had written:

> There are men who crave for mortification, "*la mia allegrezza è la malinconia.*" But unless this desire assumes a standardized religious form—hair-shirt or hermit's hut—and can be represented as a profitable bargain for another world men dare not admit it, even to themselves. If proved beyond doubt it is described as madness. Educated men may become monks, but they must not enlist as privates in the army.[1]

There can be no doubt that Lawrence's lay cloister was at best a makeshift, a substitute for the genuine state of the religious to which he could not aspire. Lay cenobitism must always appear an anomaly, a peculiar and specious madness, and when it is practiced in the absence of faith there is a sense of straining what is essentially a useful and practical system to no better end than to justify futility. The army and the air force afforded Lawrence that submission to an absolute authority which he craved; they fulfilled his desire for atonement, and they satisfied his urgent need for fellowship. More they could not do, for he rejected the central premise which alone can guarantee an abiding peace and perfect freedom. Yet at the end,

---

[1] *England at the Time of the American Revolution* (New York, Macmillan, 1930), quoted in *T. E. Lawrence by His Friends.*

without conscious intention, he had fulfilled himself: the path of blood and flame had been walked, had consumed him, and yet left him whole. He had assumed the burden of glory in spite of himself. So under prevenient grace it must always be, and desire for martyrdom no less than desire for truth or beauty or justice must seek its fulfillment where and how it can.

At the age of forty-one, Aircraftman T. E. Shaw entered upon his most fruitful and happy years in the air force. Cattewater, or as it was later to be called, Mount Batten, is a tiny peninsula, "like a fossil lizard swimming from Mount Batten golf links across the harbour towards Plymouth Town," he said. It was protected by its own breakwater there on the eastern horn of the sound looking out upon Drake's Island, where Colonel Newcombe had once offered him a refuge. It was a closed little kingdom where the subjects lived amphibiously, somewhat in isolation, but not without some pleasurable contact with the outside world. And Cattewater was a refuge. In Wing Commander Sidney Smith, whom he had previously met in Cairo in 1921, Lawrence found a superior who accepted him at face value, was not overawed by his past, and was completely sympathetic to the difficulties of his present position. Within the limits of service regulations, he allowed him complete freedom—a privilege for which Lawrence was very grateful and which he was careful never to abuse. He acted as clerk to his new C.O. and did much of the paper work in the marine and workshops section at Cattewater. With some twenty other airmen he slept in a hut with the sea washing against the pier only thirty yards away, but he had privacy when he wanted it, in his own office over the workshops: a small room furnished with a wooden table, three chairs, one swivel and two straight-backed, and an airman's "biscuit" in one corner for sleeping—a monk's cell in all but images and aspirations.

The change from India to England was all to the good, ending as it did the long and sterile years abroad. In that first winter, as an essentially warm-blooded animal, he was to suffer terribly from the cold, but it was after all his homeland, infinitely beautiful, in which he had actually spent very little time since early manhood. Now he could come to know it again intimately in all its varying moods. There were roads to tempt him into indulgence of his only passion, so that a new motorcycle was in order: a giant black and shining Brough Superior provided anonymously by George Bernard Shaw and his wife. But peace, the ordered tranquility he craved, was not to be achieved instantly. The uproar in Parliament and out—he was burned in effigy on Tower Hill by militant Socialists—did not die down upon his recall to England, and he knew it would not die down until he had talked privately with those who were keeping it going. This he managed to do early in February, making a friend for life out of Ernest Thurtle to whom he lent a copy not only of *The Seven Pillars of Wisdom* but of *The Mint*, in order to prove that he served the air force as an ordinary airman and not as extraordinary *agent provocateur*. The bearding of Members of Parliament in the House by an aircraft hand, however celebrated in private life, was not a course which the Air Ministry could approve, however. He was reprimanded again and made to promise that in the future he would behave like an ordinary aircraft hand and not act *ex-officio* on his own initiative. Yet he won his point; the heckling ceased, as he had foreseen it would, and he was left alone to assume his duties at Cattewater.

"Cattewater is a quietly decent station, rather new but it feels promising," he wrote in April to Squadron Leader Hurley, his former adjutant at Karachi. [*Letters*, No. 377.] And later in the month to Regimental Sergeant Major Banbury of the Royal Tank Corps: "This camp stands in the sea. I think it will be lovely, if the sea gets hot and the sun too. Meanwhile I am conscious still mainly of the cold." [*Letters*, No. 380.] And it was lovely, this Plymouth coast with its juxtaposition of land and water, of cloud and sea, and soon he was to acquire another fascinating toy to play with—an American-built 100-horsepower speedboat, the *Sea Biscuit*, which had belonged to Sir Henry Segrave. The Sound and the Channel beyond were now open to him, and he was able to explore and to learn the contours of the coast as he explored and knew the contours of the roads. In his leisure hours, too, he was able to fly, often as pilot on the dual controls, in a Moth seaplane which was jointly owned by Wing Commander Smith and an army friend. These three elements, land, sea, and air, ordained to man's use, he relished and exploited equally.

The days flowed evenly by in this calm harbor which his battered spirit had found after its years of high adventure and mental anguish. His sense of physical well-being which had deteriorated in India seemed, in England, as great as it had ever been, but he felt at last that the genius had gone out of him. That his friends, who sensed his still-great, untapped reserve of power, could not agree perturbed him sometimes, but he would not admit their claim—at least consciously. The seeming futility of his life with its daily round of small tasks, performed as he was to confess later, "*faute de mieux*," came upon him starkly at times; and always there loomed ahead most terrifyingly those years in which he would somehow have to employ himself when his years in the air force were completed. Occasionally he thought and wrote bleakly of taking a job as night watchman in a bank—his sense of humor, one feels, getting the better of his neurosis even here. What he could not contemplate was a re-entry into public life. "Please don't get the public feeling that I'm different from the crowd," he wrote Ernest Thurtle. "By experience in many camps I have assured myself (so certainly that all the print in the world won't shake my conviction) that I'm a very normal sort of Anglo-Irishman." [*Letters*, No. 378.] Not everyone shared his conviction, and he was surprised and touched when, in 1934, on the eve of his retirement, a bid for his services came from a financial stronghold of the City, offering him a position of power and responsibility on the Elizabethan assumption that he was a man who could do well in any job he tackled, whether he had experience of it or not.[2]

Meanwhile, there was his translation of *The Odyssey* to complete; there were books—a surprising number read in odd half-hours, for leisure at Cattewater was not as plentiful a commodity as it had been

---

[2] It has now been responsibly revealed that the invitation came from Sir Montagu Norman, and the position was Secretary of the Bank of England.

at Karachi and Miramshah—and there was music: a new gramophone, new records.

An estimate of Lawrence's understanding of and attitude to music was contributed to the miscellany, *T. E. Lawrence by His Friends* by W. Warwick James, the dental surgeon who knew Lawrence both as a patient and as a friend, and who introduced him to Harold Samuel, the pianist. "Superficially," he wrote, "his appreciation was akin to that of many individuals who have pleasure in listening to music, and in fact he might be regarded as one of a large group of ordinary people with musical sense and cultivation." But then Mr. James was quick to say that Lawrence, not being an ordinary man, had rather a unique approach to music, for he came to it with a curiosity to be satisfied: he wanted to see what effect a given work would have on himself and on others of different temperament. He wanted to penetrate its emotional content, to analyze it—not as a musician analyzes music, for apart from some early piano lessons he had no musical training—to understand why it affected him or failed to affect him.

There is an early description of his reaction to music which shows how sensitive too he was to the circumstances under which he listened. It happened once, when Hogarth and the Fontanas were staying at Carchemish, that they sat after dinner around the hearth blazing with olive logs, and listened to two musicians sent by their old friend Busrawi Agha to entertain them with Kurdish war songs, with the accompaniment of a shepherd's flute and a two-string viol. Suddenly a great thunderstorm broke out over the Euphrates littoral. The rain came down heavily and "rattled over the shingles in our courtyard like the footsteps of a great crowd of men." [*Letters*, No. 90.] The thunder shattered the music; in the brilliant lightning which illuminated the open door and window apertures, they caught glimpses of the sculptures outside.

> I remember particularly [he wrote, recalling the incident to his mother in 1916], the seven foot figure of a helmeted god striding along an inscription towards the doorway: and the dripping jaws of the two lions on the pedestal which seemed in the alternate glare and shadow of the flashes to be grinning at us through the window. The musicians did not stop but

> changed their song for a wild improvisation which kept time with the storm.

It was, he admitted, the most wonderful time he had ever had. The war songs of the Arab army on the march moved him strongly too, but this was exceptional music. In Cairo and later in Jerusalem he would sit quietly, hands folded, eyes closed, while Sir Ronald Storrs played to him, and to his friend Vyvyan Richards he recounted one of his unwritten Eastern experiences: that of awaking in a Palestinian, stone-floored hall after a heavy bout of fever and unconsciousness, to the sound of a Beethoven Sonata being played on a grand piano by an unknown woman missionary who had taken him in to care for him.

In later years music was a sure and strong palliative, bringing him the richest of all gifts: self-forgetfulness. Yet in *The Mint* he says that rarely in listening to music was he able to lose himself completely in the perfect consonance of musical sound; and more, that if those rare and exquisite moments when he did succeed in giving himself up utterly to nuance or phrase were to last, he could not endure them, so sharply did they catch at his heart and drain his life's blood from it. The truth was that hearing, like all his other senses, was acutely developed and he was able to come to music relatively late in life and to bring to it a rich awareness, a freshness that many a more seasoned listener might have envied. At Bovington he longed so for music that a soldier's one-fingered picking at tunes and rhythms on the canteen piano set his blood on fire, yet he would not permit himself to go over to Poole where his friend Henry Lamb would have played for him, lest he be completely undone by music. Whenever he could he went to concerts, to the "Proms" at Queen's Hall, to the Three Choirs Festival, and on occasion, out of curiosity, exposed himself to more esoteric fare. "I heard the Dolmetsch crowd once playing what they called viols, and thought them pretty foul," he remarked to James Hanley. But of necessity, gramophone music was his staple, and his enormous-horned Ginn gramophone at Clouds Hill brought him reasonably faithful reproductions of the greatest in music.

Mozart and Beethoven were perhaps the two composers whose

idiom was closest to his ideal, but his tastes like those of any music lover fluctuated considerably. The catalogue of records at Clouds Hill at the time of his death comprised fourteen compositions by Bach, including the B Minor Mass; thirty-two by Beethoven, twenty by Mozart, ten by Brahms, and eight by Schubert. Of the more modern composers, Delius was represented by ten works, Elgar by ten, Prokofiev by three, and there were two volumes of Hugo Wolf songs. The one notable composer with whom he appears to have felt no affinity whatever, and none of whose works were included in his collections of records, is Frederic Chopin, Polish patriot and *enfant gâté* of the French salons. The antipathy is understandable.

But literature remained for him the queen of the arts, the star and crown of man's creative effort, the satisfaction of intellect and spirit to which none other could compare. But it was for the persistent, the continually evolving craftsman that his highest admiration was reserved, and not for the sudden propagator of literary flukes—as he himself was. Literary flukes were well enough as far as they went; they did not nor could not constitute proof of literary worth, however. "Writers are people who go on spinning their experiences into books for sheer love of it, or inability to refrain," he told Sir Edward Marsh in 1929. [*Letters*, No. 374.] And earlier he had written Edward Garnett: ". . . the born writer is the real fact, and without such ichor in his veins a man only makes a journeyman's job of book-writing: and my critical sense makes me not covet the creation (even while I enjoy it) of those who do so, by pain, make literature." [*Letters*, No. 183.]

But he did covet the creation, and he sought to satisfy his coveting vicariously by devouring the works of other men, journeymen and giants alike. In the period of his Indian exile, no less than fifty-three titles of books, novels and nonfiction prose works, come by reference into his letters—not all of them read in India, of course, though many of them were. Writers and writing is the dominant theme of his correspondence in later years, and of writers his judgment was always well considered—though not all will be in agreement with it—and his critical comment often pungent. Indeed, his pinpoint evaluations of writers and painters are always provocative.

> I have not met G.K.C. [G. K. Chesterton] [he wrote in 1932 to G. W. M. Dunn the promising airman-writer]. Shaw always called him a man of colossal genius. I cannot read his journalism, which is perhaps a good sign. T. S. Eliot I have not met. His poetry is good, if rather sparing. His prose is pompous. His criticism mock-profound. His range of interests very queer and spotty . . . John [Augustus] is in ruins, but a giant of a man. Exciting, honest, uncanny. Barrie is too grim and hard. There are claws under his fur, obviously. G.B.S. is not a vast electric discharge. He is more like a cocktail. Very beneficent and plain to read. Slightly hard of hearing and short of sight—by which I mean, prone to imagine the whole from the incomplete part. [*Letters*, No. 473.]

(In another letter, to Hogarth, he had admitted he found Shaw "very bracing," but thought that sureness of success had closed his pores.)

He liked the primitive power of Eugene O'Neill and admired Compton Mackenzie's *Water on the Brain*. Of John Buchan he wrote Edward Garnett: "He takes figures of today and projects their shadows on to clouds, till they grow subhuman and grotesque: then describes them." [*Letters*, No. 495.] A rotten technique, but he said, his books were "like athletes racing: so clean-lined, speedy, breathless."

He had felt while at Karachi that his literary tastes were changing, were growing more simple: Wells was preferable to Norman Douglas, Kipling to Hubert Crackenthorpe—a lesser Edwardian luminary. And to Robert Graves, his later view of poetry as "a fancy craft," a luxury made acceptable only by virtue of more common tasks—like building boats or airplanes or writing popular novels—seemed especially repugnant. But this was an attitude assumed to justify and to uphold, for himself, his claim to the common touch.

Of Doughty, whom from youth up he had esteemed most fervently, he said: "Doughty's imagination was weak: his sense of scale faulty: and he had no sense of design." [*Letters*, No. 320.] This was not denigration however, and the old man remained ever secure in the full light of his devotion—a rare genius. Shakespeare, in his view, though a second-rate intellect, was "the most consummate master of vowels and consonants and the greatest poet. As a philosopher and moralist I have no abnormal respect for him: but the Elizabethan age was tempered rather than forged steel." [*Letters*, No. 182.]

In Dostoevski he discovered the greatest of the Russians, and *The Brothers Karamazov* was for him a "Fifth Gospel." His list of what he felt were the superlative books—his "shelf of giants"—varied somewhat from time to time, but invariably they included *War and Peace*, *The Brothers Karamazov*, and *Moby Dick*. Yet writing, the only art which, he said, required no special technique, was most open to abuse—to invasion by amateurs who had no right to tread the ground hallowed by a Shakespeare, a Milton, a Dostoevski, a Melville, and it was a constant self-reproach that he had trodden it himself and by so doing damned himself inexorably.

Much of Lawrence's first months at Cattewater was spent on preparations for the Schneider Cup Trophy race which was held at Calshot in September and in which, as Wing Commander Smith's clerk, he was closely concerned. This was the race which preceded the final successful winning of the trophy for Britain with R. J. Mitchell's Supermarine S.6.B. In 1929, the American team having at the last moment withdrawn, the British and the Italian teams were the sole competitors, and the cup was won for Britain by Flying Officer H. R. D. Waghorn.

From the luxury yacht *Karen* the trophy race was organized and run, and from the side of the *Karen* every evening during the week of the race, Aircraftman Shaw, qualifying for an R.A.F. swimming badge, plunged into Southampton Water, his first serious attempt at swimming since his Arabian days. It was a return to youth, a brief recapturing of an old exhilaration which the stronger excitement of motorcycling had all but displaced; and his body flashing white against the gray water gave back a poignant reflection of its earlier power and beauty, when joyously and strongly he stroked the brown and foaming Euphrates in spate. But the race brought about a contretemps which nearly ended his air force career prematurely. The Air Ministry's dictum upon his return from India had been "no publicity," and the rule was fairly and decently observed by the press at Calshot; but publicity could not be entirely avoided. Not only was Aircraftman Shaw very conspicuous on the tarmac speaking on equal terms with many of the distinguished visitors, but he was also seen chatting with the Italian flier Balbo—as it turned out, on the matter of clearing the Italian slipway which had been neglected. He was taken severely to task by Lord Thomson, the Air Minister, who called him "a self-advertising mountebank" and threatened him with a second expulsion from the air force which only his own spirited defense of himself and the intervention of friends prevented. Henceforth he was under orders not to fly in the Moth as pilot, not to visit or have any intercourse with political figures, but to perform simply the duties of an ordinary airman.

It is easy to be critical of the Air Ministry where Lawrence was concerned, but they were attempting to deal with a situation almost unparalleled in any service, and to some extent the argument was on the side of the Air Ministry. Lawrence had engaged as an ordinary airman, spurning the rank and honor that were his due, and ordinary airmen do not normally associate with cabinet ministers and Members of Parliament. That he did so seemed to the authorities to be a usurping of the prerogatives which more properly belonged to the position he scorned; and they were offended by it.

To Lady Astor, one of the banned political figures with whom he maintained a high-spirited, often frivolous correspondence, he wrote in the following January: "I was given positive orders to cease from meeting you, so far as that lay in my power: so I can't come and see you. It would not be fair to the terms on which I have been in the R.A.F. for the last eight years, and on which I hope to serve for five years more." [*Letters*, No. 403.] Lady Astor was one of the few women with whom Lawrence was able to be at his ease, and from his friendship with her and the occasional week end he spent at Cliveden, much nonsense has been said and written. Of the other women with whom he apparently had rewarding associations, Mrs. Claire Smith, the wife of his commanding officer at Cattewater seems to have been especially fortunate. He taught her German diction for her lieder singing, and the intricate business of steering the *Sea Biscuit;* and he escorted her and her lady friends over the Sound to picnics on the Devonshire coast, quietly seeing to their needs, a most benign escort, though surely bemused by his new role of ladies' man. He was the "rare beast in captivity," and it is to be hoped the ladies were fully cognizant of their extraordinary privilege; but one wonders after reading Mrs. Smith's account of these junketings, if they were, or if they simply enjoyed leading around the captive unicorn by his silver chain.

He was photographed in oilskins with the ladies, holding on to the mooring rope of the *Sea Biscuit;* perched, irregularly clad in R.A.F. uniform, white socks, and tennis shoes, on a veranda wall with the ladies beaming down at him, and in the cockpit of his boat with his patroness. He ran messages to Plymouth for Mrs. Smith—who called him Tes—picking up her vanishing cream and other *objets de toilette* from the chemist, all with a polite amiability worthy of Barrie's Admirable Crichton. It is a scene which taxes credulity—half circus, half dovecote—with the celebrated Colonel Lawrence of Arabia, notorious woman-hater to boot, willingly being put through his paces. But for all that, it was a good life: long days by the gray-green water where the flying boats rocked on their floats like monstrous sea birds, becoming eerily beautiful once they were airborne and drifting diagonally over the Martello tower with its wind sock, and banking through sun and cloud into the Western Approaches. And there were the long, quiet nights when the winking lighthouse swept its white beam at ten-second intervals through his bare monk's cell. But to make it a better life something else was needed—a more imaginative use of his skills and faculties than the stultifying routine of R.A.F. paper work—and that was soon to come.

The R.A.F. was for Lawrence the ideal, the exemplar service, yet there were reforms which he urged in the interests of reason, of human frailty, of his own peculiar recalcitrance in the matter of the propriety of military discipline in an air force. Among the minor points he raised with Wing Commander Sidney Smith, Captain Liddell Hart, and others in his last years were the wearing of bayonets at church parade—indeed, the whole dubious value of bayonets as weapons for airmen; the compulsory buttoning of the high, uncomfortable top button on greatcoats; the carrying of walking-out canes; the humiliation of kit inspection. To have kit inspection performed in the absence of troops was a measure he pressed hard to get accepted.

> It shouldn't be a parade or a beauty-show [he wrote Liddell Hart in 1929], but an inspection to make sure that our normally-invisible kit was serviceable and complete. There is no need for us standing by. That makes us hot and ashamed and the decent officers feel like nosy-Parkers, and avoid looking at us. [*Letters*, No. 390.]

As for officers and N.C.O.'s, they should be required on entering the men's mess to remove their hats as was the custom in the navy. These were small issues; there were others more important. He wanted reasonable regulations for the posting of airmen in Britain to stations within convenient distance of their homes; permission to wear civilian clothes ("It's a very valued privilege, I'm sorry to say.") in off-duty hours; sanction (denied airmen but not soldiers) to ride on motor-cycle pillions; voluntary instead of compulsory attendance at church parade. On the broader plane of humanitarian legislation, he wanted to see the abolition of the death penalty for cowardice in war.[3] "I have run too far and too fast (but never fast enough to please me at the time) under fire, to throw a stone at the fearfullest creature. You see, if I did, I might hit myself in the eye!" he told Ernest Thurtle. [*Letters*, No. 387.]

There is a belief prevalent that, once his recruit's training was over, Lawrence never actually performed the ordinary duties of a soldier or an airman. This is far from true; at Cattewater he drilled once a week, did barrack fatigues, fulfilled fire pickets more often than most airmen, and served in turn as duty crew for the boats which always stood ready to service the seaplanes and, in bad weather, rescue the crews of coastwise vessels in distress.

> There is a horrible little trawler outside that keeps on edging nearer and nearer to the rocks on the South side of the Camp [he wrote Robert Graves in May, 1929]. I suppose it's the wind, dragging her anchor. They are getting steam on her, to save the expense of a tug. If she does not get her steam going in the next hour or two, the little beast will go ashore in

[3] It was not until the Army and Air Force Bills of December, 1954, that the death penalty was limited.

front of the cookhouse, and then the duty boat (for one of whose crew I'm a stand-by this afternoon) will have to go out and do the life-saving stunt. It is humiliating to save someone's life at no risk to one's own. [*Letters*, No. 385.]

Sea, the smell of sea, the motion of sea and the salty spume of sea was to be his element for the next five years. It was the sea, the North Sea, that dominated the holiday he spent on the east coast of Scotland in September, 1930, with two ex-service friends, "Jock" Chambers, "roughest diamond of our Tank Corps hut," and Jimmy, who "jobbed horses in Aberdeen." That holiday, made necessary by an accident in which he fractured two more ribs in his chest wall, became the subject of a lengthy letter to his American publisher and friend, F. N. Doubleday. The result is a Scottish mezzotint of sand dunes and heather tussocks, rock cliffs and sea winds, mewing gulls and desolation, all made convivial by the hearty fellowship of three men. A little more work and the gloss of art would have made of it a set piece worthy of the time and attention of an editor. As it was, he composed it simply to beguile old Mr. Doubleday recovering, in America, from a serious operation.

The wind and the sea were changing him; chameleonlike, he was growing to fit his element, becoming more salty of visage, weathered like rock and as solid-looking, but with moments still of quicksilver beauty. The appearance of this short, stocky, rough-hewn, red-faced airman with his rampant fair crest growing frosty with white hairs, was a paradox and a disappointment to those who came to him expecting something else, something more delicately formed and more obviously romantic. He was too plain, too commonplace-looking to fit their idyllic vision of him. But beauty is notably in the eye of the beholder, and this is how Flight Lieutenant R. G. Sims saw Aircraftman Shaw in his first encounter with him at Bridlington when he was mistaken for a reporter.

I noticed a small man in a rough fisherman's jersey reading a blue print nearby, and although I could not see his face which he kept completely hidden with the print, I knew without hesitation who it was. I stood respectfully in front of the blue print. This was slowly lowered, and a pair of the bluest, most flashing eyes I had ever seen blazed forth, whilst a vast forehead equal in size to the terrific chin beneath, simply radiated scorn and hate at me . . . Although this reception should have struck terror, I afterwards realized that it did nothing of the sort. I was full of admiration and joy at the sheer beauty of his face.[4]

Eric Kennington who, as an artist, was trained to recognize beauty when he saw it, wrote of an earlier encounter:

. . . it was not the story telling that left the clearest impression, but the teller, with his male dignity, beauty and power. He moved little, using bodily presence just sufficiently to make brain contact. I had never seen so little employment or wastage of physical energy. The wide mouth smiled often, with humour and pleasure, sometimes extending to an unusual upward curve at the corners, a curious menacing curve, warning of danger. The face was almost lineless, and removed from me as a picture or sculpture. However gracious its attitude, it remained distant. He's like a fine Buddhistic painting, I thought. The lines have just the same harmony.[5]

Three conditions are needed for beauty, says St. Thomas Aquinas in the *Summa Theologica:* integrity which is also perfection; proportion which is also harmony, and brightness which is also clarity. These things, wholeness, harmony, and radiance, Lawrence had—not at all times perhaps, but when they were made manifest no one except a dullard could fail to perceive them. The Irish-Armenian doctor-poet, F. H. R. Altounyan has described a cold Sunday in January at Clouds Hill when his friend, through motion, made beauty manifest to him.

A huge fire was burning, and I sat down contentedly to warm myself, but he was not satisfied. I half turned to protest but he had vanished, and I was spreading my hands to the blaze when with a slight rustle he was back dragging a huge dead branch that scraped past the doorway. On this branch he danced rapidly to the accompaniment of flying twigs. The fire roared, and I found myself, still half dazed, watching him sweep up the remaining leaves with a long-handled broom till he had swept himself and them out backwards from the room. I have seen no movement in ballet more magical.[6]

---

[4] *T. E. Lawrence by His Friends.*
[5] *Ibid.*
[6] *Ibid.*

There is one more vignette by Eric Kennington, of Lawrence the motorcyclist, which is worth quoting.

> His confident ease, as he sat astride the monstrous bicycle. A few vigorous kicks on the pedal: the beginning of slow movement; a chuckle: a downward glance, and sensual grip of the rubber handles—like a cat taking its pleasure in claw-stretching: a conscious summoning of power, still latent in the horizontal machine, but active in the upright human body with its creased neck and jaw: a tortoise-like waddle, the head was raised, the eyes gazed at the horizon as if in ownership: the advance quickening snakelike, then the disappearance in a roar of dust. He was happy. He never looked back. Travelling twice as fast as his boats—nearly as fast as his brain.[7]

Ordinary things these, but it is by ordinary movements and gestures that a man reveals what inwardly he is. By 1930 Lawrence had broadened physically, become visibly heavier, but slim still. Under the close-fitting air force uniform, his body was as finely developed as an athlete's, with a rippling of muscle in arm and shoulder, and so many who knew him have testified, unknown to each other, that his entry into a room brought with it an order akin to benediction, that it is impossible not to believe it.

To older friends who saw him in these last years of his life he seemed better balanced, more tranquil, more at his ease—more of common clay? He liked to tease Robert Graves by insisting that his years of service in the tank corps and the air force had blunted his perceptions, had made him a fitter associate for garage mechanics than for men of letters. Two things impressed Graves when they met again in September, 1930, after a lapse of several years: his changed intonation which Graves felt was a mingle of North London, Midlands, and North Britain, a brogue which he associated with lorry drivers; and the conspicuous gold-filled teeth which his friend showed when he grinned. Both, he felt, were a far cry from Oxford, from All Souls. The gold, Lawrence argued, was practical; as for the accent, it was a coloration extracted from his everyday surroundings; he could and did revert to his older habits of speech and manner.

---

[7] *Ibid.*

His perceptions were as sharp as ever, his mind as keen, his memory, though occasionally faulty in details, as retentive as ever in essentials. He was able to meet garage mechanics on their own level certainly, but they were always sensible of the difference between themselves and him. "Mind not high things, but condescend to men of low estate," wrote St. Paul to the Romans, but condescend here does not mean what it has now come to mean. Rather it means a loving identification of self with those less rich in gifts of mind and spirit. This Lawrence achieved through his servitude, and because he never patronized, never asked anything for himself—except on occasion peace and quiet—he won the devotion of those men of low estate with whom he did identify himself as completely as he had won that of the Arabs. His abstemiousness which might have repelled them was never flaunted. Stimulants he had always rejected, except for the occasional glass of port when he was out with the "fellows" and not to take something would have seemed unconvivial; or the occasional cigarette—usually on his birthday—to show he could smoke, though he found neither the taste nor the sensation pleasant. These spiced *entremets* in the banquet of life were not for him. "I find myself hard to control anyhow," he told Robert Graves. "If I let in drink or love or gluttony or wine or gaming or sport it would become too much." [8] Stimulants, he felt, were designed for the times when life went flat, and though life was for him often desperate, it was never flat.

The change that was to make his last years in the R.A.F. the most rewarding came in March, 1931. Racing and tinkering with his American *Biscayne Baby* had given him a vision of new and faster water craft for the air force, and now his prodding of the Air Ministry, over the signature and approval of Wing Commander Smith, began to bear fruit. Lawrence's mechanical training had actually began at Karachi, in the engine repair shops, when he was detailed off to follow the overhaul of engines as they progressed, and to write the history of that

[8] *T. E. Lawrence to His Biographers.*

progress—"tricky, and not either quick or easy to do. Especially for a non-technical man, very vague as to the function of a cam shaft or inclined drive," he had written Sergeant Banbury in 1927. [*Letters*, No. 302.] Cam shafts were now to become his daily bread; he was sent up to the British Power Boat Company's yard at Hythe to advise on the design and carry out the testing of a new series of motor-boats, racing in them up and down Southampton Water, the Spit, and the Solent. It was exhausting work, but it was work he relished, and for the first time it seemed to him that the air force was getting full value for money. His new work brought him in contact with the navy whose representatives he impishly delighted to shock by his unnautical language and then to dazzle by his extraordinary grasp of technical problems.

> I will never be a sailor, I'm afraid [he wrote Lieutenant Robin White, R.N.]; born too late, though my father had yachts and used to take me with him from my fourth year: but my attempted accomplishment is motor-boating, a very different art, and as difficult. Sailing has only wind and water, and the two-party system is simple to work. With power all manner of complications enter and the art becomes exquisite and subtler. Only it isn't sailing! [*Letters*, No. 442.]

Most sailors would agree; yet his inherited seamanship, as well as his engineering skill, is shown most clearly in the excerpts from a monograph he wrote on the 200 Class Royal Air Force Seaplane Tender which are included in *The Essential T. E. Lawrence*. As a technical document it was intended only for the eyes of qualified coxswains and mechanics, but as a revelation of Lawrence's versatility and as an antidote for the overornate style of *The Seven Pillars of Wisdom*, it repays careful reading.

His time was now divided between Cattewater and Myrtle Cottage, Hythe, where he shared living quarters with Sergeant (then Corporal) Bradbury, R.A.F. Marine Craft. With Sergeant Bradbury he went up to Southampton for baths, for exploration of the old town and for raids on secondhand bookshops to search for rare finds. It was a happy time and he was more deeply content than he had been for years. But the date of his retirement was edging ever closer. He had originally signed on for seven years' active service and five years' reserve starting from March, 1923, but his active service was extended while he was in India to embody the reserve period, though he had the option of leaving before the end if he wished.

Clouds Hill had long been hired out to an assortment of tenants, but in 1930 he began to ready it against his return—for good this time. His friend, Sergeant Knowles, its custodian, was sent parcels of books and sheaves of instructions. A garage was to be built, suitably disguised by the foliage so as not to be an eyesore; prize rhododendrons, Tibetan and Chinese, arrived by rail from Derbyshire for planting around the cottage, its only flowers. The fee paid for his gold Meccan dagger had reroofed and refloored the cottage earlier. Since then new chimneys had been added; and *The Odyssey* was to bring up the list of improvements and add to its growing amenities: a bath with boiler and burner for hot baths—his one concession to the weakness of the flesh. The ram which provided water for this luxuriating he had himself devised to pump water from a spring across the road fifty feet or so uphill into the cistern. To store the water, he had a pool built to hold seven thousand gallons which he would have enclosed and roofed in glass with the teakwood doors brought back from Jidda, closing the northern end of the tank and forming one wall of a glassed-in study for himself.

Bookcases were to line the lower room of the cottage with its one bow window and deep fireplace. He would have a broad-as-long couch covered over with soft undyed leather—for lounging, not for sleeping; and a white leather and lamb's wool chair with wide arms fitted to accommodate a stainless steel bookrest he was having made. Upstairs, the music room held its old leather settee and eventually the gramophone, with all his records neatly catalogued and cactus needles and a sharpener provided; and lastly a plain wooden table and chair for writing. With Clouds Hill he made his ultimate gesture to the Morrisonian hall, and hall or cottage, surely no dwelling place ever reflected so strongly the personality of its owner. The furnishings were nearly all his own handiwork, or made to his design: wrought-iron and stainless-steel fenders; dark-glazed, handleless cups and saucers patterned on those he had dug up at Carchemish; a leather curtain between room and hall to obviate the calamity of a slamming door. On the stairs, soundless rubber treads, soft to the feet as deep springing grass, catered to his love of quiet. Outside, the words "*Ou Prontis*" carved on the architrave catered to his love of classic Greece and whimsical jest, for it commemorated in smiling irony the bridegroom Hippoclides' casual disregard of reputation and propriety.[9]

These were all Lawrence's own inventions, not quite in the eccentric style of the White Knight but nearly as serio-comic and somehow poignant. Leather, stainless steel, wrought iron, wood—these were his favorite media. And they were strong masculine substances, as indeed Clouds Hill, with its lack of softness and adornment was a masculine stronghold: an emphatic denial of the existence of the female, a canceling out, on the personal level at least, of the irrefutable fact of humanity's cleavage into two mutually complementary, mutually antagonistic elements: a well-calculated snub for Adam's rib, and for Adam himself, cold disapproval that he should ever have desired the cleavage for the sake of love and multiplicity. "My Dorset fastness" he called it, and in the hot, dry summer of 1934 wrote: "I hear that heath fires are raging at Clouds Hill, and am sad and afraid for the little place. I've grown to love it, I fear. What fools we become!" [*Letters*, No. 529.]

The work on *The Odyssey* progressed far too slowly to suit him and, as is inevitable with a piece of writing which is spread over a period of years, he was becoming satiated with it. "I am tired of all Homer's namby-pamby men and women," he had written Edward Garnett in December, 1930. [*Letters*, No. 429.] A year later he was ensconced, during his annual leave, in his Barton Street eyrie making a last desperate effort to complete it by working seventeen hours a day. It was finished in August, four years after being started. As a translation of a notable classic it has been stringently criticized and even condemned outright by scholars and by some who were not scholars. It is easy to make comparisons of extant translations with that of Lawrence and to prefer a different treatment of the Homeric legend.

[9] See Herodotus, Vol. 3, Book VI, p. 129. (Loeb Classical Library.)

More recently a vogue has grown for retelling Homer's tales in a rationalized, modern language, and these admittedly have more affinity for the modern taste than Lawrence's work, but they are not, properly speaking, translations of Homer, and Lawrence's *Odyssey*, for all the liberties he took with it, is.

> About the Odyssey [he wrote Sir William Rothenstein], I fully agree with you. My version is fustian: but so is Homer, I think. The more I dwelt on the Greek and struggled with it and its story, the more possessed I became with the view that here was something too artful for decency. It tried by surpassing pains and skill to simulate the rule-leaping flood of authentic greatness. All the talent in the world never approaches genius: the two are incompatible. The Odyssey is a creeping work. [*Letters*, No. 469.]

So much for Homer.

His letters to Bruce Rogers justifying his treatment of technical problems—such as the shooting through the axes in the trial by skill—are revealing of a resurgence of confidence in his own power, of that *amour propre* which he certainly possessed.

> . . . I am in as strong a position *vis-à-vis* Homer as most of his translators [he wrote in January, 1931]. For years we were digging up a city of roughly the Odysseus period. I have handled the weapons, armour, utensils of those times, explored their houses, planned their cities. I have hunted wild boars and watched wild lions, sailed the Aegean (and sailed ships), bent bows, lived with pastoral peoples, woven textiles, built boats and killed many men. So I have odd knowledges that qualify me to understand the Odyssey, and odd experiences that interpret it to me. Therefore a certain headiness in rejecting help. [*Letters*, No. 431.]

This is better understood read as a companion piece to the letter he was later to write to Liddell Hart [10] enumerating his war skills and how they had been acquired, and yet there is in it an unmistakable echo of the proud confidence which, conjoined to his flippancy, had in Egypt prejudiced some soldiers and civil servants against him. He knew too much and was too assured in his knowledge.

Had he in fact done all these things? Many of them certainly, and the rest are unimportant; he had lived close enough to them to

[10] See pp. 295–296, quote from *Letters*, No. 491.

accurately gauge their spirit and elucidate it. In this sense at least one can accept his claim.

After the false polemics of *The Odyssey*, the puling courtship and strife of the suitors, the sly coquetry of Penelope, and the wooden filiation of Telemachus, it was a relief to turn to speedboats and the sea again with their long, entailed hours of coastal voyaging, eying gauges and needles while spume flew wide over a tilting prow. Here was work that was worth while; the other had been a cake-and-jam labor undertaken to earn a bonus to his airman's pay of 3/9d. a day and guarantee him some little security, now that his tenure of service was drawing to a close. Other writing, for himself, by himself, he adamantly set mind and heart against and would have none of it. Yet in 1933 he could still say:

> Writing has been my inmost self all my life, and I can never put my full strength into anything else. Yet the same force, I know, put into action upon material things would move them, make me famous and effective. The everlasting effort to write is like trying to fight a feather-bed. [*Letters*, No. 479.]

The Mint, in typescript having gone the round of a few selected friends and one or two Air Ministry officials, including Lord Trenchard, who understandably found it most unpalatable, was given into the keeping of his youngest brother, Arnold, with instructions that no publication of it should be undertaken before 1950. The fragmentary notes on service life which he wrote subsequently were never developed and never accumulated to the main body of the manuscript.

Wing Commander Sidney Smith was posted to the Manston R.A.F. Station in July, 1931, and soon after his departure what, according to Mrs. Smith, Aircraftman Shaw had called the "Golden Reign," came to an end. He had done meritorious and useful work on the new R.A.F. target boats, but suddenly there was a fresh epidemic of press speculation about his activities, and the authorities, always sensitive, took fright. It had started with his testimony given in London at an inquiry into the crash of an Iris III flying boat in 1931 at which, as an airman who had seen the accident and taken a leading part in subsequent rescue operations, he was a key witness. "Lawrence of

Arabia" had turned up again after more than a year of obscurity, the headlines read, and his work with the R.A.F. target boats began to attract attention. It was said that the boats were designed and built by him, which was quite untrue: the engines were Scott-Paine's, though the skill that nursed them to perfection was Lawrence's. Once again, regrettably, his role had been exaggerated in the interest of good copy, and he was made to assume a greater proportion of credit than was actually due to him. No one deplored this treatment of his exploits more than Lawrence himself, and no one tried more earnestly to deflate these swollen cartoons of himself and collapse them to their proper size. Critics who set themselves to explode the Lawrence myth, to denigrate his character, or to reduce his historical role should remember this.

He was returned to his base at Mount Batten after thirty-two boats had been completed, and charged once more to perform the duties of an ordinary airman. At first the change seemed not unwelcome for the work on boats had tired him with long hours and exacting seamanship, but as time passed he grew more restive: this vegetating, this dull descent from day to day into equilibrium—like running down a gently sloping hill into limbo—was not the way he desired to spend his last years in the air force. Better that the end should come at once painfully and abruptly than this slow marking of time while root and branch wasted away. It was a judgment, a prophecy delivered on the whole of his life, not just that portion of it belonging to the air force.

In March, 1933, formally invoking the release clause of his R.A.F. contract, he requested his discharge to become effective the following month. At first it was accepted and then there were questions: had the airman any grievance, the authorities asked? None; but he made it clear he had requested his discharge because there seemed no prospect of his being employed on other than routine station duties. Soon the Under Secretary of State for Air, Sir Philip Sassoon, was involved, and as usual when Lawrence stirred and set into motion a chain of events, positive action was the result. He was immediately ordered posted to the marine craft section at Felixstowe where he was to be attached to contractors' yards to advise on the further development of high-speed boats, watch over the Air Ministry's interests, and make reports on engine trials and runs. To avoid publicity he was ordered to wear civilian clothes except when on Air Force property: thus the wheel turned in full cycle. He had donned the R.A.F. uniform in the first instance as a protective covering and a wholly efficient disguise; he was now to take it off for the same purpose. Nevertheless, he had got his own way: the downhill run would be a sharp, exciting race to the finish.

Arabia with its numinous landscape, its visions, its violence, and its poetry; Damascus where the immemorial dust swept, harbinger of the desert, across "the burgeoning green of tilth"; even Uxbridge with its bleak pains, were distant memories now. Archaeology was even farther removed, and the Syrian paradise of his youth had passed into the realm of misty legend. This was the postdepression era, the end of a reign of cold terror, brief but devastating, which had affected Lawrence in his lay cloister but little, though some of his friends had suffered from it. It was the period of the great Howard Coster portrait-photographs which show him rugged-visaged, solid of neck and shoulder, but with a haunting sadness behind the deep-set eyes. The metamorphosis from the long-haired Carchemish youth in shorts and Kurdish belt, from the white and gold fury of Arabia, was now completed in this stocky, red-faced man in dark jersey, oil-stained overalls, and gum boots. But the metamorphosis was as much one of mind as of body. To read through his published letters is to experience this mutation of personality down through the years: from the energetic, romantic, wayward, vain young man, sure of himself, though less certain of his motives, to a man fearfully embarked on middle age, disillusioned by himself and his motives alike.

In the earlier letters his experiences are graphically defined, his reactions explicit; of emotion he shows little except where he is stirred by an image or an idea—as by Chartres Cathedral or a first glimpse of the Mediterranean. Later his experiences contract into terse, sharp vignettes; he uses words more sparingly, with increasing economy of impression, and all thought and feeling become implicit, charged with emotion, yet the emotion of a man afraid to give himself away, with despair held tightly in check. ("The 'fear of showing my feelings' is my real self," he confessed to Edward Garnett in 1927. [*Letters*, No. 299.]) This shrinking from too clear a revelation of himself involved him in some curiously contradictory attitudes. There was his seeming dishonesty about himself with others which has disconcerted some and given rise to the charge, partly true, of deviousness. There was a strong impulse in him always to elude too clear an elucidation of himself and his motives; always to let fall metaphorical red herrings along the trail, to confuse the chase and then, if pursuit came close, to drop down into a convenient hole. A perusal of his notes and letters and reported verbal statements to Robert Graves and Liddell Hart reveals his fine skill in juggling facts, events, and mental attitudes in order to present different facets of himself to his two biographers. To interpret this as simple dishonest intent is to lose its real significance. A flaw of character it most certainly was, but its nature is consonant with his self-distrust, his fear of being seen, for what he was in his own eyes, in too clear a light.

His dishonesty with others about themselves was in part due to his wish to gratify—one might almost say to flatter—his friends in a way that he knew they would most enjoy being gratified. Thus he was to tell E. M. Forster in 1924 that no one else had bothered to write him pages on his war history, when the truth was that Edward Garnett had been writing him consistently about it since 1922. And in *The Mint* he wrote warmly of the impromptu banquet which the inmates of Hut 4, using the cleanest sheet as tablecloth, gave him on the occasion of his being posted to Farnborough, and remarked that no one had ever before offered to feast him. He had, and he knew he had, been banqueted at Oxford in honor of his Crusader Castles thesis, but it seemed to him far more of a privilege and an honor to be feasted by the airmen of Hut 4 than by all the Oxford savants put together. And so he chose to regard it as a unique, never-before-experienced pleasure. These are minor flaws in the character of the "seagreen incorruptible" and seen in their proper perspective, they are unessential ones. Lawrence was a man of feeling—at times of deep and intense feeling, and there was nothing cold or calculated in his attitudes except when he set himself deliberately to deflate pomposity or unmasked meanness. It is in any case far more difficult to be honest with self than with friends; and in the practice of bitter, searching self-honesty which few can really face, and then for a brevity of time only, he has few peers.

It is a mistake and an oversimplification to ascribe Lawrence's postwar malaise, the unmistakable sadness which overlay his latter years, to disillusionment with the Arabs or with the political settlements. He never had any illusions about the Arabs—not after first contact at least. As for politics, he had recognized it early as a hard-headed business to which it did not do to bring too many scruples; and he washed his hands of it as quickly as possible. Self was another thing altogether; for no matter how catholic a man's tastes, how broad his interests, how far he retreats from the perilous shoals of solitude, all his interests, his beliefs, his ideas, must ultimately be caught up in the web of introspection, in the midst of which sits the mysterious "I" in everlasting contemplation: selecting, rejecting, sifting, and arranging the puzzle pieces of existence; wrapped in its conscious and unconscious soliloquy to the end, though what that end might be no living man can know. The "I" that was Thomas Edward Lawrence was, he said, a standing court-martial on itself. Why? Misuse of power; loss of inner harmony; sexual defilement: all of these are potent reasons, and to them should be added the very natural grief he felt at the loss of such friends as Hogarth and Hardy.

Harsh ragged objects were concealed,
Oppressions, tears and cries,
Sins, griefs, complaints, dissensions, weeping eyes
Were hid, and only things revealed
Which heavenly Spirits and the Angels prize.
The state of Innocence
And bliss, not trades and poverties,
Did fill my sense.[11]

---

[11] "Wonder," by Thomas Traherne.

Such is youth, such is the state of innocence. And for Lawrence both were long overpast.

For the next year and a half he had a room in Birmingham Street, Southampton, while he moved about the country on the Air Ministry's boat business, taking the new target boats on trial runs, making reports, meeting up with seamen and boat-builders in increasing numbers. At Felixstowe, as at Mount Batten and later at Bridlington, he was called "Mr. Shaw" and treated with the respect due not to his former reputation but to his present manner and knowledge, his ability rapidly to size up any situation and take a decisive and correct initiative. It was sometimes difficult for fellow airmen to remember that his rank was a mere A/C 1; it would have been so easy to call him "sir." Noncommissioned ranks who found themselves readily doing his will defended their actions by saying it seemed natural to take orders from Mr. Shaw. For officers, the relationship with Aircraftman Shaw was not so simple, but many of them found it reasonable and rewarding to act upon his advice in matters where he was so obviously better informed or more completely master of the situation. This is not to imply that Lawrence as Aircraftman Shaw went around giving advice gratuitously or imposing his ideas on fellow airmen and superiors alike. He did not; and many of his superiors have testified to his correctness and punctiliousness as a serving airman. But punctiliousness did not prevent his winning a point by sheer mastery of personality when the occasion warranted. Flight Lieutenant Sims, who went one afternoon to the R.A.F. Marine Section, Bridlington, to pick up Aircraftman Shaw for a week-end visit, found him with a high-ranking officer and a group of Air Ministry officials in the engine shed. Here is his description in *T. E. Lawrence by His Friends.*

> At first it seemed nothing stirred or lived there, but when the eyes and ears lately confronted with sights and sounds of the busy world became more used to the gloomy silence, a faint light was visible at the far end, and a low murmur became audible. On tip-toe I approached. Surely, one thought, a ceremony is taking place. A slight upright blue-clad figure

stood high up in the bows of a boat with one electric light burning his hair to gold. He was giving a masterly lecture on the major features of the boats. The officer was listening in rapt silence . . .

The hours were long, the work sometimes most arduous, especially in rough weather which never deterred him; but it was work he thoroughly enjoyed, and it kept him ever on the move: Plymouth, Birmingham, Wolverhampton, Felixstowe, with occasional week ends snatched at Clouds Hill. Perhaps this restless journeying up and down Britain was not the least attractive aspect of his duties; it kept him from thinking too much.

Boats, engines, the sea, the coast of England; books, poetry, and an ever-increasing volume of personal correspondence were the strands which wove the pattern of his last years. And the pattern had broadened grandly. His fame, however inconvenient to him, had served to bring him to the attention of the great and near-great, and to give him access to the richest minds in the realm. The wide ring of his friends and acquaintances encompassed many of the best prose writers and poets in that golden period of English letters, as well as sculptors, architects, statesmen, and musicians. At the same time that he was rubbing shoulders with engine fitters from Birmingham and Wolverhampton he was corresponding with George Bernard Shaw, Henry Williamson, Cecil Day Lewis, W. B. Yeats, Sir Edward Elgar, Noel Coward, James Hanley, John Buchan, Robert Graves, Eric Kennington, Augustus John, Lady Astor, and Sir Winston Churchill. He was, in fact, and had for some years been leading an incredible Box and Cox existence in which, under the name of T. E. Shaw, he was continually sought after and cherished as T. E. Lawrence, his old identity, never really discarded and always readily assumed when his companions were discerning and sympathetic. Irish he was in spirit, despite the dilution of blood with other strains (he allowed himself to be elected to the Irish Academy of Letters in 1932), and with George Bernard Shaw he was always Irish in temper and humor. ("You've forgotten that I'm Irish, or that Irishmen persuade only the rest of the world," he had written to Shaw in 1923. [*Letters*, No. 235.]) Nowhere does his Hibernian humor proclaim itself more clearly than in this dual role played with such gusto on a stage wide enough to include such diversified scenes as the Power Boat Company's sheds at Hythe, the Union Jack Club on Waterloo Road where he got a cubicle with bed at 1/9d. a night on his visits to London, and the stately homes of England: Fleete, Mount Edgcumbe, and Barnwell Castle, where his lordly hosts were flattered by his presence if somewhat puzzled by his attitudes. His delight was to roar up on the Brough Superior at the door of a famous general or a peer and throw butlers and maidservants off their balance by his appearance, at the front door, in airman's uniform, the speech and manner of a gentleman only adding to the general confusion. But would he have enjoyed it so thoroughly had he really been plain Aircraftman Shaw? It is perhaps unfair to ask.

In 1929 Captain B. H. Liddell Hart, then the military correspondent for *The Daily Telegraph*, was approached by Jonathan Cape to do still another biography of Lawrence, this time a historical appraisal of his value as a soldier, a strategist, and a leader of men. While condemning the project, Lawrence was as quick to offer his assistance to Liddell Hart as he had been to Robert Graves. "These people all exaggerate so, and make of me more a mountain than a man," he complained to his mother and elder brother in China. "I read his [Liddell Hart's] proofs and knocked out a good deal of stuff that wouldn't do. Unhappily I had to put in something, each time, to replace what I knocked out." [12] And he dreaded the wave of interest in himself and the inevitable publicity which another book might raise.

> I am trying to accustom myself to the truth that probably I'll be talked over for the rest of my life: and after my life too [he had written Flight Sergeant H. A. Ford, a Cranwell acquaintance, in 1929]. There will be a volume of "letters" after I die and probably some witty fellow will write another life of me. In fact there is a Frenchman trying to write a "critical study" of me, now. They make me retch—and that's neither comfortable nor wholesome. I have thought of everything, I think: to join a newspaper (they do not eat each other, the dogs) but what a

[12] *The Home Letters*, p. 384.

remedy for the disease: to emigrate—but those colonies are as raw as wood alcohol: to commit some disgraceful crime and be put away:—but I have some people whose respect I struggle to keep. [*Letters*, No. 379.]

It is clear now that his dissatisfaction with Robert Graves' book made him hope for a book from Liddell Hart that should more closely correspond with his own idea of what an exposition of himself by another should be. What is not clear is what precisely that idea was. Robert Graves has said that Lawrence wanted him to write an elegy that would give some coherence to his diversities, and a validity on a poetic, nonhistorical plane. But the first was impossible, and the second had been done already—by himself in his own history of his part in the Arab war. Liddell Hart's book, when it reached the public in 1934, was a sincere, though to some, overenthusiastic evaluation, but it did not satisfy him any more than Robert Graves' biography had satisfied him: there was, he complained, too much of himself in it. But this was inevitable, considering the lone hand he had played in Arabia. Liddell Hart had set out to "clear away the dust of legend" that had covered Lawrence's war exploits and to put them into a perspective with the main campaign in Palestine. He had found, as he studied his subject, that the events in Lawrence's wartime actions which had significance possessed that significance because of his conception of those events; thus he found himself writing not an objective analysis, as he had proposed, but a subjective study of the man who had moved through the events he described. "But for him," he wrote, "the Arab Revolt would have remained a collection of slight and passing incidents. Through him it had an important bearing on the course of outer events both during and since the war. Also on the course of warfare." [13]

There was one thing, Lawrence thought, that Liddell Hart as a military expert could do for him.

Will you . . . strike a blow for hard work and thinking [he asked in 1933]. I was not an instinctive soldier, automatic with intuitions and happy ideas. When I took a decision, or adopted an alternative, it was after studying every relevant—and many an irrelevant—factor. Geography,

[13] *Colonel Lawrence, the Man Behind the Legend*, Preface, p. v.

> tribal structure, religion, social customs, language, appetites, standards—all were at my finger-ends. The enemy I knew almost like my own side. I risked myself among them a hundred times *to learn*. The same with tactics. If I used a weapon well, it was because I could handle it. [*Letters*, No. 491.]

And he went on: "Do make it clear that generalship, at least in my case, came of understanding, of hard study and brainwork and concentration. Had it come easy to me I should not have done it so well."

This is all of a piece with his defense of his *Odyssey* translation, but the last sentence is the key to his success with war and with motorboats: he was a brilliant amateur in both fields, with more than a touch of genius. The claim to study, the brainwork, the concentration, are not irrelevant; when a subject interested him sufficiently, he pursued it with such vigor and intensity that he mastered its essentials without the necessity of grounding, or even involving himself in details. And conversely, when his interest was sated, or when he had got from it all he wanted, he was done with it. This is a course which makes for brilliant performance and diversity, but not for the solid achievement which is normally the corollary of success.

> Have I done my best, do you think? [he asked Edward Garnett anxiously]. My prime is past. In it I worked my hardest at digging Hittites (that labour went unrecorded down the stream), at the war (history is written after 100 years), at *The Seven Pillars* (which I feel is partly theatre), at *The Mint*, which was my purest achievement, though stillborn. May I rest now? All the heat in me is gone out, and the endurance that was tougher than other men's. [*Letters*, No. 496.]

But was it gone? Talking to him in June, 1934, at the conclusion of a party given by Colonel Newcombe for the Emir Abdulla of Transjordan, Liddell Hart felt that Lawrence's attitude was changing even more than he himself realized. He had been catechizing him about his future: would he consider taking the leadership of a movement—any movement? The answer was still a firm "No," but Liddell Hart was not convinced. Oswald Mosley's Fascists, he knew, had been after him, but then so had the Socialists. Ernest Thurtle for one had wondered what effect he might have on a meeting of workingmen, could he be induced to address such a meeting. Would it ignite the latent flame in both audience and speaker, rousing Lawrence to give of himself unstintingly again to a cause, to splinter inertia and raise up a new fervor of devotion and dedication under his rare leadership?

The stigma of fascism was attached to Lawrence by his association with Cliveden, and this approach by the League of Ex-Service Men was enough to damn him in the eyes of left-wing intellectuals for years to come. But this is simply an echo of the teacup storm of 1929 after which he had written to John Buchan: "The labourites think I'm an imperial spy and the Die-hards thought I was bolshie." [*Letters*, No. 410.] To be blackened by both sides is a sure token of neutrality. But quite apart from party lines, there were some in England in those debilitating years just before World War II who dreamed of an era of power and prosperity under a strong hand—a benevolent, an ingenious hand. Is it possible that in odd moments Lawrence saw himself, smilingly, as Lord Protector under a new dispensation? He had governed once for three days over Damascus; could he not govern effectively over Britain? That the new Lord Protector should step out of a shabby lodging in Southampton, dressed in battered flannel trousers and a fisherman's jersey, fresh from the lowest ranks of His Majesty's Air Force, would doubtless have tickled his fancy for the odd, the whimsically incongruous. But if the choice had been offered him would he have accepted it? His prescience showed him the choice would not be offered; he prepared for his retirement from the air force sadly, planning for the future occupation of body and brain, but never fully believing in it. That he was saved mercifully from another trial of power is something for which all who admire him should be grateful.

The summer of 1934 was gloriously sunny and most gratifyingly hot, from Aircraftman Shaw's point of view, with the sun patterning Southampton Water with lozenges of sapphire and tufts of gold. It was a busy, luxurious summer for him, reveling as he did in heat, and it was his last. The daytime hours were fully occupied with target boats and bomb-dinghies as he hastened to complete a set program before his retirement in the following March. Time permitting and his eyes, which irritated by wind and glare had begun to trouble him again, he read. Clouds Hill stood, a hill of dreams—the "Well at the World's End"—in its sea of rhododendrons, waiting to receive him: its books now all assembled, its pictures hung—sketches of Allenby and Feisal by John and Kennington; Mrs. Altounyan's water-color impressions of Carchemish. Drought had stilled the ram, cut the water down to a trickle, and kindled the heath around it, but it was still eminently desirable, and he did desire it. Yet it was not his appointed rest, his native country, or his natural home.

In November Aircraftman Shaw in "civvies," as sparse as ever as to luggage, presented himself as a guest at the Ozone Hotel in Bridlington, where he was to remain with two warm rooms for his comfort throughout the tenure of his service at the R.A.F. target boat station.

> My room is a tower room [he wrote Henry Williamson in December], over the harbour wall, and the waves roll all day like green swiss rolls over the yellow sand till they hit the wall and run back like spinning rope. I want to walk out in the wind and wet, like at Clouds Hill, and can't, for my landlady's sake. [*Letters*, No. 546.]

Bereft of summer visitors and pounded by the North Sea, Bridlington presented a melancholy face in winter, but Lawrence would have liked it less had the summer visitors been there. At the Marine Craft Detachment, he worked with Lieutenant Commander H. E. E. Weblin, R.N., and with Flight Lieutenant W. E. G. Beauforte-Greenwood, head of the Marine Equipment Branch of the Air Ministry with whom he had worked and sailed at Hythe almost continuously from the autumn of 1930 to the autumn of 1932. With airmen and officers his relations were equally pleasant, and both were impressed by his kindness, his gentleness, and his consideration for others.

> Every time we saw him [wrote Flight-Lieutenant R. G. Sims for himself, his wife and small son], he would give us fresh cause for admiration, respect and love, and although sometimes he was obviously more troubled about some problem of his own than at others, he was invariably the

> courteous, wise, understanding and utterly regal youth in whose presence the foolish became profound, the ugly beautiful and the unattractive charming.

It was Flight Lieutenant Sims who delighted in telephoning the Marine Craft Detachment only for the pleasure of hearing the quiet, beautifully articulated voice at the other end of the line say: "Bridlington R.A.F. Detachment, A/C Shaw speaking."

Eternally youthful to Flight Lieutenant Sims, he seemed to other more astute observers now to be showing clear signs of middle age; and so the candid and disturbing photo-portrait taken at Bridlington shows him, aging, haunted, and very tired. Yet his mental iridescence could still be a brilliant exhibition: a mercurial flashing over the stream of human thought like the darting flight of a kingfisher, while with eyes more steady but alert still, and intuition poised and swift-striking, he sought out unerringly the mood and reaction of a *vis-à-vis*. Greek architecture, Sumerian sculpture, medieval warfare, the Cooperative Movement, John Buchan's characters, all would be swept up in a single conversation, discoursed on with an authority and an illumination as indisputable as they were memorable. And the impulse for fantastic invention was not yet stilled. He spoke to G. W. M. Dunn of constructing a chute from the window of the little workroom across the road from his cottage at Clouds Hill to the pool below, so that he could slide down each morning into the water—as at Carchemish. Access to him would only be by water, freeing him from the annoyance of unwelcome visitors; and books and papers in waterproof bags would reach him in his study via a clockwork boat!

And though he could find little good in himself, Lawrence brought a sense of well-being to others.

> Giving happiness is a feminine quality [wrote F. Yeats-Brown of him]. T. E. was entirely masculine in outlook and appearance, but with all his strength and courage he had also a woman's sensitiveness. His mind, so critical of himself, so charitable to others, had more bright facets than any other I have known. To be with him was to feel that one had bathed in some mountain spring.[14]

[14] *T. E. Lawrence by His Friends.*

There were no more parades; no more fire pickets, no inspections. Working hours at Bridlington were from eight to six, and the chiaroscuro of East Yorkshire days and nights, with their silver and gray monotones of rain and wind, of drafty boat sheds, deserted quay and storm-wracked cliffs beaten and washed over by the surf, wore a melancholy, brooding air that somberly conformed to his own mood of forboding sadness. He would like to have seized time by the forelock or, by some incredible feat of mind, lived outside its tyrannic and irresistible march. Yet he was growing undeniably weary of ordered days and nights.

> I have done with politics, I have done with the Orient, and I have done with intellectuality. O Lord I am so tired! I want so much to lie down and sleep and die. Die is best because there is no reveille. I want to forget my sins and the world's weariness.

So he had written in that fragment of a letter copied down by Colonel Isham which David Garnett dates as 1929 and others as three years later. But the zest for adventure was not entirely stilled. At Bridlington he dived one day in full diver's equipment from a salvage contractor's vessel, releasing a snarled rope from an anchor on the sea bed, as assured and as deftly as though he had been diving for years. The brilliant amateur again.

In this world of a mechanic's "bits and pieces" he was contented only as long as he was occupied, when, covered with grease, he was stripping down an engine or taking it out in its hull for trial runs. It was a world which, he had once told Robert Graves, satisfied him the more because no women could or would want to intrude themselves into it. But it was more: it was a world of forgetfulness where introspection and self-condemnation, born out of guilt and a sense of failure, could be quieted and submerged in the objective activity of hands and brain. And with a gesture, not of bravado but of disinterested contempt, he would himself take out the target boats on bombing practice, to the alarm and distress of his friends.

Suddenly his work at Bridlington was finished, and with it his days in the Royal Air Force. At his instigation, Sergeant Bradbury, his erstwhile companion at Myrtle Cottage, Hythe, had already been posted to Bridlington to take over from him. It was February, 1935, nearly seventeen years since the end of the war and twelve years since he had first enlisted; and it was the year of King George V's Jubilee, of the Italian invasion of Ethiopia, and the beginning of a time of stress which his former chief in the Colonial Office, Sir Winston Churchill, was later and portentously to call "The Gathering Storm."

There was a party one evening before he left Bridlington of officers and airmen: a visit to a bar where Aircraftman Shaw ate the cherries from his companions' cocktails; the theater with a Galsworthy play at which the guest of the evening, willing for once to submit to a mild lionizing, autographed chocolate boxes for the program girls and clowned in a bowler hat in the foyer after the performance. The night before he left Bridlington, Sergeant Bradbury helped him to pack his kit bag, feeling his own and his friend's desolation in the ungrateful labor. The next day Aircraftman Shaw came to make his farewells to the officer in charge; they talked briefly, and then after a second's distraction the officer looked up to find him gone. Riding an ordinary bicycle, he made his way south by road. On the road the news of the death of Frederic Manning, whose writing he had admired and whom he meant to visit on the way, reached him—"one rare thing the less in our setting," he commented, sadly.

"My losing the R.A.F. numbs me, so that I haven't much feeling to spare for the while," he wrote on February 28. "In fact I find myself wishing all the time that my own curtain would fall. It seems as if I had finished now." [*Letters*, No. 567.] Prophetic, perhaps; but he had been even more strikingly prophetic in 1928.[15] Clouds Hill was barred to him, besieged by vigilant pressmen who trampled down the ground around the cottage, threw stones that broke the roof tiles, and kept a stubborn watch for his coming. So he went to live for a few weeks as "Mr. E. Smith"—one last incognito—in Belvedere Crescent, S.E.1., trying meanwhile to persuade the brotherhoods of newspaper writers and photographers to desist. They left, only to return when he returned. The most importunate of them earned his wrath and a

[15] In an unpublished letter to Colonel Isham he had spoken of his eventual retirement to Clouds Hill and his sojourn there *until 1935*.

black eye for his pains which may or may not have been valued for the fist that inflicted it. After that he roamed the south country on his bicycle—the Brough Superior being still unlicensed—homeless and in despair. Oxford and the Ashmolean Museum came within his haunting orbit in these restless, unhappy days of being barred from the one place where he felt he had a chance of finding peace.

Once more he sought out the Newspaper Society and the press photography agencies, promising them never to warrant another newsworthy paragraph as long as he lived if only they would call off the hounds and leave him in peace. Early in April he was back at Clouds Hill again, confined to his cottage during the day while the local police patrolled it, and reprieved only with oncoming darkness which cloaked his movements. "I hope you will find me here some day: not yet, for all is sixes and sevens, as in a besieged town," he wrote H. S. Ede. [*Letters*, No. 573.]

It was a trial of stubborn wills, and in the end his prevailed. Other more fertile fields beckoned, the press decamped, and quiet came once more to the heath. Only now there was a ceaseless and distracting tap, tap at his window: a tit fluttering fruitlessly and helplessly up and down against the glass pane hour after hour, aggravating his nerves which had tautened again against the invasion of the press. "My time passes between swearing at him, cutting brushwood and inventing odd jobs," he wrote Flight Lieutenant H. Norrington [*Letters*, No. 575.] who with Flight Lieutenant Beauforte-Greenwood presented him with the stainless-steel candlesticks which stand now on the mantelpiece of the upper room at Clouds Hill. It was, he confessed, "a queer lapse into uselessness after that long-drawn series of jobs that made up my life." How would he employ his time? There was the biography of Roger Casement, the Irish nationalist executed for treason in 1916. He had considered writing this for some time now, but he had been refused access to the confiscated Casement diaries without which he felt a life could not properly be written. And there was the old idea of the printing press revived again; perhaps he would print *The Mint* after all. His retirement from the R.A.F. reduced his income by half, but if need be he could augment it: or he could reduce his living standards. There was the motorcycle—"the ancient of days" he called it with delicious irreverence—now licensed: was it essential to his well-being? He would soon discover. Disturbingly uppermost in his mind was a bid from Sir Winston Churchill to undertake the organization of Home Defence. Should he accept it? Was it his duty to try?

Meanwhile he set about making his living quarters more comfortable. The little upstairs bedroom was now lined with aluminum foil, and with its porthole window and bunk, was quaintly suggestive of a ship's cabin: the sea again. Food he kept under three glass bells, tokens of a lonely and fastidious, though not pernickety, nature which would not tolerate cookery and its consequent odors in the cottage. Square meals, if he wanted them, could always be had in one of the soldiers' cafés at Bovington. The old sleeping bags embroidered "*Meum*" and "*Tuum*" were still usable.

> The cottage is all right for me [he told Eric Kennington], but how on earth I'll ever be able to put anyone up baffles me. There cannot ever be a bed, a cooking vessel, or a drain in it—and I ask you —— are not such things essential to life —— necessities? [*Letters*, No. 579.]

On May 6 Jubilee bonfires blazed all over his beautiful Dorset Heath and he counted twenty-six of them from his window. On that night he sat down to write to Eric Kennington:

> You wonder what I am doing. Well, so do I, in truth. Days seem to dawn, suns to shine, evenings to follow, and then I sleep. What I have done, what I am doing, what I am going to do, puzzle and bewilder me. Have you ever been a leaf and fallen from your tree in the autumn and been really puzzled about it? That's the feeling. [*Letters*, No. 579.]

E. M. Forster was to have been one of the first guests at Clouds Hill, welcomed jointly by himself and Pat Knowles, his friend and neighbor across the road. But Henry Williamson, whose *Tarka the Otter* had brought him the friendship of T. E. Shaw, would also be an early visitor. Burning with the problems of a disintegrating Europe—a time sadly out of joint—fretted by domestic trials and on fire suddenly with a vision that should unite under the magical aegis of "Lawrence of Arabia" all those who had fought the war to end wars, he wrote to say he was coming. On a chill May morning when the northeast wind veered a cutting edge across the heath and shattered the blossom of the prize Philpotts-Hardy rhododendrons, the "ancient of days" was wheeled out of the shed and the man whom Williamson felt possessed the genius of friendship, rode into Bovington Camp to send off a telegram of welcome. It was dated May 13, 1935, and dispatched at 11:25 A.M. Before it had reached its destination in Devon, the flame Henry Williamson had hoped to fan to a blaze was quenched.

There are some people who believe that the accident on the road between Bovington Camp and Clouds Hill that May morning was deliberate and suicidal, though there is nothing in the facts to bear this out. The road then was a narrow country road, and in a dip near Clouds Hill as he came down it at fifty miles an hour on the return journey, he unexpectedly confronted two boys riding bicycles in single file. To avoid hitting them was impossible in the space left between them and his roaring machine, unless he swerved dangerously. It was their life or his, and in that split second of infinity allowed for such decisions, he made the only choice he could make. Once made, nothing could save him, for he wore no protective crash helmet, and after roughly swiping the cycle of the last boy and unmounting him, Lawrence was thrown clear over the handle bars, hurled through the air for a distance, and then flung head down on the road, splitting his skull in a fatal nine-inch gash from front to back.

Yet a veil of mystery did overcast the scene. A corporal of the Royal Army Ordnance Corps, who watched from a vantage point of a hundred yards away in a camping ground near Clouds Hill, saw the motorcycle overtake a large black car traveling in the opposite direction just before hearing, though without seeing, the crash that followed. But the two boys, strangely, had no memory at all of a black car passing them on the road. It was, said the coroner at the inquest afterward, a most unsatisfactory situation, but it did not alter the essential circumstances of the accident.

Bleeding and unconscious from his injuries, Lawrence was carried into Bovington military hospital by a passing army lorry, and in the absence of his two brothers who were both abroad, his friends Colonel Newcombe and Viscount Carlow took up a shared vigil beside him until Arnold Lawrence, the nearer brother could fly from Spain. For a week he hovered between the living death, paralyzed and without faculty of speech or memory, that would have been his had he recovered, and the release he had hoped for. Another with his injuries would have succumbed more quickly, but his body's endurance held to the end. In these last days the popular press reclaimed him for the world: No. 338171 Aircraftman Shaw was gone and the identity he had tried so hard to slough off was his again, though *The Times*, more circumspect, called him Mr. T. E. Shaw to the end. Ironically, he had broken his pledge to the press not to earn another newsworthy paragraph less than two months after it had been given.

Doctors and surgeons and friends waited, and waited too until word of the accident could reach his mother and elder brother sailing up the Yangtze River. In those cold and showery days of 1935 the English earth showed forth in all its miraculous witness to life, to fertility, to hope; it was a singularly inauspicious time for dying. Then early on Sunday, May 19, under the double onslaught of shock and lung congestion, the pulse grew feeble and for the first time his strong heart seemed to falter. Oxygen and adrenalin were administered, and then artificial respiration, but to no avail. Shortly after eight o'clock he was dead, never having regained consciousness since that moment five days before when it must have occurred to him, in a last coherent and limpid thought, that this indeed was the end.

"All over," he wrote laconically at the conclusion of his 1911 diary and his ordeal with Syrian heat, dysentery, fever, toothache, and blisters, and in May, 1935, all was over for him: the pilgrimage, not long in duration but most eventful, was finished. The body which had moved through life with such verve and energy was quite still, and the eternal mystery of life was once more consummated in death.

In his grave habiliments he seemed, to Sir Ronald Storrs, to have returned once more to the Arab, to have assumed again the white robes, the *kuffiya*, and the *agal* of a Bedouin chief to which his features, strong and most serene, were at last reconciled. To the funeral on the following Tuesday the world of art and letters and politics thronged by road and rail, cramming the little country church at Moreton and overflowing into the churchyard among the press photographers. To a few who on that overcast, rain-threatened day assembled earlier at Clouds Hill, it seemed impossible to believe that the spirit which had stamped its image so powerfully on the cottage was irrevocably removed; and the sensation is no less strong today so many years later.

A swarm of black flies—"like a delegation from the East," said Liddell Hart afterward—hovered over the grave at the interment. At the end the bearers, Colonel Newcombe, Eric Kennington, Sir Ronald Storrs, Pat Knowles, Sergeant Bradbury, and ex-Private Russell of the Royal Tank Corps, stepped aside, and the coffin, seeming very small to the onlookers, was lowered into its bed of leaves and the rest which, in life, his body had rarely known. He had reached at last the Sunday that should have no end.

What is his real significance?

> He will always have his detractors [wrote Field Marshal Lord Wavell], those who sneer at the "Lawrence Legend"; who ascribe his successes with the Arabs to gold; who view the man as a charlatan in search of notoriety by seeming to seek obscurity; who regard his descent from colonel to private as evidence of some morbid *nostalgie de la boue*. They knew not the man. Those who did, even casually and sporadically, like myself, can answer for his greatness.[16]

The truth is his significance does not lie in heroics, in what he may or may not have accomplished on the historical plane, but in the man himself—in what he was.

> People like Lawrence are in fact an obvious menace to civilization [Robert Graves had written in *Lawrence and the Arabian Adventure*]; they are too strong and important to be dismissed as nothing at all, too capricious to be browbeaten, but then too doubtful of themselves to be made heroes of.

[16] *T. E. Lawrence by His Friends.*

This was written with an insight which cannot today be improved on; but there is still more to it than that. Not the least provocative aspect of Thomas Edward Lawrence is that, born in the reign of Queen Victoria and with both feet planted solidly in the Middle Ages, he was nevertheless a spirit so modern in vision and temper that his century has not yet caught up with him. Sir Ronald Storrs has described him as the artist-man-of-action who overthrows all accepted ideas and sets up in their place the irresistible challenge of youth which can pull a Rolls-Royce engine to pieces, test and race speedboats like an expert, and yet do all these things with a Greek Homer in his pocket and a fastidious taste for Beethoven string quartets.

So he is, and so he will remain a challenge to the imagination for men who are young in spirit and whose minds are not become atrophied by dogmatic theories and the shibboleths of twentieth-century materialism. The brightness of his image does not dim with closer acquaintance; for the more he is revealed through his own words and the impressions of others, the more his mystery, in the spiritual sense, and his personal fascination deepen. Like an iceberg, the greater part of him is always submerged, but like an iceberg, he turns over and displays a myriad of dazzling shapes and contours, though the inner matrix is forever hidden. In the end perhaps the greatest challenge is in this gesture of a man who gave up utterly comfort, renown, and fortune for the sake of his scruples and out of desire for personal atonement; but it is not a challenge which many are fitted to take up.

Except in the political sense, neither martyrs nor martyrdom make any appeal to modern tastes, and for some—even those who set him down as part fraud—there will always be something repugnant in this withdrawal of Lawrence from the world of affairs and action. It will be ascribed to his deep and incurable neurosis, but there is a point at which motives, even neurotic motives, subserve a higher law; and the perfect economy which orders the procession and recession of living experience and in which wastage is only apparent, employs whatever substance is at hand to shape its own purpose. The road from Tremadoc to Moreton was not a *via triumphalis*, but a *via crucis*, and few will voluntarily follow in such a way. It is the way of the Celt which in his blood was a compulsive element; the sweet wooing of pain and defeat incomprehensible to those who have not experienced it. And it is the way of a pilgrim.

> . . . I have sought
> For a home that is not gained;
> I have spent, yet nothing bought
> Have laboured but not attained;
> My pride strove to mount and grow,
> And hath but dwindled down;
> My love sought love and lo!
> Hath not attained its crown.[17]

So it is and so it must ever be, whether the goal beyond the striving, the crown of all seeking, be called the Beatific Vision or the Ideal Standard always out of reach.

"I cannot doubt some deep religious impulse moved him . . . some craving for the perfect synthesis of thought and action which alone could satisfy his test of ultimate truth and his conception of life's purpose," said Lord Halifax when he unveiled Eric Kennington's bust of T. E. Lawrence in St. Paul's Cathedral. Perhaps, he speculated thoughtfully, Lawrence came nearer to the answer when he lay at Bovington between life and death suspended and saw his life whole, not parti-colored and in fragments, before him. Perhaps then the castles of Normandy and Syria rose up to gladden him again; perhaps he saw the Valley of the Euphrates and tasted again all the joyousness it once had brought him; the naked, serrate hills of Arabia shimmering in their heat haze, and the gardens of Damascus quenched and nourished by their ever-murmuring streams. But Lord Halifax liked to think "that he saw again the spires of Oxford, unearthly in their beauty, set in the misty blue of early May, until at last he reached no earthly city, but that city of his vision where he might see no longer as in a glass darkly, and know at length as he was known."

---

[17] "I Will Lift Up Mine Eyes Unto the Hills," by Christina Rossetti.

BIBLIOGRAPHY

Lawrence, T. E., *Revolt in the Desert.* George H. Doran, New York. 1927.

Lawrence, T. E., *The Seven Pillars of Wisdom.* Doubleday, Doran, New York. 1935.

Lawrence, T. E., *Crusader Castles.* 2 Vols. The Golden Cockrell Press, London. 1936. (Edition limited to 1000 numbered copies.)

Lawrence, T. E., *The Letters of T. E. Lawrence.* David Garnett, Ed. Doubleday, Doran, New York. 1938.

Lawrence, T. E., *T. E. Lawrence to His Biographers.* Robert Graves. Doubleday, Doran, New York. 1938.

Lawrence, T. E., *T. E. Lawrence to His Biographers.* B. H. Liddell Hart. Doubleday, Doran, New York. 1938.

Lawrence, T. E., *Secret Despatches from Arabia by T. E. Lawrence.* Published by permission of the Foreign Office. Foreword by A. W. Lawrence. The Golden Cockrell Press. [London] [1939]. (Edition limited to 1000 numbered copies.)

Lawrence, T. E., *Men in Print. Essays in Literary Criticism.* Introduction by A. W. Lawrence. The Golden Cockrell Press, London. 1940. (Edition limited to 500 numbered copies.)

Lawrence, T. E., *Oriental Assembly.* A. W. Lawrence, Ed. E. P. Dutton, New York. 1940.

Lawrence, T. E., *The Mint.* Notes made in the R.A.F. Depot between August and December, 1922, and at Cadet College in 1925 by T. E. Lawrence (352087 A/cRoss). Regrouped and copied in 1927 and 1928 at Aircraft Depot, Karachi. Note by A. W. Lawrence. Doubleday, New York. 1955. (Edition limited to 1000 numbered copies.)

LAWRENCE, T. E., W. G., F. H., *The Home Letters of T. E. Lawrence and His Brothers*. M. R. Lawrence, Ed. Macmillan, New York. 1954.

ABDULLAH, *Memoirs of King Abdullah of Transjordan*. Edited by Philip Graves with an introduction by R. J. C. Broadhurst. Cape, London. 1950.

ALDINGTON, RICHARD, *Lawrence of Arabia, A Biographical Enquiry*. Collins, London. 1955.

ANTONIUS, GEORGE, *The Arab Awakening, The Story of the Arab National Movement*. G. P. Putnam's Sons, New York. 1938; reprinted and revised 1946.

BELL, GERTRUDE, *The Letters of Gertrude Bell*. Selected and Edited by Lady Bell. Boni and Liveright, New York. 1927.

BRAY, MAJOR N. N. F., *Shifting Sands*. Foreword by Sir Austen Chamberlain. Unicorn Press, London. [1934].

CARRINGTON, CHARLES EDMUND (pseud. of CHARLES EDMONDS), *T. E. Lawrence (of Arabia)*. D. Appleton Century, New York. 1936.

DOUGHTY, CHARLES M., *Travels in Arabia Deserta*. With an introduction by T. E. Lawrence. 2 Vols. New and Definitive Edition. Random House, New York. 1937.

DUVAL, ELIZABETH W., *T. E. Lawrence, A Bibliography*. Arrow Editions, New York. 1939.

GARNETT, DAVID, Ed., *The Essential T. E. Lawrence*. Selected with a Preface by David Garnett. Doubleday, New York. 1951.

GLUBB, BRIGADIER JOHN BAGOT, *The Story of the Arab Legion*. Hodder and Stoughton, London. 1948.

GRANT, CHRISTINA PHELPS, *The Syrian Desert*. Macmillan, New York. 1938.

GRAVES, ROBERT, *Lawrence and the Arabian Adventure*. Doubleday, Doran, New York. 1928.

GURNEY, O. R., *The Hittites*. Penguin Books, London. 1952.

HITTI, PHILIP K., *History of the Arabs*. Macmillan, London. 1937.

HOBHOUSE, CHRISTOPHER, *Oxford As It Was and As It Is Today*. Batsford, London. 1939.

HOGARTH, D. G., *The Ancient East*. Henry Holt, New York. 1915.

HOURANI, A. H., *Minorities in the Arab World.* Issued under the auspices of the Royal Institute of International Affairs. Oxford University Press, London. 1947.

JARVIS, MAJOR C. S., *Arab Command.* The Biography of Lt. Col. F. G. Peake Pasha, C.M.G., C.B.E. Hutchinson, London. 1942.

JONES, THOMAS, *A Diary with Letters 1931–1950.* Oxford University Press, London. 1954.

LAWRENCE, A. W., Ed., *T. E. Lawrence by His Friends.* Doubleday, Doran, New York. 1937.

LEARY, LEWIS GASTON, *Syria the Land of Lebanon.* Mcbride, Nast, New York. 1913.

LIDDELL HART, B. H., *Colonel Lawrence, the Man Behind the Legend.* Dodd, Mead, New York. 1934.

LLOYD GEORGE, DAVID, *The Truth about the Peace Treaties.* Golancz, London. 1938.

MACPHAIL, SIR ANDREW, *Three Portraits.* John Murray, London, 1929.

NICOLSON, HAROLD, *Peacemaking 1919, Being Reminiscences of the Paris Peace Conference.* Houghton Mifflin, New York. 1933.

PHILBY, H. ST. J. B., *A Pilgrim in Arabia.* Robert Hale, London. 1946.

PHILBY, H. ST. J. B., *Arabian Days. An Autobiography of H. St. J. B. Philby.* Robert Hale, London. 1948.

RASWAN, CARL, *Black Tents of Arabia.* Creative Age Press, New York. 1947.

RICHARDS, VYVYAN, *Portrait of T. E. Lawrence: The Lawrence of the Seven Pillars of Wisdom.* Jonathan Cape, London. 1936.

RICHARDS, VYVYAN, *T. E. Lawrence. Great Lives.* Duckworth, London. 1939.

ROBINSON, EDWARD, *Lawrence the Rebel.* Lincolns-Prager, London. 1946.

SHAW, T. E., (COLONEL T. E. LAWRENCE), *The Odyssey of Homer.* Newly Translated into English Prose. Introduction by John Findlay. Oxford University Press, New York. 1932.

SHAW-EDE, *T. E. Lawrence's Letters to H. S. Ede 1927–1935.* Foreword and running commentary by H. S. Ede. The Golden Cockrell Press, London. 1942. (Edition limited to 500 numbered copies.)

SHAW, T. E., SHAW, CHARLOTTE, *Letters*. British Museum Additional MS. 45922 and 45903,4.

SMITH, CLARE SIDNEY, *The Golden Reign; The Story of My Friendship with Lawrence of Arabia*. Cassell and Company, London. 1940.

STIRLING, COLONEL W. F., *Safety Last*. With a foreword by Siegfried Sassoon. Hollis and Carter, London. 1953.

STORRS, RONALD, *The Memoirs of Sir Ronald Storrs*. G. P. Putnam's Sons, New York. 1937.

THOMAS, LOWELL, *With Lawrence in Arabia*. The Century Company, New York. 1924.

WAVELL, COLONEL A. P., *The Palestine Campaigns: Campaigns and Their Lessons*, Ed. Major General Sir Charles Callwell, K.C.B. Constable, London. 1928.

WILLIAMSON, HENRY, *Genius of Friendship 'T. E. Lawrence.'* Faber, London. 1941.

WOOLLEY, C. LEONARD, *Dead Towns and Living Men*. Oxford University Press, New York. 1929.

WOOLLEY, C. LEONARD AND LAWRENCE, T. E., *The Wilderness of Zin*. With a chapter on Greek inscriptions by M. N. Tod. Introduction by Sir Frederic Kenyon. Charles Scribner's, New York. 1936.

MISCELLANEOUS: Report on the Excavations at Djerabis on behalf of the British Museum conducted by C. Leonard Woolley . . . and T. E. Lawrence. Parts 1–2. The British Museum. 1914–1921; Military Operations, Egypt and Palestine, 1914–1918. His Majesty's Stationery Office. 1928–1930; Hansard; The Annual Register; Air Ministry News Letters; various histories official and unofficial of the Royal Air Force; newspaper and magazine articles and letters.

INDEX

Aaron's tomb, 99
Abdulla, Emir, 102, 108, 109, 128, 129, 166, 169, 296
Afghanistan, 238, 245, 247, 258–59, 261
Ageyl, 129, 131
Aigues-Mortes, 51
Ain Ghadian, 99
Ain Gharandel, 100
Al Akle, Fareedah, 56, 57, 78, 83
Aleppo, 57, 67, 72, 74, 81, 86–87, 89, 90–91
Alexandretta, 148
Ali, Emir, 109, 129
Allenby, Lord, 110, 117, 126, 131, 132, 143, 147, 155, 178, 216
Altounyan, F. H. R., 280
Amanullah, Amir, 247, 258–59, 261
Amery, Julian, 111
Amman, 167
Antonius, George, 110, 157
Aqaba, 98, 110, 112, 117, 125, 169
Arabia, 57–102, 104–45, 147–58, 160, 165–71, 238–39, 246, 253, 259, 271–72
Arles, 50
Ashmolean Museum, 23, 26, 58, 74
Astor, Lady, 255–56, 276
Auda abu Tayi, 110, 116, 128, 137
Azrak, 115–19, 122, 142, 160

Bacha-i-Saquao, 258–59
Bair, 134, 140
Baker, Sir Herbert, 172, 207, 252
Baldwin, Stanley, 220
Banbury, H. H., 212, 269, 283
Barker, Sir Ernest, 28
Beauforte-Greenwood, W. E. G., 298, 302
Beersheba, 97, 125, 132
Beeson, C. F. C., 37, 48
Bierut, 54, 57, 72, 92
Bell, Gertrude, 86, 90, 219, 254
Bible, 19, 53
Birijik, 65, 67, 71, 79
Blake, William, 258
Bovington, 210–26, 272, 303–04
Bradbury, W., 283, 300–01
Brémond, General, 110
Bridlington, 292, 298–301
Brodie, Samuel, 131
Brook, W. H. (Stokes), 145
Brough, George, 208
Buchan, John, 224, 226, 234, 274, 297
Busrawi Agha, 91, 96, 271
Buxton, R. V., 114, 135, 140, 220, 245

Caerphilly, 39
Cairo, 103–06, 145, 147, 154–56, 165–66
Campbell Thompson, R., 57, 61, 63, 69, 90
Cape, Jonathan, 207, 210, 219, 232–33, 241, 249, 294

Carchemish, 57–97, 101, 160, 271–72
Carlow, Viscount, 305
Cattewater (Mount Batten), 268–83, 288, 292
Ceram, C. W., 81–82
Chaigon, Mme, 40
Chamberlain, Sir Austen, 262
Chambers, Jock, 210–11, 279
"Changing East, The," 113
Chapman, Thomas Robert, 20–22
Chase, H. A., 127
Chateau Gaillard, 39
Chaundy, T. W., 19–20, 29
Christopher, Canon, 19
Churchill, Sir Winston, 165, 170, 176, 177, 236, 303
City of Oxford High School for Boys, 19
Clayton, Gilbert, 104, 106, 126
Clemenceau, 149, 151, 158
Clifton, Violet Beauclerk, 86
Clouds Hill, 63, 213, 218–19, 223, 226, 232, 272–73, 280, 284–85, 293, 298–99, 301–04, 306
Cockrell, Sir Sidney, 207, 223
Constantinople, 56
Coster, Howard, 208, 289
Cox, Canon Ernest W., 19, 24
Crac de Chevaliers, 54
Crane, C. H., 152
Cranwell, 194–95, 228–29, 242
Curtis, Lionel, 138, 161, 173, 193, 199–200, 213, 216, 225, 232, 237, 241, 243, 250, 267
Curtis Brown, 207
Curzon, Lord, 157, 164, 167

Dahoum, 62–63, 72–73, 77–79, 81, 87–88, 96–99, 117, 135
Damascus, 57, 72, 101, 141–43, 145, 148, 166
Darb al-Hajj, 57
Der'a, 57, 115, 119–22, 136, 139, 142, 160, 171, 173, 179–80, 200, 222, 254
Dinard, 17, 40
Dorset Heath, 211
Doubleday, F. N., 279
Doubleday, Doran, 233, 241
Doughty, Charles M., 46, 51–52, 66, 130, 137, 155, 161, 167, 174, 196, 233, 274
Dowson, Sir Ernest, 103, 104
Dunn, G. W. M., 274, 299

Ede, H. S., 242, 251, 302
Egypt, 66, 74, 103–06, 145, 147, 154–56, 165–66
El Ayubi, Shukri, 143
Euphrates, 59–61, 75, 78, 83, 89, 97

Fauaun Island, 98–99
Farnborough, 198, 203, 206–10, 290
Fay, Sir Samuel, 147
Feisal, Emir, 106, 109–11, 117, 124, 129, 142, 147–54, 160, 165, 169
Felixstowe, 288–89, 292–93
Ffoulkes, Charles, 72
Fontana, Mrs. Winifred, 67, 81–83, 271–72
Ford, H. A., 294
Forster, E. M., 175, 196, 219, 223, 244, 246, 249, 253, 258, 262, 290, 303
Fougères, 37, 39
France, 17, 36–37, 39–40, 47, 50, 105, 146–58, 166, 170

Galilee, 53
Garnett, David, 37, 172, 194, 206, 209, 245, 300
Garnett, Edward, 173, 175, 188–89, 196–98, 202, 204, 207, 211, 219,

Garnett, Edward (*Continued*) 224–26, 233, 235, 242–43, 247–49, 260, 273–74, 285, 290, 296
Gennesaret, 53
Goslett, Raymond, 127
Granville-Barker, Harley, 222
Graves, Robert, 25–26, 27, 48, 64, 66, 80, 81, 84, 135, 150, 160–61, 164, 165, 174, 199, 203, 204, 211, 213, 217, 218, 233, 234, 241–42, 254, 264, 266, 274, 278, 281, 282, 290, 294, 295, 300, 306
Greece, 58, 105
Green, Leonard H., 58
Gregori, 57, 62
Guweira, 131

Haifa, 57
Haj Wahid, 62, 73, 87, 89, 96–97
Halifax, Lord, 308
Hall, E. F., 199
Hamoudi, 62, 66, 72–73, 78, 96
Hardy, Thomas, 211, 217–18, 223, 265
Hardy, Mrs. Thomas, 143
Harran, 70
Hauran, 117, 119
Hedley, Coote, 103
Hejaz, 102, 143, 147
Hejaz railway, 100, 109, 115–17, 128, 166–67
Herbert, Aubrey, 104, 106
Hillingdon House, 184
Hoare, Sir Samuel, 224, 262
Hogarth, D. G., 26, 52, 57–59, 61, 63, 65, 69, 73–74, 79, 81, 86–87, 90, 95, 104–05, 109, 132–33, 148, 154, 161, 164, 199, 220, 223, 243–44, 271–72, 274
Holdich, Colonel, 104
Holmes, Miss, 57, 72
Homer, 255, 285–86
Hopkins, Gerard Manley, 258
House, Colonel Edward Mandell, 151
Hudson, W. H., 208
Hurley, W. M. M., 230, 237, 239, 269
Hussein, Sherif, 102, 104–05, 167
Hussein, Ali ibn el, 123–24, 128, 166
Hythe, 283, 294, 298

Ibn Saud, 171
Idrisi of Asir, 105
India, 227–62, 273, 284
Iraq, 165, 170–71, 190, 240
Ireland, 20, 210, 293
Isham, Ralph H., 233, 266, 300

Jaffa, 125
James, W. Warwick, 271
Jarvis, C. S., 168, 169
Jebeil, 56–58, 72, 78, 87
Jerablus, 57, 59, 65–66, 69, 71, 73, 87
Jericho, 133
Jerusalem, 125–28, 166
John, Augustus, 160, 176, 207–08
Johns, W. E., 179–80
Jones, B. V., 227–28, 230, 236
Joyce, James, 193

Kabul, 247
Kafka, Franz, 194
Kafr Ammar, 66, 74
Karachi, 230–38, 242, 244–47, 250–51, 260, 282–83
Kennington, Celandine, 255
Kennington, Eric, 128, 129, 140, 161, 164, 168, 176, 195, 202, 208, 220, 229, 280, 281, 303, 308
Keynes, Lord, 172
Khalil Pasha, 106
King, H. C., 152

Knowles, Sergeant, 213, 218, 284
Knowles, Dick, 238, 241, 252
Knowles, Pat, 303
Kut, 106

Lamb, Henry, 272
Langley, 17–18
Lansing, Robert, 154
Lawrence, Arnold W., 23–24, 28, 30, 33, 40, 45, 48, 57, 86–87, 113, 154, 177, 256, 258, 287, 305
Lawrence, David Herbert, 210
Lawrence, Frank H., 24, 28, 33, 49–50, 85, 159
Lawrence, M. R. (Bob), 18, 24, 28, 30, 33, 40, 49–50, 136, 177
Lawrence, Sarah, 16, 18, 21–23, 27, 84–85, 160, 177, 207
Lawrence, Thomas Robert, 16, 18, 20–22, 47, 154
Lawrence, W. G. (Will), 24, 28, 33, 49–50, 64, 67, 85, 90–91, 94–96, 159
Lawrence and the Arabian Adventure, 241
Lawrence and the Arabs, 241
"Leaves in the Wind," 230
Lebanon, 52–53, 56, 87, 148, 152, 157
Leeson, B. E., 209
Liddell Hart, B. H., 32, 39, 41, 107, 135, 144, 150, 177, 220, 244, 265–66, 277–78, 286, 290, 294–96, 306
Lincolnshire, 228–29
Lloyd George, 146, 149–51, 158
London, 147, 155, 161–64, 172–81, 201–03, 207, 224–26, 261–62, 270, 285, 287, 294, 301, 308

McMahon, Sir Henry, 104, 150–51, 156, 169
Malet, Louis, 149
Manning, Frederic, 301
Margab, 54
Marsh, Sir Edward, 238–39, 273
Mecca, 109
Medina, 103, 108–09
Mesopotamia, 54, 60–61, 70–71, 90–91, 106, 147–48, 151–52, 157–58, 170, 260
Messham, Florence, 27, 83
Mint, The, 188, 192–96, 200, 204–06, 213–14, 224, 226, 228, 230, 235, 247–50, 272, 287, 290, 302
Miramshah, 227–28, 238, 242, 244–47, 250–53, 259
Moab, Hills of, 57
Mont Saint-Michel, 39
Morris, William, 39, 46, 48–49, 64, 88, 158, 250, 284
Mount Batten (Cattewater), 268–83, 288, 292
Mount Carmel, 57
Murray, Sir Archibald, 104, 110

Namier, Sir Lewis, 267
Nasir, Sherif, 110, 116, 128–29, 142
Newcombe, F. S., 97–98, 103–04, 110, 153, 163, 177–78, 196, 229–30, 296, 305
Nicolson, Harold, 150
Norrington, H., 302

Odeh, Rev. N., 52
Odyssey, The, 250, 252, 255, 260, 270, 284–87
Oxford, 18, 19, 25–29, 31, 34, 42–43, 47–49, 96, 156, 159, 243, 302, 308
Oxford Union Library, 26
Oxford University, 16, 40, 43–45, 54, 57, 59, 158, 160–61, 164, 177, 290

Palestine, 53–54, 97–101, 104–43, 157, 165–71, 272

Palestine Exploration Fund, 97, 101
Palmer, "Posh," 213, 226, 233
Paris, 146–53, 155–59
Peake, Colonel F. G., 112, 140, 167–68, 171
Peshawar, 244, 245–46, 247, 259
Petra, 100
Petrie, Flinders, 66, 74
Philby, St. John, 168, 169
Picot, F. Georges, 148
Pirie-Gordon, H., 54
Plymouth, 261, 268–69, 277, 293
Polstead Road, 18, 26–28, 34, 41–43, 54, 96, 136, 158, 177
Port Said, 229–30, 260
Provence, 50–51

Rahail, 125
Reading, 161
Revolt in the Desert, 163, 197, 207, 219, 229, 232–33, 241–43
Rhys, Sir J., 54
Richard Coeur-de-Lion, 37, 38, 39, 126
Richards, Vyvyan, 47–49, 67, 73, 89, 123, 133, 135, 158, 255, 272
Rieder, Mrs., 57, 101
Rogers, Bruce, 174, 250, 286
Rolls, S. C., 140–41
Rome, 154–55
Ross, John Hume, 179–210
Rossetti, Christina, 47, 86
Rothenstein, Sir William, 208, 243, 265, 286
Royal Air Force, 179–211, 221, 227–301
Royal Artillery, 40–43, 45
Royal Tank Corps, 210–26
Rum Kala'at, 71, 83
Rumm, 125, 137

S. A., 135
Sahjun, 54
St. Aldates Church, 19, 44
Saint-Malo, 17, 37
St. Trophime, 50
Saklatvala, S., 261
Samuel, Harold, 271
Sandwich, Lady, 234
Sara, 135
Sassoon, Sir Philip, 288
Sassoon, Siegfried, 256
Scotland, 16–17, 279
Scott, Lady, 80
Seal-hunting in Mesopotamia, 73
Seven Pillars of Wisdom, 30, 35, 155–56, 161, 164–65, 172–78, 197, 200, 208, 214, 219–20, 225, 232–33, 248–49, 257
Shakir, Sherif, 129
Shaw, George Bernard, 144, 199, 207–08, 220–21, 225, 233, 239–40, 249–51, 260, 269, 274, 293
Shaw, Mrs. George Bernard, 120, 254
Shaw, T. E., 210–308
Sidon (Saida), 52
Sims, R. G., 279–80, 292, 298–99
Sinai, 97, 101, 132
Sind, 231, 236
Smith, Mrs. Claire, 276–77, 287
Smith, E., 301
Smith, George, 60
Smith, Wing Commander Sidney, 268, 270, 275, 277, 282, 287
Southampton, 283, 292, 297
Stirling, W. F., 199
Storrs, Sir Ronald, 102, 122, 127–28, 272, 305, 307
Swann, Sir Oliver, 180–81, 185, 206–07, 209
Sykes-Picot Agreement, 147–48, 151, 156–57, 170

Syria, 52–97, 101, 105–08, 117, 123, 140–45, 147–58, 165–71

Tafila, 131–32
Tell Ahmar (Til Barsip), 69
Thomas, Lowell, 126–27, 161–64, 174, 219, 225, 229
Thompson, R. Campbell, 57, 61, 63, 69, 90
Thomson, Lord, 276
Thurtle, Ernest, 203, 254, 262, 269–70, 278, 296–97
Transjordan, 128, 153, 166–70
Tremadoc, 16
Trenchard, Lord, 190, 221, 224, 226, 240, 287
Turkey (Ottoman Empire), 60, 63–64, 68, 79–80, 86, 91–93, 98–102, 108–11, 115–43, 147, 152

United States, 150–52, 154, 156–58
Uxbridge, 180, 182–206, 226, 229

Wadi Ais, 109–10
Wadi Araba, 99–100
Wales, 16, 36, 39
Wavell, Lord, 110, 113, 126, 143, 155, 222, 306
Waziristan, 227–28, 245, 253, 258, 260
Wejh, 107, 109–10
Wells Cathedral, 217
White, Robin, 283
Williamson, Henry, 298, 303–04
Wilson, Woodrow, 146, 151, 156, 157
Woolley, C. Leonard, 62, 74–75, 77, 79–80, 82, 91, 95, 97–98, 101, 103–04

Yale, William, 157, 170
Yeats-Brown, F., 299
Young, Hubert, 95

Zeid, Emir, 129, 132–33
Zin, 98, 100, 131, 133
Zormara, 61, 95